Gracious Forgiveness

A Theological Retrieval

CRISTIAN F. MIHUT

OXFORD

UNIVERSITY PRESS

Great Clarendon Street, Oxford, OX2 6DP,
United Kingdom

Oxford University Press is a department of the University of Oxford.
It furthers the University's objective of excellence in research, scholarship,
and education by publishing worldwide. Oxford is a registered trade mark of
Oxford University Press in the UK and in certain other countries

Published in the United States of America by Oxford University Press
198 Madison Avenue, New York, NY 10016, United States of America

British Library Cataloguing in Publication Data
Data available

Library of Congress Control Number: 2022950221

ISBN 978–0–19–287372–9

DOI: 10.1093/oso/9780192873729.001.0001

Printed and bound in the UK by
TJ Books Limited

OXFORD STUDIES IN ANALYTIC THEOLOGY

Series Editors

Michael C. Rea   Oliver D. Crisp

OXFORD STUDIES IN ANALYTIC THEOLOGY

Analytic Theology utilizes the tools and methods of contemporary analytic philosophy for the purposes of constructive Christian theology, paying attention to the Christian tradition and development of doctrine. This innovative series of studies showcases high quality, cutting-edge research in this area, in monographs and symposia.

To

Andrea Anne

Acknowledgments

This project is now entering its teenage years. Angelic and lovable in infancy, it has become a bit recalcitrant and lanky, but also increasingly bold and adventuresome. I am glad it is blazing its own path into the world. That being said, it really took a village to get it here. I have been greatly helped by many friends and colleagues in thinking and writing about forgiveness. I owe the following people a debt of gratitude for comments on drafts or for discussion of various parts of this book: Ruth Armstrong, Mike Austin, Jeff Bain-Conkin, Ryan Bollier, Christina Brinks-Rea, Hugh Burling, Sarah Coakley, David Cramer, Terence Cuneo, Dave DeJong, John-Paul Erdel, Tim Erdel, Spencer French, Joel Gabrielse, John Haas, Bruce Huber, Angela Knobel, David McCabe, Chad Meister, Ligia Mihut, Christian Miller, Kathryn Pogin, Abby Roeder, Nancy Snow, Jim Stump, and David Wright.

Additionally, I am beholden to the two anonymous referees that Oxford University Press commissioned. Thank you to Reader 2, for encouragement and commendation. Thank you to Reader 1, for challenging me at every turn to clarify concepts, sharpen arguments, engage deeper with the relevant literature, and structure better the parts into the whole. The project is much stronger due to their incisive and insightful feedback. I am also very grateful to Thomas Perridge, the commissioning editor of the series, for his gracious helpfulness and eternal patience with a first-book author. Furthermore, I am thankful to Alexander Hardie-Forsyth, my book's editor at Oxford, and Bhavani Govindasamy and the entire copy-editing team, for all their labor and care in seeing this project through. Special gratitude to my four children Hannah, Alexandra, Jordan, and Ethan. Each of them, in their own singular ways have taught me about the grace, resilience, beauty, and love inherent in forgiving.

Two people have been so crucial to accomplishing this work that I'm afraid any praise will be underwhelming. I have benefited enormously from the careful, precise, and thorough comments Mike Rea left on virtually every page of the manuscript. Over years of discussing this work, his subtle mind and gracious spirit saved me from a legion of mistakes, pushed me toward greater precision, and raised the most fascinating objections. One would be hard-pressed to find a better conversation partner on any topic, but especially on anger and forgiveness. Anne, my wife, has been the most consistent supporter and sharpest objector. I describe her generally as possessed of twice the wit and thrice the virtue that I have. This is true in this domain. She has read several times over the manuscript, wrestled alongside of me with these ideas, and helped me refine them. The book is dedicated to her. She is a true practitioner and theoretician of forgiveness.

I am also thankful for the permission from the journal *Philosophia Christi* to make use in Chapter 6 of my work from: "Change of Heart: Forgiveness, Resentment, and Empathy," *Philosophia Christi* 14 (2012): 109–24. Formal permission was granted by Betty Talbert, the managing editor of the journal.

The initial stages of this project were made possible through support of a grant from the Character Project at Wake Forest University and the John Templeton Foundation. The opinions expressed in this volume are those of the author and do not necessarily reflect the views of the Character Project, Wake Forest University, or the John Templeton Foundation. I am thankful for the support.

Contents

1

Forgiveness and Healing

"He heals the brokenhearted
and binds up their wounds.
He determines the number of the stars;
and gives to all of them their names."
Psalm 147:3, 4[1]

It is no mystery that the Bible pictures God as a spurned lover or a betrayed spouse.[2] At the very heart of Israel's salvation story, Exodus recalls Sinai as the hallowed ground where God enters into a kind of marital union with Israel, the terms of the relationship codified in the Mosaic covenant. But there at Sinai, we also find the original betrayal, the *ur*-story of marital unfaithfulness. As the union between Yahweh and nation is formally ratified up on the mount, down in the valley below, Israel unites herself in worship with the Egyptian gods, the overlords from which she has freshly been liberated. The Prophets and the Writings will go on to thematize and rhapsodize God's loving faithfulness against the background of Israel's continued disposition toward unfaithfulness. The golden calf will not be Israel's only one-night stand, we understand. But Yahweh will keep taking back the unfaithful partner.

Israel's memory of God's faithfulness is particularly noteworthy. Consider Psalm 147, a poem recalling the pain of Hebrew deportees in the Babylonian exile. Although the exile is the consequence of Israel's adulterous attachment to other gods, Yahweh cannot help but bring compassion to *her* pain and healing to *her* wounds. The parallelism in the verses quoted above is not accidental. A myriad of stars for a myriad of wounds. For the Hebrew poet, the pain of the exile is projected onto the entire cosmos. Inscribed upon the vault of the heavens, the wounds of the deported are legion. The scars of the brokenhearted are countless, just like the number of the stars. But this acute awareness of crushing oppression is wedded to the poet's astute theology. If the national pain has cosmic scope, so does divine grace and healing. If the Creator God attends to myriad

---

[1] Except where indicated otherwise, all Scripture quotations in this book are from the New Revised Standard Version Bible, copyright © 1989 National Council of the Churches of Christ in the United States of America. Used by permission. All rights reserved worldwide.

[2] See Hosea 1–3 and Amos 4.

Gracious Forgiveness: A Theological Retrieval. Cristian F. Mihut, Oxford University Press. © Cristian F. Mihut 2023.
DOI: 10.1093/oso/9780192873729.003.0001

celestial bodies, to countless lifeless stones and fires blazing across the vast expanse, the God of the covenant surely knows and names and binds all wounds. This covenantal God is an attentive healer. God heals each broken heart, bandages each wound in its searing particularity, just as God calls each star by name.

The remaining stanzas of Psalm 147 embed this theology of post-exilic healing in a larger story of the Creator's gracious generosity. This healing God satisfies hungry people with finest wheat and wild animals with food. This God who knows all sufferers, provides for and sustains an entire ecological order with rain-drenched mountain-pastures and timely seasons, ensuring that each generation of humans and ravens will have enough. At its core, the biblical faith has affirmed an inherent link between the healing of creation and divine graciousness. The earliest Christians were so formed by the self-giving generosity of God through Christ that they established the first hospitals, turned charity to the orphan and the elderly into enduring social institutions in the western world, and opened their homes and communities to the hungry, the lonely, the wounded, and the desperate.[3]

It may seem strange to start a book on forgiveness by talking about healing and gracious generosity. But the hope is that this theological lens helps frame or reframe some of our modern intuitions about forgiveness. Like the brokenhearted of ancient Israel, we moderns are also shot through with pain and hurt. We are all wounded, wounding animals. We give and we take offense. Our responses to offenses vary: we plan revenge, we ask for justice, we demand restitution, we let bygones be bygones, we pretend it didn't happen, we forgive, we forget. These attitudes depend in part on the magnitude of the offense and in part on the nature of the relationship we have with the offender. Sometimes, of course, wounds and violations dig in so deeply that unremitting anger and dogged resentment seem like the only sensible responses. Jean Améry recalls the Auschwitz guard who ritualistically pounded his head with a shovel. He reports feeling a precise and inescapable duty to judge his oppressor and the social mechanisms that nurtured these types of horrors. For victims such as Améry, hanging on to resentments represents at once a psychological necessity and a moral compulsion to witness to the truth of the wound.[4]

Though wounds reverberate deeply, sometimes space opens up for other responses. When he emptied his gun in an Amish schoolhouse at Nickel Mines, Charles Carl Roberts IV did not foresee that the relatives of the girls he killed or maimed would forgive him posthumously. As some may remember, Roberts walked into the school, took hostages, and ended up shooting eight of the ten girls. He killed five of them before turning the gun on himself. Many observers at the time, including some of Charles's relatives, looked with shock or puzzlement

---

[3] Cf. Schmidt 2004: ch. 5 and ch. 6.   [4] See the narrated event and its gloss in Améry 1980: 70.

on these immediate and unconditional Amish gestures of grace.[5] Public opinion has remained split on whether granting forgiveness to the unrepentant, dead killer is a laudable, questionable, or condemnable action.[6] Yet the Amish reaction to injury is at the very least intriguing. As they saw it, their acts of forgiveness flowed naturally from practices that stretched back to the words and actions of Jesus. They made it clear that forgiveness is not supererogatory, but a response rooted in grasping the gift of divine grace, independent of the offender's actual or possible repentance. Ostensibly grounded in *imitatio Dei*, practiced over centuries of suffering and persecution, decidedly anti-therapeutic, and reinforced by a strong communal ethos, this type of gratuitous forgiveness is an interesting phenomenon, one ripe for analysis.

My task here is not to explore the particularities of Amish forgiveness. I am interested more in the general phenomenon of which this may be but a token. More on target, I want to mine a specific theological explanation for some gestures of gracious forgiveness. This monograph aims to retrieve a biblical image of gracious, curative forgiveness, to develop its theological genealogy, and to explore some of its psychological and relational implications. I maintain that the biblical God is, quintessentially, a healer-forgiver. God's primary response to offenses results from an essentially forgiving nature, which I understand as a set of robust dispositions to perform unmerited, preemptive, and curative grace-gestures. And because God is paradigmatically a gracious forgiver, we, mirroring God's nature, are called to incorporate this divine aspect into our practical agency and to share in the godly task of healing the world through forgiveness.

In the thought-world of the Hebrew Bible, any number of idioms can convey divine forgiveness. God cancels the debt of sin, blots out iniquity, pardons transgression, covers up impurity (*kipper*), and bears or carries away burdens (*nasa awon*). Some of these ancient, biblical idioms still have clear resonances in our contemporary, secular culture. For instance, forgiveness as acquittal or cancellation of debt continues to be popular today. Wrongdoers, we think, owe a moral debt from which only the victims can release them. Or consider the cliché, "forgive and forget" which seems to imply that forgiveness is connected to erasing the wrongdoing or the active memory of wrongdoing.

When I say that God is a gracious, curative forgiver, I take my main cue from the rich biblical imagery that pictures God as *the bearer of Israel's iniquity*. This does not diminish the importance of thinking about God as a debt-canceller or as

---

[5] Terri Roberts recalls that during the private burial ceremony for her son, about 40 Amish people enveloped the grieving Roberts family at the graveyard site to reassure them of their forgiveness and love. (Jasmyn Belcher Morris. "A Decade after the Amish School Shooting, Gunman's Mother Talks of Forgiveness." *StoryCorps*, NPR, September 30, 2016. https://www.npr.org/2016/09/30/495905609/a-decade-after-amish-school-shooting-gunman-s-mother-talks-of-forgiveness. Last accessed August 30, 2022.)

[6] Others have investigated in detail the range of public responses to the Amish declarations of forgiveness. Cf. Kraybill et al. 2007: ch. 1, sect. 5.

an impurity-coverer. Still, I focus on *bearing away sin* because this idiom is the most frequently used in the Hebrew Bible, it occurs repeatedly in the central liturgical and theological texts of ancient Israel, and, as I will show, is theologically fruitful. Intensifying some, while sidelining other images from the OT (Old Testament), the NT (New Testament) also sees God bearing away in and through Jesus of Nazareth not only the sins of Israel, but those of the whole world. This image, I explain, uniquely and centrally illuminates the teaching and work of Christ. For these reasons, we have here distinct and irreplaceable insights for conceptualizing God's disposition to curatively and graciously forgive, a divine trait that, I argue, is at the core of divine agency.

The image of God as sin-bearer is not only pervasive, interesting, and deeply resonant theologically, it is also theoretically fruitful. Underlying the metaphor, I suggest, is the idea of a robust divine inclination to forgive that involves the interplay of two central commitments. First, it involves the long-lasting divine commitment to remove sin from persons, to separate, as it were, the sinner from the sin. The second divine commitment is to absorb into God's own self the consequences of transgression. Many will worry that this proposal has some controversial implications. It suggests that in forgiveness, the offended party not only refuses retaliatory measures but identifies in some respect with the plight and condition of the offender. I have things to say in reply to this worry, but for now I note that an articulation of the metaphor will not be plausible, much less compelling, unless embedded in a broader conceptual framework.

In a juridical framework, where divine transcendence is expressed through a strict moral law, human desire is inherently transgressive, and persons are fitting targets of God's prosecution, absorbing into Godself the consequences of sin *does* seem anomalous. At best, it appears as a kind of well-meaning, epiphenomenal regret after divine justice has done its work; at worst, a completely eliminable quality. But in a covenantal-relational framework where sin is a cosmic sickness, where transcendence is expressed through expansive divine commitments to redress brokenness, and where humans are seen as targets of divine healing, bearing away sins and absorbing the consequences of cosmic sickness makes perfect sense. Retrieving one biblical image is then inextricably tied to the artic-ulation of a larger theological framework of concepts, images, and symbols in which this metaphor is intelligible.

A final aim is to show that this theological conception of forgiveness has ethical, interpersonal, and psychological depth. Consider a consequence for moral psy-chology. If human forgivingness—the engrained disposition to forgive—is mod-eled on God's disposition, it involves a sensibility, finely tuned to multiple salient practical conditions, that expresses itself in something like the two interlocking commitments of forgiveness I sketched above. Consider some of the ethical implications. The view developed here implies realism about traits of character. And if forgivingness is an admirable trait, then sometimes gratuitous and preemptive acts of forgiveness are morally praiseworthy. The penance of offenders is not always a necessary condition for extending forgiveness. The view also allows the possibility that a range of reactive attitudes, such as anger and resentment, can coexist with forgivingness. My understanding of curative forgivingness will have some startling normative upshots. It ends up supporting, instead of stifling, some of the virtues necessary for liberatory struggles against oppression. Although I develop it in a broadly Aristotelian framework, I suggest that due to its non-trivial connections to mercy and lament, forgivingness does not aim essentially at happiness or at flourishing, as traditionally understood.

Philosophical and Methodological Assumptions

Before I summarize the main argument of the book, let me spell out some of my philosophical presuppositions. First, following current philosophical and psychological orthodoxy, I assume that a person's character is constituted by stable and enduring traits, grounded in distinctive cognitive, affective, and conative dispositions. These traits play various functional roles connected to understanding, explaining, predicting, modeling, and evaluating an individual's behavior.[7] Additionally, in a person of moral character, these traits are responsive to various considerations that lay normative claims upon her life, their differentiated saliency determining distinct courses of action in specific situations. Standard in the literature is also the assumption that moral traits or virtues exhibit cross-situational consistency, meaning that they are exemplified "across a wide variety of trait-relevant situations, even where some or all of these situations are not optimally conducive to such behavior."[8]

Second, though not a human person, the biblical God is certainly a *person*, possessing a unique personality and character. Since God has agency, we can expect that God's actions flow from and are explained by some consistent set of divine traits or dispositions. While the Scriptures consistently portray God as the paradigmatic *moral* person, one who responds characteristically and consistently in praiseworthy fashion to a variety of moral demands, some remain skeptical of this.[9] I grant the importance of the skeptical challenge, and though I cannot do it full justice here, I make some mitigating suggestions throughout.

Third, I assume that God's moral identity and character can be described independently of God's metaphysical nature. I do not claim that God's moral character *is* independent of God's metaphysical nature. The ultimate properties or relations constitutive of divine nature will also explain God's moral properties. Worries about our species' reliability regarding recondite metaphysical objects or

---

[7] See Miller 2013: 12–13.   [8] Doris 2002: 18.   [9] See Curley 2011 and Fales 2011.

transcendent beings aside, explorations of God's metaphysical nature seem to me valuable in their own right.[10] At the same time, I am convinced that the Scriptures have an unmistakable practical orientation. They seem more interested in recounting a moral and relational vision of God with us than in theorizing about its metaphysics. The descriptions of divine forgivingness embedded in the narratives and poetry of the Bible provide psychological depth, explanatory power, and normative salience, even absent a theory of their ontological basis. Generally, we can theorize about divine agency without a clear story of how it fits with *perfect being* theology or any other worked-out metaphysics of divine personhood. Nevertheless, I suspect that, implicitly or explicitly, there is a two-way interaction between the two pictures: our view of divine agency cannot help but be shaped by our metaphysics of God, and vice versa. And so, it is a minimal desideratum that the two pictures of God should not be inconsistent. It is, however, beyond the scope of this project to make explicit an account of the metaphysical nature of a forgiving God.

I also take for granted that biblical narratives and poetry provide the primary and best evidence from which to make inferences about the divine moral character. No doubt, it is irresponsible to theorize in blissful ignorance of the rabbinic or patristic traditions, or without concern for the deliveries of our ethical intuitions. But whatever inferences we draw from tradition and intuition, they must answer, in the end, to these ancient stories and poems. Our conjectures or claims about the agency of God are, at best, incomplete unless they faithfully capture the distinctive cadences, idioms, and motifs of the rich narrative contexts that frame divine action, unless they represent truthfully the story-world, the *mythos* of the ancient Hebrews.[11] In her defense of narrative knowing, Eleonore Stump claims that some understandings of persons cannot (or only with great difficulty can) be articulated in non-narrative form.[12] Perhaps Stump is right that we cannot know or cannot express certain aspects of God unless we attend to the relevant stories, and, more generally, to the relevant forms of biblical literature revealing God as a unified agent of action. More modestly, I propose that our understanding of God's

---

[10] The Church Fathers are in wide agreement that God's nature is that of a simple and unchangeable immaterial spirit. Since bodies have parts and are changeable, God cannot have a body. For a diametrically opposed view, consider the first lines of Benjamin D. Sommer's award-winning book: "The God of the Hebrew Bible has a body. This must be stated at the outset, because so many people, including many scholars, assume otherwise. The evidence for this simple thesis is overwhelming, so much so that asserting the carnal nature of the biblical God should not occasion surprise. What I propose to show in this book is that the startling or bizarre idea in the Hebrew Bible is something else entirely: not that God has a body – that is the standard notion of ancient Israelite theology – but rather that God has many bodies located in sundry places in the world that God created" (Sommers 2009: 1).

[11] I use the terms "mythos" and "narrative" akin to Kevin J. Vanhoozer to convey more than a strict story form, to refer to "all the ways in which diverse forms of biblical literature represent, and render, the divine drama" (Vanhoozer 2012: 7).

[12] Cf. Stump 2012: esp. ch. 3.

character is sharpened and deepened as we attend to the particularities and details of biblical narrative and poetry.

Relatedly, I believe that central aspects of God's character are distinctly and irreducibly conveyed through ancient liturgies and rites. Liturgical knowledge, perhaps as a species of narrative knowledge, gives us unique insight into God's moral nature. Liturgies and rites make known through scripted action-sequences and through patterned juxtaposition of images and symbols aspects of God's agency that would hardly be intelligible or graspable in their absence. I argue in Chapters 2 and 3, for instance, that the two main rites enacted on the Day of Atonement give us quintessential, programmatic, and unique clues about divine forgiveness as ancient Israel understood it. Concretely, I show how the scripted sequence of actions in the scapegoating rite illuminates the forgivingness of Yahweh in the OT, and the forgiving works of Christ in the NT.

An important methodological implication of the last two points is that this project does not make totalizing claims about the meaning of all scapegoating rituals, the universal nature of human desire, or even about the subversion of all human violence through ritual. Consider a contrast: René Girard's theory of atonement centers on three essential claims.[13] First, according to Girard, human desire is essentially imitative; all our desires are essentially borrowed desires from other humans. Second, the competing sets of imitative or mimetic desires set up an inherent rivalry among people that would end up destroying communities and civilization unless a special individual (weak or powerful) absorbs the accumulated collective violence. This individual is killed, lynched, or exiled, and subsequently, everyone in the community breathes easy, until communal violence needs to be released by yet another scapegoat. Finally, Girard claims that while all cultures are founded upon this scapegoating ritual, the Judeo-Christian tradition subverts it from within. God upholds the innocent victim. Against all the crowds who abandon the innocent victim to death, against Jewish and Roman witnesses alike, against fair-weather friends and hardened foes, God takes a stand for Jesus Christ, the innocent victim, and subverts the scapegoating mechanism from within.

As I have noted, I do not make grand claims about the essentially mimetic nature of human desire, and certainly cannot adjudicate about a ritual underlying *all* cultures. Although I certainly believe that God stands *with* vulnerable victims and *for* Christ as the Suffering Servant, I do not see the Resurrection story as reducible to a single meaning. More importantly, I theorize about sin-bearing and the institution of the scapegoat within the particular Hebraic system of signs and symbols, relying on the metaphor and ritual peculiar to Israel's own history and theology. As Chapters 2 and 3 spell out, the Hebrew scapegoating ritual recalls

---

[13] Cf. esp. Girard 1987 and Girard 2001.

different biblical dramas, constituting an apt vehicle for conveying forgiveness. Shockingly, God incorporates and completes the Hebrew scapegoating ritual in God's own being, instead of repudiating it. And if there is ritual subversion in the cross and the Resurrection, it is a subversion relative to the symbols and mythos of the Hebrew people.

Finally, I want to defend the methodological focus on a single image of forgiveness. Indeed, I unapologetically retrieve a conceptual and theological genealogy of *one* key biblical metaphor of forgiveness and attempt to press that image as far as it will go into an account of divine forgivingness. Like-minded philosophers have developed theories suggested by or grounded in other biblical images.[14] It is obvious that in theorizing about divine forgivingness and other kindred virtues, this is not the only way to proceed. I want to briefly sketch four main approaches that are distinct from mine. For lack of better labels, I will refer to them as the *whiggish*, the *tory*, the *homogenizing*, and the *kaleidoscopic* ways.

According to the *whiggish* way, we map the contours of forgiveness by prioritizing modern moral intuitions and by downplaying the relevance of ancient medical, ritualistic, social, or economic contexts. In the language inherited from Immanuel Kant, forgiveness proper is to be understood as a kind of morally appropriate response to wrongdoing, a transaction between autonomous agents. Since ancient metaphors of impurity, debt, or disease are mostly idle in conceptualizing our modern, scientific-technological notion of harming or giving offense, they fail to properly describe qualities and relations befitting of autonomous, rational selves.[15] The upshot here is that in thinking about divine forgivingness, we would begin from a stock of current folk-psychological notions, perhaps sieved through and purified by our equally modern conceptions of what moral perfection entails. As examples, consider the emotion-transformation theories of divine forgiveness or punishment-forbearance views, which rely heavily on modern intuitions about what a perfect rational agent would or would not resent (or find punishable).[16]

According to the *tory* approach, the starting point should be the theological reflection on the dominant models of atonement, since God's forgiving character shines forth most brightly in the systematic reflection on the work of Christ. If a theory of atonement (whether Penal Substitution, Satisfaction, *Christus Victor*, or Moral Influence) best explains most the phenomena or the problems raised by the death of Christ, the view of divine forgivingness implied or suggested by this all-explanatory atonement model has priority. Theology is the queen of sciences. And so, both contemporary ethical intuitions and ancient images have to bend the knee

---

[14] Cf. Margalit 2002: ch. 6 and Allais 2008. Also, see my discussion of Miroslav Volf and Anthony Bash at the beginning of Chapter 3.

[15] In my opinion, David Konstan comes close to holding this kind of view. Cf. Konstan 2010: ch. 1 and ch. 4.

[16] See Warmke 2017.

to her. Modern moral intuitions and the salience of various biblical images are measured by their fittingness with the best theory of atonement. On this approach then, the most suitable conception of divine forgiveness is derivative from the best theologizing of the atonement. The best atonement model controls which biblical metaphor of forgiveness is most salient.

Next, the *homogenizing* way extracts from the various ancient biblical pictures some structural or abstract features that would then be employed in a general theory of forgiveness. Unlike the *whiggish* or the *tory* ways, that either dismiss the ancient images or prioritize one at the expense of others, this approach simply homogenizes or flattens the various forgiveness images, reducing their historical and metaphorical content to the lowest common denominator. Consider for instance how a functional view of forgiveness, such as openness to reconciliation, could flatten different metaphors of forgiveness.[17] We may talk of reconciliation when a longstanding debt between debtor and lender is paid, or when a victim drops the charges against the victimizer, or when the judge shows clemency, or when a formerly contagious person is returned whole to his community, or when a father is united again with a runaway son. But in each of these cases, reconciliation means different things, is accomplished by different methods, and inheres in different kinds of relationships.

Finally, the *kaleidoscopic* approach argues that Scripture has a plethora of images of divine forgiveness, and that it is necessary to preserve the richness and diversity of all of these images without prioritizing any of them, without homogenization, conceptual unification, or coordination.[18] Since I deal in detail with an exemplar of this approach at the beginning of Chapter 3, I will not belabor the analysis or evaluation here.

Whatever their virtues, be they simplicity, diversity, or theoretical unification, these four approaches also incur costs. The *whiggish* way unduly restricts the articulations of forgiveness within the contemporary framework of idealized rational agency, when the phenomenon of forgiveness may very well have richer psychological, medical, mythical, or even cosmic resonances. Similar worries arise for the *homogenizing* approach. Different biblical metaphors of forgiveness presuppose different contexts—juridical, relational, psychological, medical, cultic, and economic—so a homogeneous theory of divine forgivingness would tend to flatten richer descriptions and their distinctive functions in search of common ground. If the *homogenizing* approach flattens the rich biblical imagery, the *kaleidoscopic* way allows for too much richness and diversity among the metaphors. It seems at once hasty and supine to let a thousand flowers bloom, without attempting some theoretical coordination. What if there are good narrative, exegetical, hermeneutical, practical, and theological grounds to prioritize some

---

[17] For a recent functional account of forgiveness see Strabbing 2020.   [18] Cf. Green 2006.

metaphors over others? What if some images of forgiveness cohere well together or can be naturally coordinated into a more unified account?

What about the *tory* approach? I do not have the space to submit it to a full critical investigation. Some have worried that we cannot construct a coherent, unified theory of the atonement. In the backdrop of the different atonement models we find irreconcilable metaphors and pictures that pull in different directions and can hardly be stitched together into a single coherent account.[19] Others argue that the patristic theorizing about the death of Christ intends to solve a range of distinct, and not obviously related problems—overcoming sin, defeating the devil, destroying death, and undoing human ignorance—and so focusing on one of these problems at the expense of the others, as the dominant atonement models seem to do, is from the start a problematic strategy.[20] As I see things, by holding fixed one theory of atonement in order to settle the reference of divine forgiveness, we beg substantive questions regarding biblical metaphor and imagery that should not be taken for granted. Atonement-theorizing itself depends on a rich network of charged biblical images and concepts that need clarification and articulation.

In short, though in many ways fruitful, each of the methodologies sketched above suffers from weaknesses that my approach intends to remedy. The *whiggish* way dismisses the biblical metaphors, the *tory* way arbitrarily prioritizes one image of forgiveness at the expense of others, the *homogenizing* way compresses or drains out some rich contents latent in the relevant biblical metaphors of forgiveness, and the *kaleidoscopic* way allows too much cluttered, heterogeneous content.

My approach narrows the lens to focus on one central metaphor, for a host of compelling, non-arbitrary biblical and theological reasons developed in Chapters 2, 3, and 4. A more complete account than mine would tell a story that coordinates somehow with the remaining central biblical images. But that is not a task I can undertake in this monograph. As a consequence, I make no grand claims about theoretical completeness. Perhaps the biblical phenomenon of forgiveness is essentially untidy and amorphous, and the different biblical lenses we have at our disposal pick out at most a "cluster concept."[21] But even if the concept is resistant to a full analysis in terms of necessary and sufficient conditions, we could still conceptualize forgiveness by reference to various features that tend to naturally gravitate together around one or another biblical image of forgiveness.

---

[19] Michael Rea seems to hold this, though, as far as I know, the view has not made it into print yet. Consult his "Lectures on the Atonement." Delivered at *The Summer Seminar in Philosophy of Religion*, University of St. Thomas, 2012.

[20] See Peter W. Martens. "Reconsidering Gustaf Aulen's *Christus Victor*: Toward a New Account of the Patristic Doctrine of 'Atonement'." Delivered at the *Logos Conference*, University of Notre Dame May, 2014.

[21] Mike Rea suggested to me in conversation this way of partially containing the ostensible untidiness of divine forgiveness.

This project mines only one central image in the cluster, in the hope that it coordinates well with theorizing about other central images in the same conceptual nexus. As I show in Chapter 2, the genealogy of covering iniquity (*kipper*) reveals that sin essentially attaches to and pollutes not only people but also the divine presence in Israel's camp. The genealogy of bearing burdens (*nasa awon*) shows that sin essentially burdens human beings. Perhaps in the Levitical imagination the two images are connected through the idea of a contagious disease. Fruitful new vistas would open up if we attended to the ways in which the biblical understanding explores and expands the connection between these two metaphors. I am doing this for sin-bearing, since I believe it is one of the more enduring and apt biblical pictures. Others may engage in a similar project, that of retrieving the metaphors of sin-covering or iniquity-blotting. If some of these pictures turn out to be more apt, enduring, and fruitful than others, we can also pursue coordination. But the task of identifying and conceptualizing theologically deep and fruitful metaphors is foundational. This, then, amounts to a confession and a promise. I theorize "in the grip" of one of the better pictures of forgiveness.

Overview of the Book

In this study, I motivate, articulate, and defend a Christian account of gracious, healing forgivingness. Chapter 2 argues that the Hebrew Bible sees God fundamentally as a gracious, healing forgiver. Curative forgivingness—the settled disposition to aim at healing offenders through gracious gestures—is center stage in understanding and explaining God's character. Starting from the dominant image of God bearing Israel's burdens, I show that due to its idiomatic frequency, theological significance, liturgical and ritualistic depth, and literary resonances, we can retrieve a two-pronged theological refrain: sin is an infectious disease that weighs down wrongdoers and their communities; God's reliable response to burdened humans is grace and a readiness to carry their loads. I articulate this gracious divine readiness as the interweaving of two divine commitments: the commitment to separate the offender from the offense, and the commitment to absorb into God's own being the consequences of the offense. I show how the story of Jonah not only subverts retributive justice, but affirms the centrality of a gracious, preemptive, and continuous divine disposition to absorb and neutralize iniquity. Since my account implies that God expresses forgiveness through image and ritual, I sketch an answer that relies on a joint, double-agency account of human-divine action. This idea is developed in more detail in the chapters that follow.

Chapter 3 continues the theological retrieval begun in Chapter 2 by focusing on the nature and work of Jesus Christ. I show how key parts of the NT look to Jesus as the ultimate continuant of God's drama of bearing burdens and of healing sinners. As the quintessential divine agent, Christ keeps loyalty with Israel and beyond, continuing God's healing work by embodying divine presence among blighted persons and by enacting and completing the scapegoating ritual of Yom Kippur. As the human representative of a new Israel and a new Adam, Jesus keeps loyalty with Yahweh even in times of apparent divine abandonment. Christological forgiveness seamlessly fulfills both divine commitments of gracious forgivingness: on the one hand a new humanity, separate from the sin-sickness, is reworked from within, as it were, in Christ's own humanity; on the other, as God's unique representative, Christ absorbs into his being the sin-sickness of others, without passing on the contagion. Embodying God's gracious character, completing temple-related rituals, and acting as a double-representative, Christ's actions and dispositions also paint for believers an ambitious normative ideal for responding to evil.

Chapter 3 concludes by tracing two significant theological implications. The first is an expression of the doctrine of the Incarnation. In Christ, God does not offer forgiveness from afar, neither by fiat nor by declaration alone. God accomplishes this through embodied immersion in the sin-stricken, chaotic environments and histories of sinners. Contrasting the mindreading account of sin-bearing, I propose a ritualistic, representative, recapitulationist, and physically immersive interpretation of Christ's work. The second theological implication sketches a framework for human participation in Christ's work of forgiveness by incorporation into divine agency. Just as God incorporates his agency into ours through the rails of the Hebrew sacrificial system, we are incorporated into the agency of God when we lovingly immerse our imagination into the grace-filled narratives of Christ's actions.

Chapter 4 extends the thesis that forgivingness is at the heart of God's agency by focusing on various conceptualizations of divine justice. I interrogate some of the important assumptions that too often ascribe biblical, theological, and philosophical centrality to divine retributivism. More positively, I argue that curative, gracious forgivingness supports and is supported by a non-retributivist conception of divine justice. I sketch an account that makes sense of divine wrath and hard treatment as reprobative communications which are teleologically embedded in a larger restorative-justice framework. Because it is a hybrid framework, I call it *communicative-restorative* justice. I provide several relevant episodes from the biblical narrative that corroborate this theoretical framework: the Eden story, the giving of the Torah, the Prophets, and Christ's cleansing of the temple. The Appendix at the end of the book is an addendum to Chapter 4. It examines the book of Lamentations due to its strong divine retributivist language and imagery. On a closer look, I suggest, the book does not lionize or affirm it, but ends up mounting a *reductio ad absurdum* of divine retributivism.

In several respects, Chapter 5 is the centerpiece of the project. I articulate and illustrate a two-level account of curative forgivingness. I follow Robert C. Roberts some of the way in articulating forgivingness as involving *a sensibility* attuned to various blame-reducing, beneficence-maintaining conditions. But I go beyond it, to show that curative forgivingness also involves *a conception* of one's life as a trusting participation in the story of a transcendently good God who cauterizes and contains our individual suffering. I then explain three modes of such participation: the appropriation of a teleological meta-narrative, participation in grace as an aesthetic phenomenon, and developing a lifelong friendship with Christ.

Finally, the main question I take up in Chapter 6 is this: Can we recommend curative forgivingness to people living under oppression? Wouldn't virtuous anger be overall a more fitting response to wrongdoers whose actions express and perpetuate systemic evil? In response, I survey and clarify several ways in which anger can be taken to be virtuous. I then articulate a model of practical selfhood—the dramatic/dialogical model—that aims to accommodate both forgivingness and the virtue of anger for individuals living in non-ideal circumstances. I show how the dramatic/dialogical model responds to a serious worry about anger-entrenchment. I suggest a theological meta-narrative that makes sense simultaneously of the virtues of anger and of forgivingness. This is an important point, because we have a dilemma on our hands. One lesson I draw is that anger is less likely to be a virtue in persons with power and privilege, and more likely to be a virtue in the dispossessed. But then, it would seem that anger could not be had at all by a being with maximal power. God could not show righteous indignation. In response, I argue that divine anger is a sustained and deep divine affective pattern of echoing the pain and rage of oppressed people. The picture that emerges is this: the virtuousness of anger cannot be assessed piecemeal, in separation from larger psychological forces active in one's agency. These in turn depend on the larger meta-narratives, and one of the stories available to those oppressed expresses God's own responses to systemic injustices.

The chapter and the book end by suggesting not only that curative forgivingness is compatible with virtuous anger, but that they can be brought closer together through the concept of normative hope in persons.

2

Bearing Burdens and the Character of Yahweh

"It was no messenger or angel but his presence that saved them;
in his love and in his pity he redeemed them;
he lifted them up and carried them all the days of old."

Isaiah 63:9

A popular conception of God's character is neatly captured in Michael L. Morgan's summary of Judaic thought:

> The biblical God is a lawgiver. Sin is transgression of divine law: it is disobedience to divine command and an affront to God, an act of rebellion. The normative response of God to sin is anger and retribution. The biblical God is a just God, and this justice is a feature of divine life and cosmic order that is canonized in the book of Deuteronomy and expressed extensively throughout the Bible.[1]

Let us refer to this as the classical picture of divine character. If God is primarily a legislator and retributive concerns have pride of place, what should we say of divine forgiveness? Some in the Rabbinic and Christian traditions have proposed that forgiveness is at most a release valve for divine wrath.[2] God necessarily has the disposition to forgive, they opine, but its characteristic function is to temper retribution. According to the classical picture, forgiveness belongs to a framework of mainly forensic concepts: God is essentially cosmic legislator, sin tears the normative fabric of the world and offends God's being, and so, retribution uniquely anchors God's concerns into the universal moral order while forgiveness softens the punishment sinners deserve. Morgan adds:

> Whether or not this compassion results in a reduction of punishment or stay of execution, as it were, there is more to God's response, and this supplement is

---

[1] Morgan 2012: 139.

[2] For a terrific summary of the plurality of positions held by the rabbis on the relationship between divine justice and forgiveness see Urbach 1975. For a sense of how the Christian tradition articulated what I called the classical view see Edwards 1741. Also, one hears echoes of this in the *Westminster* and the *Heidelberg Catechisms*.

Gracious Forgiveness: A Theological Retrieval. Cristian F. Mihut, Oxford University Press. © Cristian F. Mihut 2023.
DOI: 10.1093/oso/9780192873729.003.0002

what forgiveness involves…Forgiving is a surplus that includes a change of attitude, a sense of goodwill, and an overcoming of the sense of being violated, humiliated, or diminished. The Bible does not thematize this surplus, but it does hint in its direction.[3]

On the classical picture then, God's default motivations seem rooted in righteous anger. Forgiveness, "a surplus," dials down retribution, and involves a change in God's self-perception and other-regarding attitudes. As a supplemental, secondary impulse, forgiveness assures that God's majesty remains intact, and that God can continue to show goodwill to sinners.

Contrasting the classical view, I argue here that the Hebrew Scriptures suggest a more ambitious role for divine forgiveness. Forgiveness is not an anomaly at the outskirts of a retributive motivational profile. It is not chiefly the tamer of punitive justice, and not a kind of therapy God needs to get over the sense of being violated. To see the unplumbed and far-reaching extensions of this idea, we shall focus on God's entrenched disposition to forgive: forgivingness. Divine forgivingness implies a stable outpouring of graciousness toward offenders, not to be conceptualized as a mere "surplus" left over after justice has debited most of God's efforts. Forgivingness—the settled disposition to forgive—is an enduring, preemptive, other-focused, deep-seated trait that interacts meaningfully with other gracious divine dispositions, one that explains divine action.[4] And the Bible does thematize it. Diverging from Morgan, we might very well say, *the biblical God is a gracious, curative forgiver. Sin is a burden that weighs down and diminishes offenders and their communities. God's normative response to burdened humans is primarily mercy and a readiness to carry their load.*

My aim in this chapter is to flesh out a conception of divine forgivingness beginning from the image of a sin-bearing God. After considering some central metaphors of forgiveness in the Hebrew Bible, I argue that bearing away iniquity (*nasa awon*) has a unique theological centrality due to its idiomatic frequency, paradigmatic iteration, liturgical depth, and fruitful semantic overtones. Next, I sketch a preliminary account of sin-bearing forgivingness that involves two divine commitments: the commitment to remove the offense from the offender, and the commitment to absorb the consequences of the offense. I show how God absorbs rebellion, using the story of the prophet Jonah as an example. The chapter ends by tackling a lingering objection.

[3] Morgan 2012: 142.
[4] Whenever I use "forgivingness" it always refers to the entrenched disposition to forgive. Forgivingness, the virtue, is conceptually distinct from the act, the process, or even the non-entrenched disposition to forgive. See Roberts 1995.

Hebraic Images of Forgiveness

The Bible speaks in different ways, idioms, and metaphors about divine forgiveness. Among these, three metaphors take the explanatory lead. God is said to cancel the debt of our sins (and the conceptually-related blot out iniquity), to cover the stain of our sin (*kipper*), and to bear away the burden of our sin (*nasa awon*).[5] We should take these seriously. Each image expresses more than a manner of adorning the concept, or a way to make it accessible. Instead, these partially constitute the content of the concept to which they point. They enter the very kernel. These ancient biblical images are primed to sharpen our intuitions and deepen our modern conceptions of forgiveness. A rich metaphor is likely to illuminate forgotten aspects of divine forgivingness, aspects that would remain hidden, unless we quarry its riches.

Before we turn our attention to the centrality of sin-bearing, let us make some preliminary genealogical and contrastive remarks. Even when dislodged from their ancient contexts, these metaphors still abide with us, each in their own way motivating distinct and sometimes competing sets of modern intuitions that seek articulation in various contemporary forgiveness models. Additionally, the images of debt-cancellation and stain-covering bring to light different aspects of forgiveness than those derived from that of sin-bearing, the image whose virtues I want to highlight.

The first image suggests that forgiveness involves the annulment of an economic or legal obligation. Famously, the prophet Isaiah imagines the sin of Israel as a huge national debt accrued toward God, and the Babylonian exile as payment for it.[6] God alone, as the wronged party, has the power to cancel the debt or to forgo litigation: "I, I am He who blots your transgression for my own sake, and I will not remember your sins."[7] Some think this metaphor comes dangerously close to conceptualizing forgiveness as forgetfulness. For instance, Avishai Margalit argues that when faced with a choice between *blotting out* and *crossing out* iniquity, the latter concept seems psychologically and normatively preferable to the former. When a victim blots out a moral debt accrued against her, she commits to forgetting the wrongdoing. On the other hand, crossing it out "leaves traces of error under the crossing-out line."[8] Psychologically, blotting out seems to require of the forgiver, unrealistically, to actively forget or edit one's memories of wrongdoing. Furthermore, it is not intuitively clear how even more passive forms of forgetfulness could be compatible with the divine attribute of omniscience.

---

[5] For *debt-cancellation*, Deuteronomy 15 argues that not canceling debts on the Year of Jubilee incurs guilt. In the NT, see Matthew 6:12. Gary Anderson claims, for instance, "in the New Testament the metaphor of sin as debt was ubiquitous" (Anderson 2009: 31). For *blotting out* see Psalm 51:9. For *kipper* see Psalm 85:2–4, where the idiom occurs side-by-side *nasa awon*. For another central occurrence see Exodus 34:7.

[6] See Isaiah 40:1–2.   [7] Isaiah 43:25.   [8] Margalit 2002: 197.

Additionally, from a normative standpoint, it seems more noble to aim at overcoming the reactive attitudes occasioned by the remembered offense rather than at forgetting the offense. Understanding forgiveness as crossing-out or covering of wrongdoing seems overall preferable to blotting it out.

Unlike the image evoking a legal or economic backdrop, the context for the second metaphor is cultic, rooted in the expiation rite of the Day of Atonement.[9] Once a year, the high priest enters the Holy of Holies and purifies the holy space and objects therein by sprinkling them, covering them (from the Hebrew verb *kipper*) with the blood of a sacrificial goat. Sin is seen here as a pollutant that desecrates holy spaces and the objects therein, so if God is to continue living in the midst of his people, sin must be expunged. As noted, Margalit finds this biblical metaphor fruitful. Covering iniquity, he says, implies crossing-out instead of deleting, and this suggests that in forgiveness the victim faces the offense while forgoing retaliatory pursuits. She continues *to believe* the offense puts a blotch on the history of the offender, but does not allow that stain to figure into her practical deliberations about that person.[10]

Though also rooted in Israel's cultic life, the third image of forgiveness is primarily curative. Surely enough, God is a cosmic judge, and surely enough, God is the transcendent Holy Other. But as emphatically, dominant biblical narratives and liturgies present God as a healer. God heals and unburdens a broken people. Later on in the argument I spell out some important differences between bearing burdens and covering stains, but for now I want to make explicit my motivations for starting from *nasa awon*. I claim that the image of a sin-bearing God reveals neglected but essential aspects of the biblical concept of forgiveness. And because of this, I claim that bearing burdens is important for conceptualizing divine forgivingness. I offer below four main reasons for the centrality of this image.

The Centrality of *Nasa Awon*

I begin with *idiomatic frequency*. *Nasa awon* is used more frequently than any other image of forgiveness in the Hebrew Bible. The English translations rendering it as "forgiveness" obscure the literal Hebraic expression of "carrying burdens away." According to Gary Anderson, the most common way of expressing human

---

[9] See Leviticus 16.

[10] Nicholas Wolterstorff's account also seems to rely upon this biblical metaphor (Wolterstorff 2011: ch. 15). In his view, to victimize another puts a blot on one's personal *and* moral history. In forgiving, we no longer hold the offense against the wrongdoer in the sense that *we treat him as if* the offense put a blot only on his personal history but not his moral history. The blot is covered but not erased; the transgression is remembered but no longer effectual in the practical deliberations that involve the offender.

sinfulness in the First Temple Period is in terms of a burden or a weight, and the idiom of bearing away a sin "predominates over its nearest competitor by more than six to one."[11]

Theologically, even more significant than the recurrence rate is what I call *paradigmatic centrality*. The most intimate portrait of God in the Hebrew Bible is revealed at Mount Sinai. It is here that Yahweh claims Israel as God's own. It is here that Israel falls for another deity, the proverbial golden calf. It is here that Moses asks to see God's face in the aftermath of something akin to marital betrayal. It is here, as God shows up robed in divine glory, that Moses hears the declaration of divine attributes, "God, showing-mercy, showing-favor [grace], long-suffering in anger, abundant in loyalty and faithfulness [truthfulness], keeping loyalty to the thousandth [generation], bearing iniquity, rebellion and sin, yet not clearing, clearing [the guilty], calling-to-account the iniquity of the fathers upon sons and upon sons' sons, to the third and fourth [generation]."[12]

Biblical scholars refer to this list of divine self-attributions as the "grace-formula."[13] Because *nasa awon* makes this list, God's readiness to bear Israel's rebellion and guilt is part of God's keenest self-disclosure. Crucially, the grace-formula is rehearsed throughout the entire Hebrew Bible, in the Law and the Psalms, in the major and the minor Prophets.[14] This refrain of coordinated attributes structures and encodes the Hebraic self-understanding and their understanding of the kind of deity that is Yahweh.

God's readiness to bear iniquity, alongside graciousness, faithfulness, mercy, and slowness to anger are introduced at *the* foundational moment in Israel's history as a nation. These qualities are uniquely revelatory and explanatory of God's action in the context of Israel's original betrayal. Yahweh is singularly faithful, compassionate, and forgiving. If God bears away transgression here, God will do it anywhere.

Different traditions have narratives that distinctively reveal the moral excellences of these cultures.[15] As Robert C. Roberts notes, some narratives become not just illustrative but constitutive of a people's self-understanding and moral identity.[16] Roberts illustrates this point by reflecting on the way the Hebraic moral identity is constituted by the Exodus story:

---

[11] Anderson 2009: 17. He finds 108 instances of *nasa awon*, 17 instances of *salakh*, and 6 instances of *kipper*.

[12] Exodus 34:6–7 in the translation of Fox 1997: 455.

[13] About the provenance of the notion "grace-formula" see Wöhrle 2009: 6–7, footnote 9.

[14] See the various iterations and interesting developments of this refrain in *The Law*: Numbers 14:17–19; *The Psalms*: Psalm 103:6–14, Psalm 145:8–9, Psalm 86:5, and Psalm 85:2–4; *Major Prophets*: Isaiah 63:7–9; and *Minor Prophets*: Joel 2:12–14; Jonah 3:9, 4:2; Nah 1:2b, 3a; Mal 1:9a; Hos 4:10; Joel 4:21; Micah 7:18–20.

[15] Cf. Roberts 2012; MacIntyre 1984; and Nussbaum 1990.   [16] Roberts 2012: 179–80.

If an ordinary narrative displays the self-understanding of its characters, this one structures a self-understanding in its believing reader or hearer. This narrative does not just exemplify a moral tradition, in the way that, say, the characters of Alyosha and Father Zossima in Dostoevsky's *The Brothers Karamazov* exemplify Russian Orthodox Christianity and the virtues of its most exemplary adherents; it founds one or at least constitutes a crucial stage in its founding... The Hebrew sense of self that is involved in one way or another in all the Jewish virtues—hospitality to the foreigner, generosity, trust and humility, the praise of God, just treatment of fellows, contrition, truthfulness, marital fidelity, honoring of parents, and so forth—is in essential part the sense of belonging to the people whom God made his own in this special way.[17]

I want to extend Roberts's point. In the Exodus story, God's claiming Israel as his own at Sinai, the subsequent betrayal, and God's response to it are, if not *the* constitutional events in the Hebraic self-consciousness, then surely among its most significant markers. But they are also paradigmatic episodes for grasping how Israel sees God's moral character. It is not incidental to the story that Israel abandons Yahweh subsequent to being claimed at Sinai. The dispositions the grace-formula ascribes to God are no mere rhetorical flourish. Sin-bearing, mercy, eternal faithfulness, and short-lived anger define essentially God's moral self in relation to fickle Israel. These are not disposable, contingent, or revisable qualities. They are *the* interpretative lenses that will filter Israel's subsequent history with Yahweh. Though the molten golden calf in the shadow of Sinai recalls the national disposition toward idolatry, God remains faithful and bears away their rebellion. And when successions of rebellions, idolatries, and exiles will threaten to unravel at once the sense of God's presence and the very fiber of Hebraic identity, Israel will deepen, sometimes in innovative ways, the memory of a loving and forgiving God.[18]

We have surveyed the idiomatic frequency and theologically paradigmatic centrality of sin-bearing. Thirdly, forgiveness understood as God bearing away iniquity has *liturgical and cultic depth*. We have just seen how, iterated in the theologically central grace-formula, sin-bearing points to a nonnegotiable moral quality of Yahweh. But some of the singular and irreducible meanings of the image are additionally unveiled on the Day of Atonement (Yom Kippur), the yearly ritual enacted for the forgiveness of sins. The ritual reinforces in distinctive and fruitful cognitive and emotive ways Israel's experience of divine forgiveness. That is to say, the ritual deepens the theological and existential meanings of *nasa awon*.

I have mentioned some theological resonances of *kipper*, the cultic image of forgiveness associated with the first rite of Yom Kippur, the sacrifice of the

---

[17] Ibid. 180.
[18] See in footnote 14 a sample of the biblical texts that recall the initial grace-formula.

expiatory goat. As it is well-known, the second rite involves a scapegoat. In the cultic action, the high priest places the sins of the people upon its head, then, weighed down by them, the scapegoat is driven into the wilderness. The context here suggests that the metaphor of sin-bearing is primarily curative.[19] If the expiation rite sees sin as a heavy miasma or a polluting smog "that creeps into God's presence... and wraps itself around the holy vessels," the scapegoating rite understands it as a concrete weight, a burdensome disease that blights people.[20] The language of covering stains evokes primarily a cultic context where sin is a contaminant that blocks a holy God from residing among people. By contrast, the evocations of bearing-away iniquity reveal God as the paradigmatic healer and deliverer of a blighted and burdened people. Leviticus 16 goes out of its way to announce that the cure is total: the scapegoat carries away *all* iniquities, *all* transgressions, and *all* sin.[21] Developing this cultic theme of healing, Isaiah's Suffering Servant—the paradigmatic agent of God's deliverance for exiled Israel—is said to have "borne our infirmities and carried our diseases."[22] More generally, the Psalms and the Prophets pervasively argue that God heals by removing sin.[23]

From the liturgical context of the Day of Atonement we can extract one focal similarity and four main differences between conceptualizing sin as pollutant and as burden. The similarity hints that sin is a concrete reality inherently carrying within itself the seeds of serious personal, communal, or environmental degradation. Unlike the idea of debt, which is an abstraction, both pollution and disease are concrete realities that affect people, their social interactions, and even the natural environments in which they live.[24]

At the same time, the salient differences between sin-as-burden and sin-as-pollution motivate distinct nuances and extensions of divine forgiveness. First, regarding the target object, pollutants affect the presence of God (they pollute holy places and infect holy things) while burdens affect people. Second, regarding phenomenology, the subjective experience of sin as a burden and a disease *feels differently* than experiencing sin as a stain. A person may enjoy the benefits of an unburdened moral conscience, though the same person may be treated as a pariah in her community. Alternatively, we may enjoy an untarnished social recognition, while afflicted by broken relationships or a guilty conscience. Third, regarding the nature and consequences of sin, Leviticus understands non-intentional and casual wrongdoings to generate impurities; by contrast, deliberate and wanton transgressions *burden* communities and individual transgressors. Finally, regarding the vehicle and direction of sin-removal, it is a consecrated and therefore pure animal

---

[19] See Carmichael 2006.   [20] Hamilton 2005: 274.   [21] Leviticus 16:21.
[22] Isaiah 53:4.   [23] Cf. Psalm 103; Psalm 51; and Isaiah 43.
[24] See Chapter 3 where I give an argument that "bearing burdens" could be taken as a more fundamental metaphor for sin than indebtedness.

that covers iniquity, as its blood disinfects the spaces closest to the heart of God's action in Israel: the Holy of Holies. But the scapegoat becomes impure and accursed, as it hauls wantonness far from the holiest place back to its source in the netherworld.[25]

In light of these differences, an argument could be made that *nasa awon* works at a more fundamental level than *kipper*. Instead of merely concealing successive accumulations of impurities that essentially remain there, the scapegoating rite decisively removes the most egregious wrongs from the camp. For my current purposes, I do not need to defend this stronger thesis. My argument does not require *nasa awon* to function more fundamentally than *kipper*. All I need to show is that bearing-away sin points to a distinctive and irreducible mechanism for expressing divine forgiveness on Yom Kippur. And the cultic evidence I presented bears this out.

I must deal at this point with an important objection. Some will grant the uniqueness and irreducibility of the mechanism, but object that the scapegoat cultus provides *the wrong* explanation for forgiveness. Avishai Margalit argues, for instance, that the picture is bad on two fronts, one cognitive and one emotive. The scapegoat picture is cognitively bad because it "suggests theurgist magic—the art of compelling the gods in some supernatural causal way to do what the magician wants them to do, in this case to displace human sins onto the head of the goat."[26] As Margalit sees it, the badness of the ritual lies in causing and intensifying superstition. The worry is that the participants in the ritual come to accept the false belief that Aaron's action and the goat's vanishing in the wilderness are *causally efficacious in enacting forgiveness*. And why is the scapegoat picture emotively bad? Margalit explains:

> In the case of the scapegoat, the picture is misleading because we tie the wrong emotions to it. A goat is not an appropriate model for the forgiveness of sin because it is not a creature that we see as expressing innocence, even if it actually is an innocent creature. The "servant of God" of whom Isaiah says "The Lord laid upon him the guilt of us all" is compared not to a goat but to a lamb or an ewe. These are animals that, unlike the goat, are seen as representing innocence. One must separate the sheep from the goats. The scapegoat has entered Western culture as a creature that people blame and punish for sins it did not commit— sins that were actually committed by those doing the blaming and the punishing. But the scapegoat, even if totally blameless, is not a symbol of innocence. It

---

[25] Gary Anderson helpfully notes: "As Jacob Milgrom, the great scholar of the book of Leviticus, has argued, the goat that has been burdened with these sins 'is in reality returning evil to its source, the netherworld.' Because this area was thought to be beyond the reach of God, the sins would fall outside the range of his supervisory powers. Once God could no longer see them, it is as if they ceased to exist" (Anderson 2009: 23).

[26] Margalit 2002: 187.

generally represents radical otherness—the different, the totally strange and threatening. This is why it is so easy to place blame and sin on it. This change in the picture of the scapegoat upon entering Western culture is not a coincidence. It shows that the goat was always a bad model for the idea of forgiveness and carrying sins.[27]

Margalit sums up the challenge: "There are two different levels on which we test a picture. One is the cognitive level: Does it represent or strengthen illusions? The other is the emotive level: Is it linked to appropriate feelings? The picture of the scapegoat fails both tests."[28]

I respond, first, by questioning Margalit's unduly restricted etiological interpretation of the scapegoating rite. By focusing on the literal transfer of human sins onto the scapegoat, Margalit obscures its richer cognitive and affective meanings. He underestimates the extent to which in Israel's collective imagination this act may have been more indicative or symbolic rather than causative and constitutive. It would be surprising if Aaron's actions or the goat's vanishing were taken to obscure or replace the ultimate agency of God. The mature participants perceive Aaron placing sin-burdens on the head of the goat, and the goat rushing toward the wilderness. But it's unlikely they attribute the main causal responsibility for being forgiven to Aaron or to the goat. Instead, these actors are seen either as parts of a larger process of forgiveness enacted by God or symbols of that reality. To restate this idea in Aristotelian jargon, if the participants grasp at all the point of the practice, they see God as the efficient, the formal, and the final cause of the atonement ritual. So even though Aaron, the goat, and their acts are components in the total causal story, they fulfill only the material conditions of the process by which God, the main causal contributor, takes care of sin.

Another way to conceptualize the ritual is to distinguish between essential and contingent elements in this curative framework. The essential elements may be these: sin is a concrete burden or disease affecting persons, God unburdens persons from their sins by a concrete way of transfer, God is the ultimate agent dispensing away with sin. Among the contingent elements: Aaron saying a prayer, the high priest placing his hands on the head of some goat, some goat running toward the wilderness. As I argue in Chapter 3, these contingent elements, significantly, point forward toward the Messiah, God-embodied, the only one who has the standing and authority to dispense with sin.

The scapegoating ritual then does offer us fruitful ways to conceptualize the providential provision and the generous causal involvement of God in sin-bearing. Additionally, it offers ways to anchor fitting affective reactions in response to God's actions. When the participant perceives the scapegoat vanishing into the

---

[27] Ibid. 188.   [28] Ibid.

wilderness, she grasps spatially the reality of being separated from God, and this image helps her feel in her guts, as it were, the weight of sin and the angst of exile. Because she *grasps* that God's grace is responsible for her sin-divested, guilt-free status, she *feels* gratitude. Thankfulness is intensified as she enters imaginatively into the skin of the laden-and-displaced animal that bears away the consequences of *her* own transgression. Due to an unduly narrow etiological framing, Margalit is inattentive to the symbolic order that gives the scapegoat ritual rich cognitive *and* emotive content.

But perhaps this first reply is too general or speculative to satisfy Margalit's challenge. Let me briefly consider some particular interpretations of the rite. I do not have to argue in favor of a single best symbolic interpretation. The rite lends itself to different (and sometimes incommensurable) interpretations. A reductive spirit is ill-suited to dealing with metaphor and ritual. Nonetheless, there are worthy candidates that fruitfully unpack this liturgical picture. One main family of symbolic interpretations focuses on the pedagogical function of the rite. Instead of assigning meaning to the discrete ritual pieces by setting them in a coherent narrative frame, this first strategy recommends drawing a practical or pedagogical lesson from an abstracted, reified picture of the ritual. As Maimonides says, "... but these ceremonies are of a symbolic character, and serve to impress men with a certain idea, and to induce them to repent; as if to say, we have freed ourselves of our previous deeds, have cast them behind our backs, and removed them from us as far as possible."[29]

More concretely, an alternative family of interpretations takes the scapegoat rite as commemorative. The ritual recalls seminal narratives or historical events that ground the practice of repentance. Recall Margalit's worry that the goat expresses the radical other, the totally strange and the threatening, making it a symbol inappropriate for pegging our aspirations of forgiveness. On some commemorative interpretations, the goat evokes a specific cognitive content, referring to a precise event or sequence of events, in a way that elicits *appropriate* emotive reactions. Two examples illustrate this. One interpretation argues that the scapegoat reenacts the transgression of Israel's sons against their brother Joseph.[30] Recounting the deceptive use of a goat by their forefathers, the rite intends to induce the participants to abandon deception and to confess transgression in search of divine forgiveness.

Another commemorative interpretation recalls the Exodus deliverance. It harks back to Israel's being freed from Egypt in order to worship God in the wilderness.

---

[29] Maimonides 1956: 366.

[30] Calum Carmichael says: "It seems to me that the sinbearing goat going into the wilderness to Azazel is primarily a rite of remembrance. It harks back to the brothers' deception in a number of ways. It points to their location in the wilderness where they perpetrate their offense. It recalls both the placement of the offense upon the goat, and the transformation of this domestic animal into a dangerous one" (Carmichael 2002: 177).

Here the goat represents a perpetually incorrigible Israel who goes out into the wilderness to meet Yahweh the liberator, the God who graciously carries her and relieves her burdens.[31] It makes sense, of course, that on the Day of Atonement a rite would recall the historically-laden, collective disposition toward backtracking and rebellion. The goat is a mnemonic device that helps the participant contextualize her own personal history of sin within the larger, national narrative of fickleness and transgression, a narrative that simultaneously reenacts by striking contrast, Yahweh's faithfulness and forgiveness.

To sum up these observations, if the rite functions pedagogically or commemoratively, then the participant has any number of interesting ways to reconcile *the perception* of a goat running toward the wilderness, with *the belief* that God is the one who carries the burdens of his people, with *the desire* to confess transgressions, desire accompanied by appropriate *feelings* of remorse and guilt. And that is to say that Margalit's dual-challenge fails.

A final response. Regardless of how the original worshippers frame the scapegoat rite, biblical writers reflecting back on Yom Kippur express that God is the main agent disposing of Israel's iniquity. Consider prophet Micah voicing an iteration of the grace-formula:

Who is a God like you, pardoning iniquity and passing over the transgression of the remnant of your possession? He does not retain his anger forever, because he delights in showing clemency. He will again have compassion on us; he will tread our iniquities under foot. You will cast all our sins into the depths of the sea.

(Micah 7:18–19)

Micah envisions God as Israel's quintessential sin-bearer. The image here is functionally equivalent to the goat dispensing Israel's sins into the godforsaken wilderness. Sin is explicitly conceptualized as a concrete burden to be hauled and dumped into a domain representing chaos, oblivion, and the absence of God. Strikingly, not a goat, but God's own self, carries out this mission.

Similarly, consider Psalm 103, another creative improvisation on the grace-formula:

The Lord works vindication and justice for all who are oppressed.

He made known his ways to Moses, his acts to the people of Israel.

The Lord is merciful and gracious, slow to anger and abounding in steadfast love.

He will not always accuse, nor will he keep his anger forever.

---

[31] Cf. Pinker 2007. Pinker argues that the Yom Kippur ritual suggests God was originally approached both in the Tabernacle and the wilderness, because Yahweh was conceived to inhabit both places.

He does not deal with us according to our sins, nor repay us according to our iniquities.

For as the heavens are high above the earth, so great is his steadfast love toward those who fear him;

as far as the east is from the west, so far he removes our transgressions from us.

As a father has compassion for his children, so the Lord has compassion for those who fear him.

For he knows how we were made; he remembers that we are dust.

(Psalm 103:6–14)

As in the Micah text, God is the agent carrying transgression "as far as the east is from the west." The imagery in the last couple of stanzas quoted implies that sin is a burden, though the larger context of the psalm assumes a legal background where sin is a debt owed to Yahweh, the righteous and compassionate judge. There are at least two noteworthy observations here. First, the characterization of God's separating people from their sins evokes the spatial separation that the scapegoat puts between sinners and their transgressions. But equally significant is Bradley C. Gregory's observation that "the psalmist uses the spatial sense in order to give expression to the legal concept."[32] This suggests that the scapegoat imagery is so ingrained in the poet's repertoire, and it references divine forgiveness so perspicuously, that he uses it as the given on which to hook the explanation for why God forgoes legal action against the people. *The image of sin-bearing and the cultic action of scapegoating explain and justify why God drops the case against Israel.* We also get a glimpse inside God's motivational profile. The God who identifies with his people's burdened condition unravels the demands of the prosecution through an action that strongly resembles or enacts the scapegoating rite. The sentence is commuted because, fundamentally, God is a compassionate healer more than an exacting judge. But I am getting ahead of myself.

In sum, I have given two main reasons for the liturgical depth of *nasa awon*. First, I argued that it expresses an irreplaceable and irreducible mechanism for divine forgiveness on the Day of Atonement. Second, I argued that this rite, which distinctly deepens the metaphor, reenacts fertile scripts of forgiveness. Even while bypassing explicit belief formation, the image in its cultic context evokes rich cognitive and emotive contents that make present and concrete to the audience the reality of divine forgiveness. Through dense symbolism and scripted action-sequences, the ritual immerses participants in rich narrative contexts of forgiveness.[33] Participants feel what it is like to betray a brother, and then to be received in mercy by him; they experience what it is like to wander lost and

---

[32] Gregory 2006: 551.
[33] For an insightful description and analysis of liturgical immersion see Cuneo 2014a.

rebellious in the wilderness, only to be met by a faithful guide; they understand experientially that their burdens have been lifted and their transgressions dispensed with. The unifying thread of these scripts is that God is the main agent of forgiveness. God, like old Joseph, shows grace to treacherous brothers. Yahweh meets a fledgling and recalcitrant Israel in the wilderness and carries him to safety. So, when a worshipper is burdened by personal or communal sin, he gains experiential knowledge of a God poised to carry all treachery to a place of no return.

In this section, I have given three reasons for the centrality of *nasa awon*: its frequency, its theological significance in Israel's foundational episodes, and its liturgical depth. To conclude this section, I mention a fourth reason: some of its semantic and conceptual overtones. The metaphor has a rich imagistic and conceptual range, denotations mined creatively in various liberationist contexts in the Law and the Prophets.

Sin-bearing evokes a broad and deep divine disposition to deliver Israel not only from their own sin, but also from the oppression of others. Using the same idiom, several texts emphasize that God has been carrying Israel away from Egypt and throughout their wilderness trek as if "on an eagle's wings."[34] God bears away Israel prior to their capital sins of idolatry and grumbling. God is the kind of deity that lifts up his people away from the oppression of others, just as he lifts up transgression from them.

The depth of God's dispositions to redeem Israel by lifting them up can be explained through the interaction between divine empathy and sympathy. Some texts emphasize that God's deliverance is rooted in God's pathos for his people. Consider how the prophet Isaiah, in an iteration of the grace-formula, makes empathetic suffering the causal explanation for divine deliverance: "So He became their Savior. In all their affliction He was afflicted, and the angel of His presence saved them; In His love and in His mercy He redeemed them, and He lifted them and carried them all the days of old."[35] From the Egyptian slavery to the Babylonian captivity, God is so intimately attuned to Israel's suffering, that he saves, redeems, and carries them all along. The beloved's suffering has a direct impact on God's own motivations.[36]

---

[34] Cf. Exodus 19:4–6 and Deuteronomy 32:10–11. The context implies that a standard disposition of Yahweh is to carry Israel, even apart from transgressive contexts.

[35] Some may worry here that the simple reference to God as the bearer of Israel's suffering is complicated by the term "angel of his presence." A couple of responses. First, given this particular translation (NASB), God seems to be the direct subject who experiences Israel's suffering, as well as the one who loves, shows mercy, and bears her. The angel of his presence appears as the direct subject of the act of redemption. Second, even if God's identity is more fluidly connected to the angel of his presence, clearly the latter's agency is an expression of God's agency. The angel does not perform actions that God would not perform. Finally, and most interestingly, apparently the original Hebrew is ambiguous. Alternative translations render it as a contrastive intensification: "It was no messenger or angel, but his presence that saved them" (NRSV). If this is the original intent, saving and carrying Israel proceed from the very center of God's being.

[36] As many have noticed, God experientially knows the pains of Israel in Egypt. Cf. Exodus 2:23–5 and Exodus 3:7–8: God "hears," "remembers," "sees," "knows" their groaning pains. Cf. Judges 2:18.

God's empathetic, suffering *alongside* Israel is vividly embodied in the sufferings of the Hebrew prophets—God's representatives and messengers.[37] But we must point out another significant resonance of divine sin-bearing: *its substitutionary and representative dimensions.* If God carries Israel's burdens *alongside of* them, God also carries their burdens *for* them. Terence Fretheim helpfully points to two stages of transfer and representation. First, he sees representative suffering as pervasively interwoven in Israel's cultic and religious life. The scapegoat, the priest, the prophet, and the Suffering Servant are all representatives of Israel that bear the sins *for* the people.[38] Second, he argues that these special individuals can engage in substitutionary suffering only because they are representatives of God. They fulfill a role God had been effecting and carrying through all along. God is the ultimate sufferer *for* the people.[39] I pick up this theme in Chapter 3 when I argue for the essential double-representative role of Jesus.

Sin-bearing also evokes the glory of God. The Hebrew word for glory (*kabod*) means literally weight or weightiness. Ancient kings would show their glory, their weight, as they flashed their armor in the streets at the outset of a military campaign. When Moses asks God to reveal his glory at Sinai in the prequel to the grace-formula episode, he perhaps expects a dazzling display of martial majesty. What Moses gets instead is a list of divine attributes, concluding with the picture of God weighed down by Israel's transgression. Perhaps the narrator is telling us that "the weight" of God distinctly consists in the readiness to be weighed down by the burdens of others, especially those of the most vulnerable. And if the connection between divine glory and the fate of the vulnerable is merely suggested here, it is surely developed elsewhere in the Bible.[40]

Finally, sin-bearing evokes a restoration and elevation of one's deepest identity. When the high priest enters into the Holy of Holies, he is weighed down by a golden breast plate covering his heart on which the names of the sons of Israel are inscribed.[41] Exodus mentions another essential piece of the priestly wardrobe, a gold-plated attachment to Aaron's turban, to carry the guilt of the people of Israel.[42] The idea seems to be that in order for "the sons of Israel" to be elevated restored and consecrated into God's presence, the priest must absorb and be weighed down by the burden of their guilt.

We have seen how sin-bearing evokes thus a number of theologically profound responses: God lifts up his people from oppression, God suffers alongside *and* on behalf of his people, God restores and consecrates through a representative the very identity of his people, and perhaps God's very glory is directly implicated in

---

[37] For a resonant example of empathetic, prophetic suffering see Jeremiah 4:19.

[38] Fretheim 1984: ch. 9 and ch. 10. Cf. Exodus 28:29; Leviticus 10:17; and Ezekiel 4:4–6.

[39] "The servant of God thus assumes the role which God himself has played. Just as it entailed suffering for the servant, it must have entailed suffering for God. By bearing the sins of the people over a period of time, God suffers in some sense on their behalf. By holding back on the judgment they deserve, and carrying their sins on his shoulders, God chooses the road of suffering-for" (Fretheim 1984: 140).

[40] Cf. Psalm 8.   [41] Exodus 28:29.   [42] Exodus 28:36–8.

the disposition to forgive. In the next chapter we will note the profound ways in which the New Testament, especially the Gospel of Mark, letter of Hebrews, 1 Peter, and some of Paul's writings, assigns to Jesus of Nazareth the divine role of lifting up the sin of Israel—and of the world—in a way that combines the scapegoating and the priestly function. This is to say that the narrative arc of the Christian Scriptures summits in the realization that the divine agent responsible for global sin-bearing is identical to Jesus of Nazareth.

From Image to Account

In the previous section I have argued that *nasa awon* is a frequent, theologically paradigmatic, liturgically deep, and semantically resonant metaphor. We are now well-positioned to garner some insights and characterize sin-bearing divine for-givingness. Observing its place in the grace-formula and drawing upon the imagery of Yom Kippur, I first define the divine disposition to forgive primarily as a distinctive mode of God's *hesed* (divine faithfulness) that involves two interlocking commitments: God's commitment to put distance between indivi-duals or communities and their sins, and God's commitment to absorb into Godself the consequences of iniquity. Second, I contrast sympathetically the *nasa awon* conception of forgiveness with one derived from *kipper*.

I begin by noting that the place of *nasa awon* among the other divine attributes in the grace-formula invites a network characterization of this divine trait. By network characterization I mean that sin-bearing forgivingness is elucidated in relation to other attributes that constitute God's character. Though I sort out divine dispositions along cognitive, volitional, and affective dimensions, these simply reflect helpful taxonomies. But the taxonomy should not be taken to carve out divine nature at its joints.

Wittgenstein argued that the grammar of a concept is given by its patterns of usage. We pick up the concept "slab" by noting how it functions in various linguistic contexts in which it is instantiated, such as when we speak of "a slab of meat," or "a slab of stone," or "a wooden slab." Similarly, says Robert C. Roberts, the grammar of a trait "which may vary from one moral tradition to another . . . determines such things as the kind of actions and emotions (*in situ*), of motives and reasons, that characteristically exemplify the trait."[43] In the grace-formula, *nasa awon* accompanies other quintessential divine attitudes such as graciousness, loving-kindness (relational loyalty), compassion (mercy), long-suffering (slowness to anger), and truthfulness. These give us at least a provisional

---

[43] Roberts 2012: 177.

map of the divine moral character. Since forgivingness is introduced alongside these attitudes (and not others), they together point to a "grammar" of the trait. I propose then that the content and function of divine forgivingness is determined in part by reference to the emblematic divine cognitions, affections, and volitions recited in the grace-formula.

Divine forgivingness is defined in part by reference to divine cognitions, such as truthfulness. This may be taken to involve a complete, compassionate, and undistorted knowledge of transgressors, of circumstances related to sin, of general and specific consequences of sin, and of God's own inner responses to sin and sinner. Divine truthfulness then is co-instantiated with, and part of the grammar of, forgivingness. God could not be forgiving without being truthful in the sense explained above.

Divine forgivingness is also accompanied by characteristic divine affections. Unburdened by the need of a philosophical defense, the grace-formula simply identifies mercy, anger, and long-suffering as divine affections.[44] Furthermore, the grace-formula confers a certain priority to favorable affections such as divine mercy and long-suffering over negative attitudes such as anger and accusation. The priority of favorable affections can be fleshed out in three distinct ways. First, favorable affections are more enduring than anger and accusation. The text implies that there is an expiration date on anger—it lasts to the third or fourth generation—but not on divine mercy, since it endures to the thousandth generation. The permanence of favorable affections suggests they are the default setting of God's sensibility, while wrath expresses a bounded and transient reaction to sin.

Second, the abidance and pervasiveness of favorable affections suggests that divine compassion runs motivationally deeper than anger. This is true in virtue of a structural, non-contingent feature of divine agency. God's long-range plans tend to align with divine mercy over against wrath. Finally, the favorable affections contextualize, modulate, and permeate the negative attitudes themselves. "Long-suffering in his anger," says the grace-formula. Divine wrath is neither an expression of personal vengeance nor an objective, uninvolved disposition to dish out just deserts. Though God's anger flares, in paradigmatic biblical episodes, divine grieving flanks its onset and divine regret and suffering its closure.[45] And if grieving and regret are aspects of compassion, paradigmatic divine anger seems framed, measured, and infused through and through by mercy and love. Drawing

---

[44] To some it may sound surprising that "long-suffering" picks out an emotional disposition. Literally "long of pinions," the expression is almost always used in the Hebrew Bible to characterize feelings, specifically as a way of describing an emotion that counterbalances or slows down anger.

[45] For instance, God's judgment before the flood is framed by divine grief (Genesis 6:6). After the flood, God also expresses a form of regret (see Genesis 8:21). Furthermore, in the renewal of God's covenant with Noah from Genesis 9, we may see an intensification of divine suffering. God commits to carrying even more of the human burdens after his judgment. Cf. on divine regret van Wijk-Bos 2005: 234–42.

on the analysis of a number of "divine wrath" texts, Fretheim even goes as far as to claim, "lament is always an integral aspect of the wrath of God."[46]

We have seen then some of its cognitive and affective dimensions, but the essence of sin-bearing divine forgivingness engages God's capacity to keep commitments, God's *hesed* (read: loving-kindness or covenantal faithfulness). While clearly engaging and reinforcing divine mercy, it is more than a mere affective inclination. *Hesed* is a stable and permanent commitment to act lovingly toward Israel. Recall the gripping iteration of the grace-formula prophet from Micah: "He does not retain his anger forever because he delights in showing clemency [*hesed*]. He will again have compassion on us; he will tread our iniquities under foot. You will cast all our sins into the depths of the sea."[47] God's favorable affections sustain divine *hesed* and vice versa in ways that outstrip human notions of interpersonal faithfulness. It is of a different order and magnitude. Any person would be within their rights to break covenant with an unfaithful partner. Yet, time and again, God is proclaimed to be everlastingly loving-kind and faithful, precisely in contexts of recurring betrayals. And precisely because Israel seems pathological in pursuing affairs with sundry neighboring deities, God's *hesed* stretches beyond the comprehensible.

I am inclined to take sin-bearing forgivingness as an expression of divine loving-kindness, because *hesed* fixes the contours of divine agency. In the jargon of Harry Frankfurt, *hesed* is volitionally necessary for God.[48] This means that loving-kindness fixes the boundaries, the limits of God's agency. Loving-kindness is a higher-order attitude that serves a regulative function in God's motivational profile. Yahweh would not be Yahweh, were he to act in ways inconsistent with loving-kindness. *Hesed* is not, as it were, just another item, not even "first among equals" in the divine psychology. Rather, it designates the very shape of God's decisional profile, the control tower advising God to throw God's weight behind some attitudes rather than others. And given the centrality of *hesed*, God is predisposed to identify with favorable affections and, as it were, dial-down negative affections. Because God is essentially loving-kind, God is the kind of agent who identifies with mercy and alienates retribution.

There is good biblical evidence to draw an intimate link between *hesed* and sin-bearing forgivingness. Return to the psalmist:

> For as the heavens are high above the earth, so great is his steadfast love toward those who fear him;
>
> as far as the east is from the west, so far he removes our transgressions from us.
>
> (Psalm 103:11–12)

---

[46] Fretheim 1984: 110.   [47] Micah 7:18.   [48] See Frankfurt 1998 and Frankfurt 2004.

I mentioned above that in the wider context of this psalm the forensic idiom of forgiveness is rooted in the cultic image of dispensing with iniquity.[49] God forgoes legal action against Israel *because* he is a God who carries iniquities. God does not extract the due legal obligation *because* God is a healer. Here I want to emphasize the poetic parallelism that expands the notion of divine faithfulness into that of forgivingness. In the poem, the vertical expansiveness of steadfast love maps onto the horizontal distance God sets between people and their sins. The poetic device urges us to take seriously the possibility of an internal connection between the two divine dispositions: either the two are identical; or forgivingness is an intensification of *hesed*; or both are different expressions of the same underlying divine commitment; or, at the very least, though distinct, the two function analogously.

In any case, it seems we have good reason to understand divine forgivingness as intimately associated with *hesed*. Can we say more about the content of this divine steadfastness? I think we can, especially when we unpack the thick descriptions inherent in the scapegoating rite and the semantic associations of *nasa awon*. These imply at least two things: first, that God sets a distance between people and their sins so that now they are de facto unburdened, rid of their diseases; and second, that God himself is now burdened with the consequences of sinfulness. I suggest, then, that the distinctive content of sin-bearing forgivingness is given by two interlocking commitments: (*Ci*) God's commitment to set a distance between individuals or communities and their sins, and (*Cii*) God's commitment to absorb into Godself the consequences of iniquity.

That forgivingness implies something like *Ci* is generally, if not universally, accepted. It is hard to see how an individual is forgiving, if she does not regard her offenders in some way detachable from their offenses. As I noted, the Bible celebrates a God inclined to see sinners in a sympathetic and empathetic light. God prioritizes the circumstances that enable him to construe offenses as peripheral to the agency of offenders, and sinners as subjects of a continual goodwill, even when the offense is ingrained in their character. As we will see in a moment, God maintains goodwill toward Jonah, even though the latter displays a nontrivial, consistent, and entrenched pattern of rebellion against God.

Interestingly, *kipper*, the image of covering sin, can also be taken to imply a specific expression of *Ci*. *Kipper* indicates that the offense is disregarded without being forgotten.[50] God covers the shame of Adam and Eve with animal skins, and the guilt of Cain with a mark intended to protect him from being killed. By covering their shame and guilt, God construes these first offenders as continued recipients of divine benevolence. But the cover itself draws attention to their offending status. In the conceptual framework where sin is understood as pollution and stain, the remaining traces of transgression require the exile of the agent.

---

[49] Gregory 2006: 549–51.   [50] Cf. Margalit 2002: 188–200.

These stories suggest then that *kipper* is part of a conceptual network that essentially involves exile and repentance. And the interpretative tradition has inferred that only repentance or remorse affords a "non-magical way of undoing the past."[51] *Kipper* implies that God's commitment to fully separate us from our sin depends upon our commitment to separate ourselves from it.

But if *Cii* informs *Ci*, then *nasa awon* suggests a more ambitious conception of forgiveness than *kipper*. The image of the high priest lifting up into Yahweh's holiest presence the names of Israel's tribes alongside the weight of their collective guilt constitutes a compelling image of God's decisive initiative in forgiveness. Though human remorse may generally trigger divine forgiveness, to claim that the latter depends upon the former is an overreach. Making divine forgivingness dependent upon the thinness, double-mindedness, and rationalization that attend (with psychological regularity) human repentance seems to me inadequate. If anything, the dependence relation runs the other way. We can only repent and lament our sinfulness due to God's robust commitment to separate us from it. Our most earnest and sustained efforts of repentance are feeble or conflicted responses to a prior and abundant divine grace.

Additionally, if divine lament for our recidivist and rebellious condition shapes divine sensibility, God remains committed to God's people even in the absence of our occurrent or dispositional remorse. Hosea 11 illustrates this. Pictured as a loving mother, Yahweh recalls teaching an infant Israel to walk, healing him when he stumbles, and nurturing him. But now, Israel has become an obstinate and deviant teenager, "bent on turning away from me." For a moment God entertains the notion to exile Israel back to Egypt and Assyria, lands that signify disintegration of identity. But that's just a passing thought. Yahweh is defined by reference to *hesed*. This loving commitment to the remorseless rebel, seemingly an expression of divine holiness, explains three interrelated divine actions: God absorbs into Godself the consequences of Israel's rebellion, God outpours compassion, God suppresses judicial action. By a holy and incomprehensible steadfast love, God would rather suffer Israel's deviancy than inflict pain on him:

> How can I give you up, Ephraim?
> How can I hand you over, O Israel?
> How can I make you like Admah?
> How can I treat you like Zeboiim?
> My heart recoils within me; my compassion grows warm and tender.
> I will not execute my fierce anger; I will not again destroy Ephraim;
> for I am God and no mortal, the Holy One in your midst,
> and I will not come in wrath.
>
> (Hosea 11:8–9)

---

[51] Ibid. 194.

Kipper then offers this paradigmatic understanding of forgiveness: God commits to set a distance between Godself and offenders, to conceal their shame and guilt, but also to have them live through the consequences of their own sinfulness. *Nasa awon* goes beyond this conception to imply that offenders no longer have to carry the moral burden of their iniquity, that God restores the identity and integrity of the sinners by removing their sin, and that God instead suffers the consequences of *their* sins. While there is overlap between the two conceptions, *nasa awon* has a distinctive content which suggests a radical divine participation in the condition of the offender.

I do not aim to provide a full analysis of the concept, but I can begin to elucidate *Cii*, God's commitment to absorb the consequences of sinfulness. I will have more to say in Chapter 3, when we turn to Jesus as the paradigmatic divine absorbent of guilt and shame. For now, it suffices to say that absorbing evil involves neither deleting the wrongdoing from the offender's life story, nor pretending it's not there, nor lessening its role in the practical deliberations involving the offender. It involves instead an infinite forbearance, a historically deep, long-suffering grace and patience with the offender. Some voices in contemporary theology resonate with this dimension of divine forgiveness. Reflecting on the status of terrorists or holocaust perpetrators, people who are commonly thought of as unforgivable, Anglican theologian Rowan Williams claims,

> And yet God holds and keeps open in his life, his 'memory', even such people. It is possible to be your own victim, too, and the violence you do to protect yourself is no less real than that which others do. So the camp commandant who has diminished and isolated himself by his violence, and compounded the injury to himself by refusing to own the memory of it, has still unwittingly left his past in the hands of God. If forgiveness is ever to be realized for him, it is not only the face of his victim which must be 'returned' to him, but his own forgotten face: the face of himself as his own victim, scarred and ruined by what he has done.[52]

As an empathetic and sympathetic creator, God suffers in his being the diminishment and isolation of all individuals, victims and offenders alike. When offenders diminish or harm their victims, in a real sense they uncreate their deeper selves, effectively causing in the Creator God the compounded pain of unrealized goodness, harm to others, and unrealized relational wellbeing. God absorbs the consequences of sinfulness in the sense that he suffers the pain of the victim and the self-diminishment of the offender, while seeking to restore both. Like an involved parent pained by the harm, insult, or unrealized potential affecting her children, the Creator God suffers whenever the wellbeing and thriving of victims and offenders is stunted or diminished.

[52] Williams 2002: 15–16.

But as we have seen in the previous section, as God of the Covenant, Yahweh commits to absorbing the suffering of the beloved through a particular love of attachment. In ancient Israel the priest, the prophet, and the scapegoat enact and reenact imperfectly, intermittently, and symbolically a suffering that is permanent and seamless in the life of the Covenant God. God holds within Godself the collective sorrowed and rebellious history of Israel, and yet God does not hurry to execute retribution. As we will see in detail in the next chapter, the Covenant God enters into an even more intimately loving relationship with Israel through Jesus Christ, and through this Christ-restored Israel, with the entire world. This means that through Jesus the God-man, Yahweh will lift up into Godself the identity, the guilt, the shame, and the pain of the entire humankind.

As we will glance in a moment, the post-exilic prophets paint a moving picture of the Covenant God. To absorb the consequences of sin like Yahweh, involves gracefully living with the pain of un-atoned harms while longing for reconciliation. It is to sober-mindedly count the wounds and yet remain open to the offender, even when there's little chance of penance, restitution, or reconciliation. Absorbing entails the continual refusal to resolve in retribution, resentment, or malice the emotional arc that begins with the offense. Instead, it involves relentlessly holding your offender's scarred face with mercy and grace before your eye. And when he is too scarred and ruined to face himself, absorbing the offense involves lamenting what the offender might or could have become.

In this section I have proposed an account of divine forgivingness derived from the picture of *nasa awon*. As a mode of *hesed*, sin-bearing forgivingness is a particular expression of God's faithfulness to Israel. And as God's loving commitment to identify with mercy and lessen retributive anger, it has a specific content. I suggested it is given by the two interlocking commitments expressed by *Ci* and *Cii*. God absorbs wrongdoing, in the sense that he continually exercises a stupefying ability for forbearance and continued grace to persons. Through Creation, Covenant, and Christ, God is so attached to scarred creatures that he suffers for and alongside them their multilayered stories of diminishment. Furthermore, God's most intimate love of attachment, especially as expressed through Jesus Christ, explains God's stupendous ability to view us in a benevolent light, to construe us as continued recipients of his graciousness. Nonetheless, forgivingness never lessens God's truthfulness, nor, as we will see in Chapter 4, does it eradicate a strong condemnation of wrongdoing. For given the contours of divine *hesed*, truthfulness is wedded to divine compassion, and moral anger to divine lament.

Bearing the Burdens of Jonah

In sharp contrast to the traditional picture of an inflexible cosmic judge, we have a vivid illustration of divine forgivingness in the book of Jonah. God is actively and preemptively involved in absorbing the rebellion of Jonah *and* of the pagans in the story. We meet Jonah as he scuttles away from God's command. Jonah's calculated withdrawals into the belly of the ship, the belly of the fish, and under the shadowy booth disclose a persistent and expansive willful separation from the concerns of a compassionate God and of afflicted humans. His only communication with the pagans in the story consists of brief sentences proclaiming first self-doom, then impending doom for them. And in his dialogue with God, Jonah oscillates between an accusatory anger and a defensive self-pity. Significantly, the prophet explains God's forgiving the Assyrians by reference to the memorable grace-formula. However, Jonah does not celebrate it or strive to model it. He *accuses* God for his forgivingness!

Jonah grasps that God is essentially forgiving, gracious, faithful, and compassionate toward Israel. Yet, in his mind, *hesed* toward Israel demands punitive measures against the devastators, the Assyrians. The God who relaxes retributive justice either does not properly attend to the ruin Assyrians brought upon Israel, or God knows it and does not care. In either case, God fails in faithfulness toward Israel. In either case, God has given up on justice and truth, and Jonah will bring it back into divine focus through any means available, be they disobedience, disaffection, minimal conformance, or tantrums. Compassion to the unforgivable, Jonah thinks, necessarily violates the truth of the victim. Behind his willful blindness, underlying his flight away from God and others, and underlying his general grumpiness and expressed death-wish, there is a gaping wound, perhaps a trauma, that, as far as Jonah can see, demands a strict, retributive god.

The story shockingly depicts a Covenant God who is lovingly committed to both repentant violator and unrepentant victim, to both the contrite outsider and the callous insider.[53] And this divine forgivingness, though motivated by grace and compassion in both cases, manifests itself in distinctive ways. Jonah had come to Nineveh wanting the divine fire to consume the pagans. Instead, a preemptive divine mercy, that is, the affective dimensions of forgivingness, arranges the conditions God knows would elicit God's pardon. God has all the initiative in the story. God sends the Hebrew prophet to the Assyrians, God intervenes to reroute him when he goes off-course, and then God resends him to the same destination. Jonah himself recognizes that kindly affections ground God's commitment to save Nineveh: "...for I knew that You are a gracious God and merciful, slow to anger and abounding in steadfast love, and ready to relent from punishment."[54] It is precisely this knowledge of God's gracious *hesed* that flings the prophet into the throes of anger and despair. Like a disgruntled lover, Jonah first accuses God of untruth and lack of loyalty, then, after losing the plant

---

[53] Some may wonder if I am not obscuring the most important category, that of unrepentant violator. I do not think so. Jonah fits the bill. He represents clearly in the story the Hebrew victim wounded by Assyrian violence. But he is also an unremorseful and repeated violator of divine commands.

[54] Jonah 4:2.

God had providentially grown as shade for him, Jonah simply reports anger-unto-death. How does God respond?

> You are concerned about the bush, for which you did not labor and which you did not grow; it came into being in a night and perished in a night. And should I not be concerned about Nineveh, that great city, in which there are more than a hundred and twenty thousand persons who do not know their right hand from their left, and also many animals?   (Jonah 4:10–11)

The priority of mercy is a metaphysical truth deeper than the truth Jonah thought God needed to relearn. Recalling the creation story of Genesis 2 where, as an artisan attached to his masterpieces, God crafts out of the dust *all* living creatures, God here includes not only the Assyrians but also their cattle in the range of *hesed*. Significantly, God explains his salvific action in part by appeal to a tremendous capacity to suffer. God acts to prevent the ruin of Assyria due to his anticipatory grief. If God is moved by the possible loss of cattle, God will certainly spring into action at the impending plight of people. The God attending to the movement of blistering winds, leafy plants, gnawing worms, swallowing fish, and many cattle, is especially attached to lives of these ignorant Assyrians.

The explanation for God's pardoning the Assyrians in the book of Jonah reveals the following pattern: God's action springs from God's active and preemptive forgivingness as a mode of *hesed*. It is precisely this sin-bearing disposition that sets in motion the chain of events resulting in the Assyrian repentance. This active forgivingness is partially expressed by God's commitment to absorb the consequences of iniquity, a manifestation of a vast and layered capacity for suffering. For one thing, God remembers exhaustively the wounds the Assyrians inflicted on beloved Israel, and still gives them grace. For another, God's anticipatory grief of losing the Assyrians is stronger than the impulse to punish them. In fact, this grief, this divine pathos, is every bit the sign of a thorough love of attachment, one that Jonah recognizes as an expression of covenantal faithfulness *toward* Nineveh. Jonah correctly grasps that God's love for Nineveh is modeled on an interpersonal covenantal relationship. No wonder Jonah is aghast that God expresses long-suffering toward the Assyrians as if they too were God's beloved people. Finally, as we will see below, God absorbs the pain of Jonah's obstinacy. This suffering is analogous to that of a father who watches a self-righteous, older son incapable of celebrating the repentance of his prodigal brother.

Now some may worry that the story shows divine forgivingness toward a collective, a group of people, a community, but not toward an individual.[55] The narrative, goes the objection, does not elucidate God's disposition to forgive

---

[55] I am grateful to an anonymous reviewer who drew attention to this worry.

individuals but only groups. There are at least two ways to respond to this worry. The first would be to argue that God's disposition to forgive communities is analogous to divine forgivingness toward discrete individuals. I will not defend this move here. The second move I will defend. The Jonah story highlights a direct expression of God's forgivingness toward an individual. Indeed, if divine forgivingness toward Nineveh, a collective, is based in an anticipatory grief, God's forgivingness toward Jonah, an individual, is based in a continual forbearance, a long-suffering that aims to subvert the prophet's retributivism. Running to Tarshish, Jonah shows he does not know his left hand from his right. No different from the Assyrians, he too is pathetically ignorant, but unlike Nineveh, Jonah perseveres in his disobedience without giving genuine signs of repentance. He is several times over the beneficiary of unmerited divine mercy and grace.

God speaks to Nineveh only through a reluctant, tight-lipped, doom-and-gloom preacher. But look at all the messengers God sends Jonah: God's own word, the sea storm, the big fish, the bush, the worm, and the blustering wind. And all of this to no avail. Jonah persists and entrenches himself in callousness. If even a weaker version of Jonah's truth applies, if even a weak retributivism rules the day, divine punishment is the only appropriate response to willful, persistent rebellion. But Jonah's truth is not God's truth. God gives long-lived grace to those wearied and diminished by wounds or trauma. God holds within Godself the history of violence Assyria inflicted on Jonah's people, *and* Jonah's own personal history of rebellion and disobedience toward God. It is telling that the story ends with God giving the entrenched offender an experience of personal grace, and a question-mark that is an invitation to show grace to the archenemy.

Some may see in the story of Jonah an instance of God's graciousness to unrepenting, traumatized victims and repentant violators, but not so clearly an expression of sin-bearing divine forgivingness. I respond in two ways. First, the fact that this story is used liturgically on Yom Kippur celebrations, together with the centrality of the grace-formula in the explanation of God's acts in the story, strongly suggests that the divine graciousness is to be understood in part through God's bearing away the transgressions of both Nineveh and Jonah. In other words, the internal narrative arc and the communal performance of the story converge on an intimate association between graciousness and sin-bearing.

Second, we see an even tighter connection if we read the story of Jonah typologically. Post-exilic readers of the book would have seen in Jonah a double-agency, each actor, in his own way, carrying certain burdens. First, as a prophet, Jonah is a representative of Israel; thereby he would have been seen to embody and represent the pain of the ten northern tribes that never returned back to Canaan from the Assyrian captivity. Given that their distinctive Jewish identity was swallowed up by the empire, the prophet proleptically embodies the trauma, the gravitas, the immensity of national loss. The burden is too much. No wonder Jonah has a death-wish. No wonder he descends toward Sheol.

At the same time, Jonah is *also* a representative of God. And as a divine ambassador, like Israel, Jonah has a distinctive global mission, indeed an Adamic co-mission to bring God's light to the nations, to be God's compassionate viceroy for the world, to bring light and life in the realm of chaos. Through his turning away, Jonah typifies the failure of Israel to fulfill its global mission to the Gentiles. Through his repeated flight from Yahweh, Jonah typifies the cycles of national estrangement and departure from the very heart and character of God. And so, Jonah carries not only his own personal guilt of rebellion against Yahweh, but an informed post-exilic reader would recognize in him a paradigmatic representative of a national guilt-burden.

Nonetheless, the ultimate carrier of burdens in this story is Yahweh. God's last speech conveys a love of attachment that carves a path of salvation for the Assyrian, that has pity on dumb animals and misguided humans, and that suffers the unrepentant prophet. In other words, God absorbs into his being at once the trauma the Assyrians would cause to Jonah's nation, and Jonah's failure to live in a way that brings light to the world. Furthermore, God does not merely put up with Jonah's rebellion. God's gracious forgivingness aims at transforming Jonah. How so?

By bearing with an unrepenting person, by providing Jonah with an experience of unmerited grace—the bush provides shade in addition to the booth Jonah built—God hopes to restore Jonah beyond retribution to a kind of generous care of the world. By bearing with him, God intends to restore in Jonah that Adamic capacity for the care of creatures and creation. And if Jonah cares for the plant that was a sheer gift, perhaps he can be stirred up to enter into a partnership with God's care for the welfare of people whose fate was entrusted to him.

In short, God expresses sin-bearing forgivingness with respect to both the trauma and the guilt of Jonah. God continually absorbs the consequences of Jonah's disobedience, and without exacting retribution, without blaming, gives Jonah grace upon grace. As a skilled diagnostician, God invites Jonah to think about the underlying causes of Jonah's retribution-drive. The reader knows that Jonah's rage is lit by an immense personal and national wound that God intends to heal. And healing will come when Jonah will be lifted back up into his vocation and function as co-creator with God, as one who brings, through the power of word and gesture, healing to the nations. But first Jonah must accept the invitation to be transformed in his perception and see a world—plants, cattle, repenting devastators, and devastated victims screaming for retribution—all held together by the pervasive mercy and grace of God.

To review, I argued that starting from the central biblical image of sin-bearing we gain fresh insights into God's disposition to forgive. I proposed that forgivingness is a profound, quintessential divine trait, a mode of *hesed* involving two interlocking commitments for the wellbeing of offenders. And I showed that the book of Jonah portrays a God in whom the sin-bearing disposition runs deeper than and subverts retributive justice. I close by briefly discussing a lingering worry.

But How Does It Work?

I have claimed earlier that the scapegoating ritual of Yom Kippur contains a fitting cognitive and affective content that solidifies the experience of forgiveness in the participant. Nonetheless, some may worry that that explanation does not go very far toward showing *how* God forgives or heals the nation through rite, liturgy, or ritual. So how *does* God effectuate forgiveness and healing through rite and ritual?

I do not believe that this is a sheer matter of stipulation and declaration. While I do think that remission rituals contain suggestive sequences of action that paint psychologically compelling pictures of forgiveness, that does not necessarily entail that God does forgive by these means. I want to venture a hypothesis that combines recapitulation, joint human-divine agency, and anticipation.

I have suggested that forgiveness rituals are compressed scripts that singularly recall paradigmatic stories of God's redemptive, healing presence in the lives of broken or sin-ravaged people. The scapegoat recalls the faithfulness of God to the castaway Joseph, even while it hyperlinks to *the* salvation story of the Hebrew Bible: the Exodus. God carries Israel and their transgressions in their wilderness-experience toward salvation. In abbreviated form, these action-sequences recapitulate and bring into the present past narratives of God's salvific and healing actions. What if God uses his own agency overlayed, as it were, on top of these specific ritual gestures? What would induce God to act in the context of such compressed scripts?

In a well-equipped, beautifully-adorned, and clearly-organized public library, children are more apt to pick up a book and read. In a smartly-furnished and well-designed classroom, students experience an environment primed and loaded for learning. I want to suggest that Israel's atonement cultus provides a locus in time and space that is primed and loaded for the experience of forgiveness. It is as if for a week or so the entire furniture in the social room has been designed and equipped to communicate forgiveness. The cultus—the sequences of gestures involving the temple, priests, holy objects, blood, goats, etc.—provides a multi-sensorial saturation with dramas and narratives of God's particularly intense, concrete, and redemptive presence to Joseph, to Moses and Israel, to Jonah. Through immersion in these narratives, by using cognitive and affective vehicles that harken back to God's forgiveness, the participants in fact avail themselves of divine forgiveness. By entering into the anteroom where the drama of God's forgiveness has continually unfolded, they *also* experience it.

I also want to suggest that the participants experience the real thing and not a simulacrum. Others, of course, have suggested a *double-agency* model of causal efficaciousness.[56] The idea is that human cultic activity is at the very same time

---

[56] Cf. Wolterstorff 1995: ch. 3; Cuneo 2010; and Cuneo 2014a.

divine activity. One way of putting it is that the rituals and rites with their saturated contents bring God's activity and presence from the past into the present, they continue to extend the history of God's salvific interaction with people, and to create, as it were, new social facts of the human-divine cooperation. You find a particularly adorable old wedding photo and show it to your spouse. That photo becomes in that moment a fitting, nonarbitrary vehicle for rekindling or intensifying current spousal love. Similarly, perhaps God joins his agency and intention to these particular gestures and not others because they are apt, non-arbitrary vehicles for mediating divine presence.[57]

I want to say more. The *double-agency* model of the effectiveness of divine forgiveness is justified not only retrospectively, not only through the abbreviated recapitulation of God's healing acts. God condescends to join his forgiving intentions to Israel's forgiveness cultus in anticipation of and because of the Incarnation. The scandal of the Incarnation is not only that God becomes man, but a Jewish man in the Second Temple Period, one whose understanding of God's forgiveness revolved around the Temple cultus. And so, if Jesus of Nazareth becomes the focal point of God's dispensing healing and forgiveness in Israel, and then the world, Jesus's actions and gestures will, in some sense, be fulfillments of the Temple cultus. Jesus's activity will at once fulfill and radicalize the old cultic functions, continue God's story of healing and liberation, and create a new social reality where others can experience even more intimately the forgiveness of God. To the articulation of these expectations, I turn in the next chapter.

---

[57] In this sense, ritual exposure can mediate the presence of God just as reading Scripture or listening to a sermon. When people claim that they encounter God through the reading of Scripture, I assume that the real thing, God's presence, is mediated to them through the apt evocation of a biblical image, story, or thought.

3

Christ and Healing with Goats

"…and he…cured all who were sick. This was to fulfill what had been spoken through the prophet Isaiah: 'He took our infirmities and bore our diseases.'"

Matthew 8:16–17

"Let us then go to him outside the camp and bear the abuse he endured."

Hebrews 13:13

A number of thinkers take the life and work of Christ either as basis or inspiration for articulating a conception of interpersonal forgiveness.[1] True to the retrieval project begun in the previous chapter, I too will extend the idea of sin-bearing forgiveness by focusing on the nature and work of Christ. I argue that the NT (New Testament) sees Jesus Christ as God's ultimate, "greater and more perfect" agent of absorbing human sin, by whose distinctive actions God heals wrongdoers. Due to its quintessential power to reveal God's character through touch, word, and action, Christ's life casts new light on interpersonal forgiveness. The first section distinguishes my approach from two seminal theological approaches to interpersonal forgiveness, that of Anthony Bash, and of Miroslav Volf. The second section presents evidence that the NT centrally sees Christ's forgiveness as a continuation, radicalization, and fulfillment of God's sin-absorbing work of healing. The third section begins to develop the relevant connection between Christ's work and human interpersonal forgiveness in two ways. On the one hand, in contrast to Eleonore Stump's mindreading account of sin-bearing, I propose a ritualistic, representative, recapitulationist, and physically immersive interpretation of Christ's work. On the other hand, in conversation with Marilynn McCord Adams, I begin to sketch a framework for human participation in Christ's work of forgiveness.

Bash and Volf on Christological Forgiveness

In his skilled and insightful recent work, Anthony Bash identifies three main idioms the NT uses for interpersonal forgiveness: (i) *aphiemi* and *aphesis* implying

---

[1] Cf., e.g., Shriver 1995; Volf 2005; and Jones 1995.

Gracious Forgiveness: A Theological Retrieval. Cristian F. Mihut, Oxford University Press. © Cristian F. Mihut 2023.
DOI: 10.1093/oso/9780192873729.003.0003

that a victim lets go or remits the debt incurred in having been wronged; (ii) *charizomai* implying that the victim gives the gift of undeserved favor to the person who has wronged her; and (iii) *apolou* implying that the victim releases or sets the wrongdoer free from the wrong he or she has done.[2] A prime example of the *kaleidoscopic* approach, Bash is reticent to develop or defend here any single model of biblical forgiveness. This is so in part because he sees the language of forgiveness, both ancient and modern, as socially constructed, in part because he thinks biblically-revealed divine forgiveness "does not appear to be entirely self-consistent with other aspects of divine self-disclosure,"[3] and in part because he sees a kind of socially-conditioned dynamic development even in the NT's conceptualization of forgiveness.[4]

While Bash focuses on Jesus's *teaching* on forgiveness, he resists making either divine forgiveness or its expression in Christ's atonement the controlling idea for illuminating human interpersonal forgiveness. This is a striking and unfortunate result. I find in his latest work two main arguments for this refusal. The first argument proceeds from the essentially metaphorical nature of any discourse about God. I quote:

> It is not surprising that the writers of the Christian Scriptures chose metaphors to explain interpersonal forgiveness...Language about God, including language about God's forgiveness can only be figurative and analogical. Indeed, it is hard to see how language about God can be explored apart from by more metaphor. Interpersonal forgiveness is a scion of divine forgiveness – not the same and not as richly textured, but nevertheless genealogically related – and so necessarily also described and explained by metaphor.[5]

The concern here seems to be a kind of semantic indeterminacy. Divine forgiveness is semantically pluripotent, so explicating any one of its images essentially involves or elicits other metaphors. Metaphorical richness creates an irresolvable semantic indeterminacy. Since we simply do not have the proper linguistic tools to fix the reference of divine forgiveness, relying on this concept to shed light on human interpersonal forgiveness is a nonstarter.

I want to briefly respond to the second step in Bash's reasoning. In short, I grant the semantic pluripotency of divine forgiveness-discourse, but also see ways in which we can avoid arbitrariness and indeterminacy. First, following Bash's own Wittgensteinian commitments, our concrete socio-cultural context already sets some boundaries around the field of metaphors we use, making salient some while

---

[2] Bash 2015: 28–9.   [3] Ibid. 66.

[4] Bash 2015: chs. 9–12 argues that while Paul's letters evidence a strong conceptual connection between forgiveness and grace, in the latter NT documents, namely the Gospels, interpersonal forgiveness is always preconditioned on repentance.

[5] Bash 2015: 30–1.

eclipsing others. Additionally, believers have at their fingertips rational criteria, such as immersion in the biblical narrative and theology, the faith practices of their own ecclesial traditions, and their own existential concerns, for discerning in their own situatedness the salience of various metaphors. As we shall shortly see, starting from a distinctively theological standpoint, in a cultural context that overvalues transaction, Miroslav Volf retrieves an understanding of divine forgiveness rooted in the metaphor of gift-giving. Furthermore, as Chapter 2 shows, nonarbitrary literary and theological signposts in biblical texts themselves highlight the particular aptness of the image of bearing burdens. This chapter deepens that argument, offering novel Christological reasons for the aptness and fruitfulness of this metaphor, while also beginning to show its relevance to interpersonal forgiveness.

If in his latest writing Bash sees human forgiveness related to divine forgiveness genealogically, in an earlier writing he draws a sharper, explicit demarcation between the two. I quote:

> From what I have been saying, God's forgiveness is one kind of forgiveness—it is *sui generis* because that forgiveness alone addresses the predicament of irreversibility. The forgiveness that you and I may offer is another kind of forgiveness—and that sort of forgiveness is enormously variegated.[6]

What does it mean to say that God alone and no one else has the capacity to address the predicament of irreversibility? Bash claims that only God can annul the act that violated the moral order, while human forgiveness merely reinterprets the relational consequences of wrongdoing. Notably, through Christ's atonement God has indeed nullified the consequences of the moral law. Bash says:

> ...God, by forgiving human beings, discharges people from their moral culpability. This is the heart of the atonement. In contrast, human beings cannot nullify what has violated the moral order. We are trapped in the 'predicament of irreversibility' and so must live with the consequences—moral, relational and psychological—of what we have done or suffered. Of course, that does not mean that we cannot seek to obviate those moral, relational and psychological consequences; what it does mean is that we cannot undo, reverse or erase the fact of having violated the moral order.[7]

To summarize the early Bash argument: forgiveness either undoes, reverses, erases *or else* it provides different *ways of conceiving of* the violations of the moral law. God alone can undo, reverse, or erase violations of the moral order, and through

---

[6] Bash 2011: 142.   [7] Ibid.

the atonement, God accomplishes this. Human beings can at most reframe or reinterpret the violations of the moral law. Thus, divine forgiveness, especially as expressed through Christ's cross, is essentially different from human forgiveness.

Several notes about this argument. Bash assumes not only that God is the sole legislator of the moral order, but that the divine act of forgiveness which reverses the moral order only makes sense in a larger conceptual framework that includes confession, repentance, and restitution.[8] A consequence of this observation is that "Jesus is *not* an example of someone who forgave the unrepentant."[9] Additionally, while human forgiveness cannot participate ontologically in divine forgiveness, that is, in forgiveness proper, it is nonetheless rooted in, justified by, and motivated by it. Consequently, Christians have a qualified duty to forgive only those who genuinely repent. A gracious view of the offender is required along with a confidence that in the eschaton God will put all things back to rights.

Worries about this earlier Bash argument abound. First, we can imagine a conversation between the latter and the earlier Bash. The latter Bash might raise a concern along the following lines: "If divine forgiveness uniquely involves God nullifying the moral law, the juridical metaphor seems to get pride of place among all other fitting images used to conceptualize forgiveness. But since we have a plethora of biblical and theological metaphors of divine forgiveness, we are now owed clear and evident criteria for enshrining one above the others."

Additionally, as the argument from Chapter 2 shows, God discloses Godself to Israel essentially as a healer, faithful lover, and gracious forgiver. What stands out is not only God's capacity to forgive penitent Israel by the terms of the covenant, but even more, God's transcendent capacity to steadily love and graciously forgive precisely when Israel breaks the covenant. If the early Bash were correct, God's gracious dispositions toward the recalcitrant Jonah or Yahweh's suffering love directed at Hosea's rebellious Israel would not be connected to forgivingness. Instead, they would either instantiate human forgivingness erroneously attributed to God, or fainter divine dispositions not entirely worthy of moral perfection, or perfect divine dispositions that are not properly forgiveness. But Israel's central theological texts tell a different story. The disposition to absorb Israel's rebelliousness *is* quintessentially an expression of divine forgiveness, and it is at the heart of Yahweh's loving character. This chapter's burden is to argue that in his life, teaching, and sacrifice, Christ not only manifests this divine disposition, but also radicalizes and deepens it. Through the life and cross of Christ, God absorbs into

---

[8] "It is possible to go further and to say that to seek forgiveness without confession, repentance and restitution is an oxymoron in the Hebrew Scriptures and in Jesus' day. The examples of forgiveness that Jesus offers or gives all take place where there has been repentance that is explicit (Zacchaeus in Lk. 19:1–10) or implicit (Lk. 7:36–50; 5:17–26; Jn. 21:11–19). John's baptism was a baptism of *repentance*: John rebuked those who looked to God for mercy because of their Jewish ancestry (Matt. 3:9) and not because of God's gracious and merciful response to their repentance" (Bash 2011: 138).

[9] Bash 2011: 146.

God's own being the sins of the whole world, of Israel *and* of the Gentiles, while the former actively rejects him[10] and the latter are oblivious to such salvation.[11]

Finally, as a response to the so-called predicament of irreversibility, the last section in this chapter also begins to construct a model according to which some human dispositions to forgive and some instances of interpersonal forgiveness participate ontologically in God's work of undoing wickedness and its consequences. God heals and restores creation in part through human capacities expanded by participation in divine curative forgivingness.

I now turn to a different account, one not at all reticent to ground interpersonal forgiveness in the divine character. In his *Free of Charge: Giving and Forgiving in a Culture Stripped of Grace*, Miroslav Volf offers a radically different theology of forgiveness than that of Anthony Bash. The organizing idea is that forgiveness, both human and divine, is essentially a kind of unconditional generosity that seeks the good of the offender *before* he or she has made any amends. Forgiveness is essentially a gratuitous gift. Volf's subtle, Luther-inspired, Trinitarian-rooted account deserves a more thorough and careful treatment than I am able to give in this brief gloss. All I can do here is sketch some crucial steps. First, divine forgiveness is the expression of an extravagant, self-giving Trinitarian generosity, whose very essence is unconditional love. Unconditional, other-directed, loving generosity is an essential property of both intra-Trinitarian and inter-Trinitarian relations.[12] God—Creator, Redeemer, and Sustainer—gives and gives and gives without condition or expectation of reciprocation. For our purposes, two Christological implications of this divine generosity are especially noteworthy:

  (i) God's self-giving love through Christ is not dependent upon the features of the beloved; Christ loves indiscriminately, Christ loves the unlovable.[13]
  (ii) God's generosity expressed through Christ's cross confers value upon persons, even upon the ignoble and the bad.[14]

Second, Christ is God's ultimate agent of forgiving human sin, and through the cross—the central event in the eternal drama of divine forgiveness—God places the burden of human sin upon Godself.[15] This self-burdening is an essential expression of God's loving generosity, since through this gift the sin-burden is

---

[10] Cf. Romans 9–12.   [11] Cf. Romans 5:6–8.   [12] Cf. Volf 2005: 71–3.

[13] Volf claims that through Christ God loves "sinners, evil persons, fools, and weaklings in order to make them righteous, good, wise, and strong" (Volf 2005: 38).

[14] "This is the love of the cross, born of the cross, which turns in the direction where it does not find good which it may enjoy, but where it may confer good upon the bad and needy person" (Volf 2005: 38).

[15] "What happened then when God 'made him [Christ] to be sin who knew no sin, so that in him we might become the righteousness of God' (2 Corinthians 5:21)? The answer is simple: God placed human sin upon God!...That's the mystery of human redemption made possible by the mystery of God's Trinity: The One who was offended bears the burden of the offense" (Volf 2005: 145).

removed. But the cross is also fittingly just. God does not place the sin-burden upon some innocent third party. And God does not pass over the seriousness of sin, since there really is a heavy burden and God bears it.[16]

Third, through union with Christ, believers are called to participate in divine forgiveness. The implications of participating in Christ for interpersonal human forgiveness are far-reaching: forgiveness for Christ-followers is an unconditional, indiscriminate, and permanent *duty*, which does not allow for situational exceptions. According to Volf, the duty to forgive requires: an initial condemnation of the injury or insult; giving the offenders the (gift of) release from their owed moral debt and incurred guilt; and a commitment to letting the offense ultimately slip into oblivion. As he puts it:

> To forgive means most basically to give a person the gift of existing as if they had not committed the offense at all. Therefore, not remembering offenses rightly crowns forgiving.[17]

Three clarificatory notes about the human duty to forgive. To begin, Volf holds that humans enact Christ-like forgiveness only through union with Christ by the Holy Spirit, and not through their own natural powers. When we forgive, Christ forgives through us. This effectively means that "we make God's forgiveness our own; God forgives, and we take that divine forgiving, and in a sense put our own signature underneath God's."[18] Furthermore, because this sky-high duty sharply confronts recalcitrant dispositions born out of our psychic drives and social mores, forgiveness also involves a purposive, intentional process of orientation and reorientation to enact the grace of God toward others. Finally, Volf draws a sharp conceptual distinction between forgiveness and reconciliation. Forgiveness is a univocal monadic gift, and Jesus requires his followers to give the gift even if offenders will never accept it. Reconciliation, on the other hand, is a transactional, dyadic, relational affair. The offended offers the gift, but the offender must repent, make restitution, or apologize for reconciliation to be possible. Consider: God has forgiven all humanity in Christ, but God has not been reconciled to those that continually reject divine grace.

Given all I have laid out in Chapter 2, it is no surprise that my account is more sympathetic to Volf than it is to Bash. While I agree with Bash that human forgiveness is an amorphous, context-dependent phenomenon, like Volf, I focus on its aspects that involve more continuity than discontinuity with the divine. Additionally, while methodologically I deal with image, ritual, and narrative, and while Volf starts from theology, we fundamentally agree on a detectable coherence in God's moral character, organized around self-giving love, grace, generosity, and

---

[16] See for instance Volf 2005: 143–8.   [17] Ibid. 175.   [18] Ibid. 202.

a forgiveness that absorbs the brunt of the offense. *Pace* Bash, for both Volf and I, divine forgiveness paradigmatically involves absorbing the wrongdoing unilaterally, independently of offender-repentance. Finally, in ways that I will articulate later on, I agree with Volf that interpersonal curative forgiveness involves a kind of union with Christ, a kind of participation in Christ.

I depart from Volf in two respects. First, as Chapters 1 and 2 suggest, the concept of *virtue* seems more fitting and fruitful than that of *duty* to capture Christ-rooted interpersonal forgiveness. Suppose there was a divinely ordained duty to forgive. That duty would seem more intelligible against a background of underlyingly reliable, enduring, and skilled dispositions to forgive, rather than in their absence. Furthermore, the nature of our participation into Christ—the emulation of divine character, the holistic (cognitive, affective, desiderative, volitional) transformation of human agency, the fact that the transformation would likely be scalar—can be more fruitfully explained and justified by the cultivation of relevant dispositions rather than by discharging duties. This chapter begins, and Chapter 5 develops more fully, an account of curative forgivingness as a kind of quasi-Aristotelian syndrome of dispositions.

Second, while I resonate with Volf's emphasis on sin-bearing as the central metaphor for divine forgiveness in the atonement, for him the terminus of the process of forgiveness is a kind of forgetting, oblivion, or erasure of the wrongdoing.[19] In another work, Volf argues that the decision to lovingly forgive our wrongdoers requires remembering not only truthfully but also healingly. And the latter requires embedding the memory of our wounds in the larger story of God's redemptive action, especially as typified in Exodus and in Christ's Passion.[20] Volf goes on to argue that when a believer takes the really long view of things, she looks forward to the formation of communities that will be so enrapt by God's goodness and mutual love that she will let the memories of wounds simply slip out of the mind:

> ...memories of suffered wrongs will not come to the minds of the citizens of the world to come, for in it they will perfectly enjoy God and one another in God.[21]

I am attracted to the idea of redemptive memories, and also hold that healing forgiveness involves embedding our wound-narratives into God's story. Yet as I see it, redeeming the memories of wounds does not require forgetting them. An alternative way to conceptualize redemptive memories is on the model of Christ's resurrected body. Presumably Christ's stigmata are a permanent *cognitive* reminder of his ordeal, but the *affective* sting of pain, betrayal, denial, and mockery has been removed and replaced with affections directed toward

---

[19] For a more comprehensive account of the role of memory in forgiveness see Volf 2006.
[20] Cf., e.g., Volf 2006: esp. ch. 5 and ch. 6.   [21] Volf 2006: 177.

restoration and communion. Though Christ's wounds should last forever, cir-
cumscribed as they surely are by a transfigured, resurrected body, they give no
cause for resentment or estrangement. The qualitative feeling of pain has been
sucked out, and through the thriving life impinging on all sides at their healed,
closed borders, the wounds themselves have become enduring icons of God's
goodness, and occasions for drawing other wounded creatures into God's healing
embrace.[22] As I see things, the memories of suffered wrongs may come to the
minds of the eschatological citizens. Through them, they would see all the more
clearly God's goodness to their singular embodied existence, and see, refracted
through the eyes of other heavenly citizens conscious of their own enclosed
wounds, abundant evidence of God's eternal healing. This interpretation suggests
that viewing forgiveness as bearing burdens is intelligible not only in light of
Christ's atonement, but also eschatologically.

I have demarcated my project from two recent accounts of interpersonal
forgiveness, one skeptical of continuities between God's forgiveness and ours,
the other celebrating them. The heart of this chapter argues that the image of God
as Israel's healer and sin-bearer uniquely illuminates Jesus's *work* and *teaching* of
forgiveness. But before we jump in, I need to clarify one more important point. As
we have seen, both Bash and Volf emphasize that the NT predominantly uses the
image of debt-remission to conceptualize forgiveness. Indeed, the preeminent
biblical scholar, Gary Anderson points out that in the NT the idiom of canceling
debts is more frequent than that of bearing burdens. He notes that in the Palestine
of Jesus's day, "the word used in commercial contexts to identify debt became in
religious contexts the most common word for sin."[23] This, in conjunction with the
observation that the NT seldom uses the idiom of sin as weight, leads Anderson to
argue that the notion of debt comes to "replace the notion of weight with regard
to sin."[24] If debt-remission completely replaced sin-bearing as the central idea for
rendering forgiveness in the NT, that would pose a formidable challenge for my
argument. Thankfully, Anderson's conclusion is too strong.

I will respond briefly to his worry in two ways. I provide first a conceptual
response. Second, I propose a linguistic-inductive argument. First, it seems that
the concept of burden can more fruitfully illuminate that of debt than vice versa.
Not all phenomena we describe as burdensome are rooted in economic indenture.
People carry relational, legal, psychological, theological, or ethical burdens. But
the concept of debt seems more intimately dependent on that of burden.
Phenomenologically, a debt typically feels weighty and burdensome to the debtor.

---

[22] I have in mind the episode in the Gospel of John where the resurrected Christ appears to Thomas.
The playful tone in Christ's invitation to Thomas to investigate his wounds indicates he is aware of
them but without the characteristic qualia of pain. Christ treats his wounds as an invitation to Thomas
to witness God's goodness, to overcome his own fears and doubts, and to join the community of
believing disciples.

[23] Anderson 2009: 7.   [24] Ibid.

Furthermore, our linguistic conventions corroborate this asymmetrical depend-ence relationship. For instance, we talk of carrying a "heavy" or "light" debt out of college, and often refer to our debts as "financial burdens." Additionally, this talk seems psychologically realistic and fitting given the serious, enduring, and varied strains that economic debt can place on the psyche of the debtor—stress, anxiety, shame, depression, guilt—and on his various relationships—with loaning agent, with family, with friends.[25] Even beyond psychology, the financial deficit can be fruitfully imagined as an economic burden transferred from an agent that cannot carry it to another agent—individual or corporate—that can. So, one response to Anderson is to say that even if the debt becomes the common idiom of rendering sin in the NT, the underlying psychological and relational work is still done by the concept of burden.

The second response is inductive and socio-linguistic. There are at least two possible ways in which older conceptual frameworks may endure despite apparent replacement by newer idioms. One way is that the older metaphors are unex-pressed in contemporary written records because they are simply presupposed. We may expect conceptual novelties to find expression in ancient writings, while older certitudes are assumed and interwoven in the unexpressed context. Another possibility is that archaic modes of thinking and feeling survive because they are embedded in cultural rituals, in social or religious liturgies that are regularly played out and reenacted. These metaphors have become engrafted in the social imagination, an essential part of the framework through which people make sense out of their actions and interactions. If ritualistic thinking conditions our social imagination, older metaphors may display considerable epistemic and attitudinal resilience despite idiomatic changes. It is more likely that the *Koine* Greek and the idiomatic Aramaic of Jesus's Palestine were overlaid on top of a conception of divine action that presupposed the symbolic, ritualistic thinking of Exodus and Leviticus, rather than that the former symbolic world simply disappeared from the social memory. Jesus's contemporaries are still recalling Levitical goats though they speak of remission of debts.

As Chapter 2 argues, Israel's distinctive mnemonic and theological tropes, specifically, its liturgies, its cultic expressions, and its Messianic expectations of forgiveness, are essentially mediated through the image of God bearing burdens, of God absorbing diseases. If this image is as deeply interwoven in Israel's cultic, liturgical, and religious life as it appears, it would be surprising if it was eclipsed or replaced by the time of Jesus. And if cultic thinking endures, then the image of bearing burdens survives *alongside* newer metaphors and idioms, perhaps even *underlying* and *guiding* newer modes of thinking. If the older, cultic thinking continues to structure the understanding of events, we expect the NT writers to

---

[25] Cf. Dew 2007 for a study highlighting a positive causal connection between consumer debt and increased marital conflict.

self-consciously reference the older image of sin-bearing with or without the idiom. And we expect that this understanding of forgiveness will be transmitted to the generation following the NT writers.

Indeed, these expectations are met. The NT sees Jesus as radicalizing and deepening the Hebraic understanding of the God who bears burdens and absorbs diseases. It does this *directly* by invoking the relevant sin-bearing idiom. But it also does this *indirectly* by evoking central ritualistic, liturgical, and theological contexts where this curative image had done the work in the past. The NT applies in creative ways a number of these narratively loaded contexts to Jesus: a new Sinai, a new Moses, and new Exodus; a new wilderness experience; new entrance into the promised land; the scapegoating rite; and the curative evocation of Isaiah's Suffering Servant. While the next section focuses on selected NT texts that illuminate Jesus's work by reference to scapegoating and curative thinking, it is beneficial to set these in a wider theological perspective. Standing on the shoulders of other scholars, I assume that the Gospels, and the NT more generally, see Jesus of Nazareth as recapitulating, compressing, representing, and embodying the history of Israel and that of the world.[26] This central Irenaean theological assumption will become especially salient in the third section.

Evidence of Cultic, Curative Forgiveness in Jesus

I claim that the forgiveness Jesus enacts and teaches is centrally mediated through the metaphor of sin-bearing. In this section, I survey some direct idiomatic evidence we find in the Gospel of John, in the letter to the Hebrews, and in 1 Peter. Subsequently, I will examine indirect evidence from Paul's understanding of the atonement. From Paul, I transition to a brief survey of the scapegoat allusions in the Matthean and Marcan Passion narratives. I conclude with an argument that cultic expiation and scapegoating, alongside other curative imagery, play a foundational role for understanding Christ's work of healing and forgiveness throughout the story in Mark.

Instances of the Idiom "Bearing Burdens"

In this sub-section I discuss three NT texts that explicitly identify Jesus as God's sin-bearing agent. We find the first instance in the Gospel of John. When John the Baptist sees Jesus coming to the Jordan, he exclaims: "Here is the Lamb of God who takes away the sin of the world."[27] While a number of scholars correctly take

---

[26] Cf., e.g., Leithart 2017; Kennedy 2008; Watts 2000; and Kynes 1990.   [27] John 1:29.

the "Lamb of God" to reference both the Paschal imagery of Exodus and that of the Suffering Servant song of Isaiah 52:13–53:12, it would be exegetically and theologically irresponsible to overlook the atoning/curative overtones of the Levitical context.[28] Although John says "the Lamb of God" and not "goats," if he self-consciously references Isaiah's Suffering Servant, then the work of Jesus Christ is set not only in an Exodus framework (the blood of Christ does indeed keep death and destruction at bay), but also in the atoning/curative conceptual frame of Leviticus, because:

(a) Isaiah's own understanding of sin as burden and disease that falls upon the Suffering Servant would be refracted through the Levitical image of sin as weight;[29]

(b) John's readers would be primed to see especially in the passion of the Johannine Christ God's Servant who silently accepts a kind of substituting redemptive suffering that is the means for the healing and justification of many;[30]

(c) just as in Isaiah's song, the theme of Christ as persecuted, rejected, and driven out of his own community is a leitmotif throughout the entire gospel;[31] and

(d) there's a universal scope of the removal of transgression rendered uniquely in both Isaiah 53 and John 1 by the use of the singular "sin," that harks back to the totalizing way Leviticus conceptualizes the burden of sin.

Beyond the scapegoat motif and the Levitical image of sin as burden, it is important to observe other Levitical atonement-related reverberations in John's narrative, such as the literary-theological sin-purgation motifs[32] along with the robust sense in which John presents Jesus as the unique high priest, especially in the events leading up to the cross.[33]

Finally, we see the curative mindset embedded in the subversive twists of the Johannine Messianic roles: Christ is at once a subversive king, prophet, and priest. Jesus is the king of Israel (John 1:49) who instead of dominating those under his authority, serves them and even washes the feet of the betrayer and the denier

[28] Cf. Bauckham 2015: ch. 7 and Keener 2003: 452–6.

[29] Cf. Isaiah 53:6 and 53:12 along with the explanation in Stökl Ben Ezra 2003: 176–8.

[30] Cf. Isaiah 53:7b, 11.   [31] Cf. Orchard 1998.

[32] God's eschatological Messiah performs the following highly symbolic actions: (a) transforms the water used for ritualistic purification from sins into the wine of celebration (John 2:1–11) and in the immediately following episode cleanses and purifies the Temple (John 2:13–22); (b) speaks of a new birth through water and Spirit (John 3); (c) washes the feet of the disciples (John 13) so that so purified and sanctified (John 17:19) they (and all who follow them in obedience to Christ) would be inhabitants of God's eschatological temple (John 14); (d) to the end that they themselves become agents of renewal, purification, and healing of the world (John 17:1–19).

[33] Cf. Heil 1995.

(John 13), loves his subjects (John 15:9–17), and shares his own glory by identifying with them (John 17:20–3). Jesus is the subversive shepherd and also the Paschal-lamb who protects his "sheep" from death and destruction (John 10).[34] Consequently, if the Johannine Jesus is the subversive high priest, the expectation is set that he might play the paradoxical roles of the immolated goat who sanctifies spaces and peoples, and of the scapegoat who carries away not only Israel's, but the whole world's burden of sin.

This last Levitical paradox, explored in John in narrative form, is systematically and explicitly treated in the letter to the Hebrews chapter 9. Jesus, the high priest, enters "the greater and more perfect tabernacle" not with the blood of an immolated goat, but with his own, and by sprinkling it, he cleanses and purifies not some external spaces, but "our consciences from acts that lead to death." After the writer establishes the necessity of the Levitical ritual, and its being fulfilled in the singular and unrepeatable sacrifice of Christ, he says this:

> But as it is, he has appeared once and for all at the end of the age to remove sin by the sacrifice of himself. And just as it is appointed for mortals to die once, and after that the judgment, so Christ, having been offered once to bear the sins of many, will appear a second time, not to deal with sin, but to save those who are eagerly waiting for him.   (Hebrews 9:26b–8)

Here we find a second explicit NT idiomatic reference to sin-bearing. To follow the logic of the passage, if God's presence constitutes the real temple, and if Christ is the greater and more perfect high priest, and if the sacrificial death of Christ fulfills and perfects the necessary role of the immolated goat, then it simultaneously fulfills the necessary role of the scapegoat. Christ is the greater and more perfect vehicle for dispensing the total burden of sin. I argue below that commencing with Jesus's baptism, the Gospel of Mark recalls this paradox and the scapegoating context, although the explicit idiom of bearing burdens is absent.

Meanwhile it is worth observing that we have a third explicit sin-bearing NT reference in 1 Peter. This text does three things at once when explicating the forgiveness that Jesus enacts upon the cross: it takes sin-bearing to involve a transfer by which the new sin-carrier is wounded and the original sin-bearers are healed; the idiom used references Isaiah's Suffering Servant while also recalling the scapegoating rite from the Day of Atonement; and in some sense, it sets up Christ's forgiveness as exemplary and normative for Christ-followers. Addressing believers described as exiles and visiting aliens, who are tempted to give up the call

---

[34] Cf. Exodus 12:23–4, 46 and John 19:36. Also, just as those who eat the paschal meal are safe from the death and destruction in Egypt, so those who eat the flesh and drink the blood of the Son of Man have an inherent connection with eternal life. Cf. John 6.

of holiness due to persecution and suffering, 1 Peter urges that they suffer affliction with the grace and nobility exemplified by Jesus Christ:

> For to this you have been called, because Christ also suffered for you, leaving you an example, so that you should follow his steps ... When he was abused, he did not threaten; but he entrusted himself to the one who judges justly. He himself bore our sins in his body on the cross, so that free from sins, we might live for righteousness; by his wounds you have been healed. For you were going astray like sheep, but now have returned to the shepherd and guardian of your souls.
>
> (1 Peter 2:22–5)

Peter's language suggests that Christ's forgiveness is a kind of praiseworthy forbearance that absorbs the consequences of the offense. In this context, absorbing the offense seems to involve a syndrome of at least four related dispositions. First, it involves an agency configuration in the victim such that hostility plays no motivational role in guiding action toward the perpetrator. Second, the cessation of hostility is partially motivated by a kind of sensitivity to the brokenness of the offending party (offenders are sick persons in need of healing and dumb sheep in need of guidance). Third, the victim has a basic trust in the providential care and justice of God, who mends and puts back together both innocent victims and guilty victimizers. Finally, it involves a kind of intimacy with God (the believers who imitate Christ's forbearance have returned back into God's bosom so to speak) that is constitutive of a real power to transform former hostility into peace, and violence into love.

In the wider 1 Peter context, we see that Christ's forgiveness is not only some psychological maneuver; it has real, ontological bite. Beneath the visible order of a Roman empire built on slavery, Peter envisions a different organic order growing through acts of self-giving suffering. In the shadow of pagan temples, fortified cities, and commanding villas built by a brutality that silences the vulnerable, grows an invisible Hebrew temple founded upon the self-giving suffering of Christ. Just as Christ absorbed their wrongdoing, healing and transforming the recipients of the letter, so by absorbing the vilification of their own wrongdoers, the real power of this Hebraic temple grows, extending the invisible but real reign of God throughout the Roman empire.

Peter references not a generic temple, but evokes the precise, ritualistic context of Yom Kippur. When he consciously redrafts the song of Isaiah's Suffering Servant, he knowingly applies to Christ the underlying cultic connotations, including that of the vilified goat carrying people's iniquities toward the wilderness.[35] From its introductory frame, the letter presupposes a familiarity with Leviticus, by invoking

---

[35] Cf. footnote 193 in Stökl Ben Ezra 2003: 117.

the blood of Christ sprinkled upon believers (1 Peter 1:2). This expiation metaphor is then reiterated at the end of chapter one (1 Peter 1:19), thus setting the
stage for the controlling image of chapter two. There, the believers who are already
familiar with Yom Kippur are invited to imagine themselves as living stones and
holy priests in the temple, already covered and sanctified by the blood of Christ,
the high priest. If Peter uses the expiation metaphor and the Yom Kippur context
to argue for moral purity amidst a pagan world, it makes sense to also apply the
scapegoating image to the sin-bearing Christ in order to advance the argument
that believers are also called to absorb the vilification of their persecutors.[36] Peter
brings together two cultically-related images of Christological forgiveness to bear
upon *praxis*, the habits and practices of his audience. Since Christ covered their
iniquity, believers are consecrated objects, like the temple-furniture purified on Yom
Kippur. And since Christ carried away their diseases, they too are to absorb the
persecution and rejection likely to befall them.

The image of bearing burdens, it appears, plays a central organizing role in the
imagination of the recipients of both Hebrews and 1 Peter. It is epistemically
foundational, shedding a singular light on Christ's cross. Additionally, it plays a
unique justificatory and motivational role: a consecrated believer's natural function is to absorb iniquities, for by doing so, she returns home into God's embrace
and extends the range of Christ's healing and peaceable reign into the world.

I move now to observe how even in the absence of the idiom, the scapegoating
image is recalled in other key theological contexts throughout the NT. Whenever
Jesus is imagined and remembered by NT writers as the scapegoat of the Day of
Atonement, there is a standing invitation to think of divine forgiveness in terms of
sin-bearing and sickness-absorbing. We find such evocations in central Pauline
texts and in the Gospels.

Scapegoating in Paul

Paul uses a variety of metaphors—social, cultic, economic, and political—to
describe the forgiveness Jesus enacts upon the cross.[37] It is not particularly
surprising that Paul sometimes mixes metaphors.[38] But some might be truly
astonished to find out that cultic metaphors do the heavy work in explaining

---

[36] The expression from 1 Peter 2:4 "...the living stone which has been rejected by men" may recall
both the Isaiah 53 context and the scapegoating context.
[37] In Romans 3:23–6 the image is clearly cultic; the blood of Christ covers our transgressions
allowing divine forbearance to "pass over" our sins. In Romans 6 the language is ostensibly fiscal or
juridical, but the theological context is Exodus. The forgiveness Jesus enacts on the cross is actually not
a payment, but a champion's trailblazing fight for freedom from bondage. Recalling the liberation from
Egypt, the cross is not an economic transaction whereby God's ledger against us gets wiped off, but an
emancipation from death and a transference into life abundant (cf. Romans 6:22–3).
[38] See Stephen Finlan discussion of Romans 8 in Finlan 2004: 227.

the *mechanism* of divine forgiveness in Paul. Stephen Finlan argues that for Paul the metaphors for the salvific role of Christ's death can be basically divided into two kinds, cultic and social. "The social images (redemption, reconciliation, adoption, justification)," Finlan argues, "make metaphorical use of transactions that move people from a negative social or interpersonal condition to a positive one: from slavery to freedom, from alienated to reconciled, from stranger to son, from condemned to acquitted."[39] But Finlan goes on to argue that even though Paul spends more time on social images, specifically on justification, the dual cultic metaphors of expiation and castigation are explanatorily foundational, "often expressing the last soteriological word in an extended argument."[40]

A first salient conclusion of Finlan's landmark study is that the rites and imagery of Yom Kippur determine the *content* of Christ's atonement but that its *benefits* for believers are unpacked through social metaphors. In his death, Christ *is* a purification offering (Romans 8:3), a sacrifice (1 Corinthians 11:25), and a sin-carrier (2 Corinthians 5:21, Galatians 3:13). Because the atonement effects a change in the ontological status of believers from impure to pure, and from sinful to blameless, the net benefits are changes in their social standing. A second conclusion, even more important for my argument, is that the scapegoating rite uniquely describes the mechanism of sin transfer and removal. According to Finlan, Paul sets up the cultic imagery of the sacrificial offering and Christ as the Mercy Seat to communicate the idea that Jesus is the blameless victim offered at the heart of the Temple. Then, in shocking contrast to this blameless, holiest agent of purification, Paul deliberately uses the scapegoating image to identify Jesus with a loathsome creature, cursed and driven away from the Holy of Holies. Paul intentionally uses divergent images in order to identify distinct and irreducible salvific processes. As Finlan puts it, "[t]he metaphysical logic of these rituals is directly opposite to each other's" for the purpose of conveying the single paradoxical idea that Jesus freely offered his righteous life as an offering for the healing of sinful, detestable others.[41]

Finlan is not alone in observing that Paul relies on the scapegoating rite to explain the mechanism of salvation. Daniel Schwartz also argues that it is the cultic background that elucidates Paul's strange notion from Galatians 3 and 4, about how the death of an accursed person can be redemptive for others. Schwartz points out the unconventional use of the verb "to send forth" (in "God sent forth his Son" from Galatians 4:2) which occurs only here for Paul. The oddity can be explained if Paul is familiar with the Septuagint where the verb is used only once in Leviticus 16 in reference to the scapegoat being sent forth into the wilderness. Pulling these strands together Schwartz explains: "In other words, Paul's thought behind Gal 3:13; 4:4–5 is as follows: Christ was hung on a tree, and so became a

---

[39] Finlan 2004: 1.   [40] Ibid. 2.   [41] Ibid. 226.

curse, and so could become a scapegoat which, by being sent forth to its death, redeemed the Jews from their curse."[42]

Scapegoating in the Passion Narratives

Even in the latest documents of the NT, the cultic mode of thinking about divine forgiving through scapegoats endures. The Gospels allude to the scapegoating rite as an explanation for the way in which Jesus deals with sin. In his monumental work on the Yom Kippur background in early Judaism and Christianity, Daniel Stökl Ben Ezra argues that the scapegoating imagery and rite lie behind the Barabbas pericope from Matthew 27. The goat ritual informs Matthew's formulation of the passage, he holds, in part due to the strong similarities with Halakha's prescriptions of Yom Kippur: the lottery of the two goats compares to the choice between two accused men; the goats are similar, both men bear the name "Jesus"; the two goats and the two men are chosen for divergent destinations; there is a confession over the goat and there is a confession over the condemned; there is a washing of hands at the end of each process.[43] Stökl Ben Ezra goes on to suggest that Matthew intentionally embellishes key elements from Mark's passion story for a theological purpose, namely, to heighten the tension and to widen the gap between God's choice and the people's choice for the Messiah. Jesus is God's true scapegoat but in choosing Barabbas as *their* scapegoat, the people misappropriate the role of God, deepen their guilt, thus becoming even more needy of Christ's forgiveness:

> The labels Jesus of Nazareth and Jesus Barabbas symbolize two aspects of the historical Jesus. Jesus of Nazareth is the Messiah, as God wants him to be, while Jesus Barabbas is the Messiah as the people want him to be. The people usurp the role of God on Yom Kippur in choosing between the two goats, Jesus of Nazareth and Jesus Barabbas. As scapegoat they choose the wrong goat, Jesus Barabbas, who is released in their midst (and consequently pollutes them), and hence as sacrificial goat, the wrong goat, Jesus of Nazareth, whose blood spilled at the wrong place, also pollutes them.[44]

Other interpreters see scapegoating imagery in the Marcan passion story, but argue that Barabbas functions as the scapegoat and Jesus as the expiatory goat.[45] For a number of reasons I am inclined to disagree with this interpretation, though I cannot go into great depth developing each of them here. First, if Stökl Ben Ezra's point is correct and the crowd does indeed misappropriate the rites of Yom

---

[42] Schwartz 1983: 263.   [43] Cf., e.g., Stökl Ben Ezra 2003: 169–70.   [44] Ibid. 170–1.
[45] Maclean 2007.

Kippur in the Gospel of Matthew, there is an even stronger case that in Mark they do the same. One of the themes in Mark is the confounding of all folksy expectations regarding the person and work of the Messiah. It would be strange if the crowds get the mechanism of salvation right when they get pretty much everything else wrong regarding the Christ.[46] Relatedly, it would be puzzling for Mark to knowingly invoke the cultic background and have a character as marginal and controversial as Barabbas play the causally efficacious scapegoat-role of dispensing with Israel's sin. Additionally, as I will show below, there are other theologically significant aspects of the Marcan narrative that can be fruitfully understood with Jesus functioning as the scapegoat. And if, as I will show, Jesus absorbs disease and sinfulness throughout the entire narrative in Mark, it would be odd indeed if this function suddenly got transferred to Barabbas at the very height of Jesus's Messianic ministry. Finally, some of the earliest Christian thinkers contemporaneous with or slightly postdating the evangelists apply the scapegoat imagery to Christ and not to Barabbas. Stökl Ben Ezra documents in exquisite detail not only that the Gospel of Barnabas, Justin, Tertullian, and Hippolytus identify Jesus with both the scapegoat and with the sacrificial goat, but also that this typology plays a theologically crucial role in their arguments.[47] It seems to me that the case for the continuity of typology is stronger than the case for discontinuity. To put it differently, regardless of the Jewish sources of the typology, if second-generation Christians apply the scapegoat metaphor to Christ in order to make sense of the passion narratives, unless we have strong reasons to the contrary, we should do the same.

Bearing Burdens and Healing throughout the Gospel of Mark

In what follows I argue that Mark intentionally frames his story of Jesus around cultic imagery and that he uses it to explain Christ's healing ministry. I begin with the claim that Mark sees in Jesus the center of God's action and presence in Israel, a kind of ambulatory, organic temple. This idea is corroborated by the way Mark distinctively invokes the Day of Atonement background at the beginning of his Gospel. I go on to suggest that Mark invokes this specific cultic background as a partial explanation in the healing of the paralytic (Mark 2) and of the woman with the bloodletting (Mark 5). Mark portrays Jesus as fulfilling the dual cultic functions of Yom Kippur, the same functions Paul sees in Jesus. On the one hand, Jesus is a stand-in for the Jerusalem Temple or for the holiest part of the Temple that is consecrated and made holy by God. Regardless of his peregrinations through

---

[46] Cf. Mark 3:22, 3:32–3, 8:11–13; and 8:28.
[47] Cf. Stökl Ben Ezra 2003: 152–9. According to him, Tertullian uses this typology to argue against Marcion that Jesus is the Messiah of the Old Testament.

Palestine, Jesus remains animated by the singular vision to move toward the center of God's action in Israel. Jesus is magnetized by the Temple, because he is the paradigmatic temple; he is the organic replacement of the bricks-and-mortar holy site.

On the other hand, we also find Jesus often at the periphery, haunting decidedly unsacred spaces, touching decidedly unsacred things, at times even entertaining the preferences of demons called *Legion*. If Mark is concerned to show that the physical presence of Yahweh, generally associated with the Jerusalem Temple, finds a new epicenter in Jesus, he might want to show that the temple-cultus finds a fuller expression in Christ. Indeed, throughout the Marcan narrative, Jesus moves centripetally toward the sites of God's presence: the Temple, the synagogue, and various places of theophany. But he also moves centrifugally, away from these, in spaces haunted by the devil, desert demons, chaos, and death. The centripetal and centrifugal movements of Jesus are explained by the hypothesis that Mark appeals to the cultic imagination of his readers, who see in the trajectories, gestures, and actions of Jesus both the purgation and the scapegoating rites.

I believe Mark applies these cultic functions creatively and subversively to Jesus. Jesus's life and work is refracted through cultic modes of thinking, but in ways that enrich, expand, or subvert our understanding of the Temple rituals. Jesus stretches the epicenter of God's presence all the way to the godforsaken wilderness where he absorbs into his sacred body the chaos and disease characteristic of polluted objects and spaces. This organic temple haunts the wilderness in search of the burdened and the sick to heal. Meanwhile the Jerusalem bricks-and-mortar Temple is where a deeper wilderness resides, as it has become at best an obstacle for the burdened to find healing and at worst the locus of continuing oppression and contagion. Consider the beginning of the Gospel. The storyline is simple enough: John the Baptist appears in the wilderness preaching a baptism for the forgiveness of sins. He tells the crowds confessing their sins by the Jordan that a greater one is coming, one who will cover them with the Holy Spirit. Jesus arrives. John baptizes him. The heavens are torn asunder, the Father claims Jesus as his son, and the Spirit descends. And then Jesus is driven into the wilderness, to be tempted by the devil, and to hang out with wild beasts. Perhaps Mark announces that a new Exodus is afoot. Called out through the waters, claimed by God only to be sent out into the wilderness, Jesus embodies a newly restored and liberated Israel. Or perhaps by framing the story with the words of the prophet Isaiah, Mark communicates that this one is God's Suffering Servant, the singular agent of eschatological restoration. Still, we should not miss the cultic undertones. Mark's readers would have known that on his mother's side John the Baptist descends from Aaron, the high priest (see Luke 1:5).[48] The confession of sins, the

---

[48] I do not mean to intend here that Mark's readers know Luke's Gospel. I mean to say that they know the information that Luke presents about John the Baptist.

covering of sins through water, a high-priest figure who performs the expiatory action, and the blameless figure who shows up right on cue, are clear signposts that Mark has framed the beginning of his Gospel as a reconstruction of the Day of Atonement. "But where is the Temple?" we may ask. After all, the physical setting here is the wilderness of the Jordan River. Enter the Marcan subversion. The answer is that though substantially and spatially distinct from the Jerusalem Temple, Jesus becomes the primary site of God's presence in the world. Surprisingly, Jesus of Nazareth is the epicenter of God's action, an ambulatory, organic temple right there, in the wilderness of the Jordan River.

An important linguistic observation supports this point. The only other time Mark uses the verb "torn asunder" (*schizo*) is to describe the ripping of the veil separating the Holy from the Holy of Holies after Jesus's death on the cross (Mark 15:38). This tear, just like the rent of the heavens in the prologue, is followed by the proclamation that Jesus is the Son of God. This time, in the muteness of the heavens, it is a Roman soldier, a distant other, that is entrusted with the declaration. Mark, I hold, carefully encloses Jesus's work of forgiveness-as-healing with two lacerations, two instances of torn-asunder, and two identity declarations. Others have noted this parallelism.[49] But what has gone either unnoticed or underappreciated is that in both cases the background evokes the Day of Atonement, albeit in creative and subversive ways.

Mark thinks cultically and ritualistically not only about the atonement, but about the entire work of Jesus, from his baptism all the way to the cross. Returning to the prologue, if Mark self-consciously employs the expiation rite as a lens for understanding Jesus's baptism, it makes much sense to think that in the next scene introduced by the sentence, "and the Spirit immediately *drove him out* into the wilderness," the writer also means to recall the scapegoating rite. If Jesus is a priest higher than his cousin John, if he has access to an even more effective sin-cleansing agent than water, namely the Holy Spirit, then Jesus also functions as a more effective vehicle for offloading diseases than the Levitical goat. Mark does in story-form what Hebrews and 1 Peter have done systematically. He introduces Jesus Christ as the ultimate holy site—high priest, purgation vehicle, and sin-offloading vehicle—where forgiveness, healing, and reconciliation between God and humans takes place. And this massive work of healing is unleashed from the beginning of Christ's ministry.

Specific curative contexts in Mark continually allude either to the image of bearing burdens or to the scapegoat rite. The first time Jesus declares forgiveness of someone's sins, he offers as evidence his curing of that person (Mark 2:9). It is not just that forgiveness of sins "goes with" healing. In this case, Jesus's divine

---

[49] France 2014.

authority to forgive sins is revealed in unburdening the paralytic.[50] Mark 5 tells the story of Jesus healing a woman with bloodletting and afflicted by doctors, as an interlude between the exorcism of a man named *Legion* and a resurrection. If Jesus functions here as an ambulatory temple that essentially engrafts the scapegoating function of absorbing affliction, its movements are reversed. Jesus moves from the periphery toward the center of religious life, from wilderness and tombs through the seashore at the outskirts of town toward the synagogue. And it is there, at the outskirts of town, in a territory of shame and social semi-isolation, in the space between the one haunted by demons and the one haunted by death, that the afflicted woman meets and touches Jesus. If Jesus is merely a person, no matter how astute, popular, holy, or powerful, if he is touched by a ritualistically unclean person, he also becomes unclean.[51] But suppose that Mark's thinking is framed by Levitical goats. Well, then, Jesus essentially co-opts and perfects the cultic functions, including the power to bestow holiness and remove uncleanliness. This would explain to Mark's readers *that* Jesus heals the woman and *how* he does it. Through physical contact a transfer takes place. Christ absorbs the woman's infirmities, while she is physically healed and relationally restored in her identity as a daughter in Israel. The story corroborates the earlier Pauline insight, that restoration to a filial status with God is grounded in the underlying work of Christ's carrying our burdens and healing our diseases.

Those acquainted with the biblical narrative know what happens when mortals unwittingly touch holy objects. Uzzah is struck down for touching the Ark of the Covenant, even though he acts altruistically (1 Samuel 6). In Mark 5 when the woman touches the Messiah, not death, but healing springs forth. And not divine condemnation, but a blessing issues forth, one crowned with a declaration of belonging: "Daughter." If my hunch about the cultic background of the prologue is on the right track, we can generalize to other healings in the Gospel of Mark. Not only for this afflicted woman, but for all those afflicted, Jesus functions as the peripatetic Mercy Seat, the paradigmatic holy site of God's presence, which has essentially co-opted and perfected the function of the Levitical scapegoat. The last time the Ark of the Covenant is on the loose through Palestine, it gets returned to sender because it spreads tumors, diseases, and death in town after Philistine town (1 Samuel 5). But in Mark, in town after town, people flock to Jesus to be touched and to be healed. In other Gospel accounts also, *healings are paradigmatically performed through physical touch*, and touching in Mark's thought-world involves transmission of stuff. What Mark implies Matthew makes explicit. Jesus draws out the disease into himself. After he recounts the healing of Peter's mother-in-law, he says: "That evening they brought to Him many who were possessed with demons;

---

[50] Like myself, David Konstan sees here, just as in the episode from Matthew 9:2–7, the older image of forgiveness as lifting-up sin. Cf. Konstan 2010: 115.

[51] Cf. Haggai 2:11–13.

and he cast out the spirits with a word, and cured all who were sick. This was to fulfill what was spoken through the prophet Isaiah: 'He took our infirmities and bore our diseases'" (Matthew 8:16–18). Matthew thus articulates what is implied but evident in Mark's remembrance of Jesus.[52] The sick and infirm who touch and are touched by Jesus not only survive, but are thoroughly healed. Jesus heals infirmities and forgives sins *because* he absorbs and off-loads them. The Holy One of Israel can remain uncontaminated in the midst of an ocean of contaminated folks for the same reason. Jesus simply *is* the spring of holiness and healing. Jesus *is* the ultimate decontaminant; he *is* the paradigmatic vehicle for absorbing, dispensing, and inoculating against the contagion of sin, disease, and death.

Theological and Philosophical Implications

I have argued so far that the image of bearing burdens provides a significant mode of thinking about Christological forgiveness in the NT. We found idiomatic evidence for it, along with instances of cultic and curative thinking that presuppose it. I have argued that Mark's account of Jesus's lifelong work of forgiveness from his baptism to the cross, as well as Paul's, Peter's, and Hebrews' respective understandings of the cross are often mediated by the cultic and curative rituals embedded in Israel's memory. I want to draw out two theological consequences of the idea that in Christ, God absorbs human disease, pollution, and iniquity. The first one is a riff on the astounding implications of the Incarnation, while the second begins to trace interpersonal ramifications derived from the forgiving character of God as expressed through Christ.

Incarnation, Bearing Iniquity, and Physical Contact

First, return to the observation that in the Gospels Jesus paradigmatically removes sin and disease through *physical touch*. In the Christian imagination, God's most complete revelation takes place in the Incarnation. In the fullest human representation of the divine we have, God does not offer forgiveness from afar, neither by fiat, nor by declaration alone. God accomplishes it through embodied gestures and actions, up-close and personal. God immerses Godself into the concrete chaos and history of offenders. Not an avatar, not the angel of his presence, not some other intermediary, but God's own self comes into *intimate contact with their skin*. In

---

[52] Cf. Matthew 11:4–6 and Matthew 11:28–30. Notice: (a) the inherent connection between afflictions and burdens; (b) Jesus is the center of healing and dispensing of burdens in Israel; (c) Jesus self-consciously endorses the role of healer and dispenser of burdens in Israel; and (d) the transaction: Jesus lifts up heavy burdens but imparts a light burden to his followers.

order to come to terms with the radical nature of this idea, consider another common ancient view of divinity:

> In the ancient pagan imagination, the high gods, the really big players, were ensconced in some heavenly realm where they – well, acted like gods. They squabbled and had love affairs among themselves; they feasted and accepted sacrifices from human beings. They might be propitiated or bribed to push events one way or the other on earth, but theirs was a *very limited engagement* with humanity.[53]

We have already noted how at Sinai, God is so moved by love and pain that he forges his name to a clan of oppressed slaves. He sees their affliction, hears their outcry, knows their pain, and astonishingly comes down to deliver them from the hands of their harsh masters (Exodus 3:7–8). But in Jesus, this God of the oppressed enters into an even more "unlimited engagement" not only with Israel, but with all of humanity. God with sinews, tendons, and nerve endings now knows not only propositionally and sympathetically, but also first-hand and experientially the *human* pain of abandonment, loneliness, despair, and broken trust. And this fleshly God not only experiences *our* pains, but by coming into physical contact with us, *lifts us out of* our fear, oppression, loneliness, self-deception, brokenness, and death.

Refracted through the Incarnation, divine forgiveness shows not so much the wrongness of the debt-cancellation or the forensic models of forgiveness as it does their shallowness. Pagan gods, or as the case may be, pagans kings, could at times be counted on to cancel debts or to remove the guilt of transgression through edicts and declarations.[54] By contrast, the Christian God removes transgression and its effects through touch. In Jesus, God comes as close as possible to offenders, absorbs the consequences of their offenses into God's own being, and transfers onto the afflicted divine healing and restoration. The Incarnation reveals *something* so assertively personal, unconditionally gracious, and somatically intimate, something that eclipses the sterile, uninvolved objectivity inherent in the idioms of debt-cancellation, acquittal, pardon, or clemency. While these latter images continue to stir the Christian imagination, a central Gospel headline is that Jesus is an intimate friend who heals, unburdens, and forgives. The Incarnation suggests that much of the judicial, transactional, and logocentric focus in classical and contemporary discussions of divine forgivingness needs to be, at the very least, balanced, expanded, and recalibrated by the personal, unconditional, and tactile. In "the Word become flesh" we see par excellence the intensification of the divine disposition to come so close that God may heal human nature through the divine touch.

---

[53] Davis 2001: 48.   [54] Cf. Morgenstern 2002 and Bleeker 1966.

But what does it mean to say that Christ absorbs human transgression and its consequences into God's own being without contaminating oneself? *How* does Jesus do it? Can we analyze deeper what we mean by God bearing away sin through Jesus? I would like to suggest an answer through contrast with a recent account defended by Eleonore Stump. According to Stump, Christ bears the totality of humanity's sin and pain on the cross through a kind of mindreading. Consider the following key passage:

> At one and the same time Christ mind-reads the mental states found in all the evil human acts human beings have ever committed. Every vile, shocking, disgusting, revulsive psychic state accompanying every human evil act will be at once, miraculously, in the human psyche of Christ...without yielding an evil configuration in either Christ's intellect or will.[55]

And:

> When Christ is in mind-reading connection with all human beings, Christ has in his psyche a simulacrum of the stains of all the evil ever thought or done. In this way, he has the sins of human beings within himself. But he has this evil in his psyche off-line, as it were, that is, without the ordinarily associated evil states of intellect and will. Through mind-reading, then, Christ can have all human sin within himself on the cross without himself being sinful, that is, without having any morally evil beliefs or states of will of his own.[56]

The mindreading model of sin-bearing has several interesting features. It has a comprehensive or universal scope, since it claims that in that single event on the cross, the human mind of Christ miraculously accesses the atemporal divine mind that contains within itself a facsimile of every single human psyche, past, present, and future. In virtue of its *sui generis* nature, the mind of Christ has a unique ability to enter into every human experience of guilt and shame, while maintaining an uninterrupted love-union with God. Apart from the divine nature, Christ's human mind would not be able to mindread all human beings at once, and apart from the human nature, Christ's divine mind could not receive in itself the moral stains of human psyches. For Stump then, Christ carries the total weight of human sin in the sense that his psyche simulates telepathically and synchronically the total shame and guilt of mankind. The total-sin-simulation event in Christ's psyche on the cross has a double effect: it is experienced as a horror which, in that moment, obstructs his psyche from a shared attention with the divine mind,

---

[55] Stump 2020: 164.   [56] Ibid. 169.

but it has no causal power to morally corrupt any of Christ's motivational and cognitive capacities.

The mindreading model has some obvious advantages. It makes coherent sense of the biblical image of sin-bearing, and explains the Pauline intuition that the Crucified was cursed, even "made sin" for us. It explains the comprehensive and universal scope of divine forgiveness. It illuminates the primacy of the divine initiative, the univocity and asymmetry of divine forgiveness—Christ has already borne the sins of the unrepented, unrepenting, even of those yet unborn—while explaining how mutual indwelling requires a willed participation of the human psyche in God—God unilaterally effects forgiveness of all mankind, but cannot unilaterally accomplish reconciliation. It also paints an evocative picture of divine sorrow in the face of human sin, and sketches a plausible way God comes close to humanity. And yet, we have to ask, is it compelling enough, especially in light of the scandalous particularity of the Incarnation? Does God come close enough to us through mind-simulation?

I leave aside theoretical worries about overreliance on a simulationist theory of mind, or about the metaphysical presuppositions of the interaction between Christ's temporal human and atemporal divine mind, or about its limitations in exemplifying and modeling interpersonal forgiveness. I focus on three worries that contain the seeds for an alternative account. The three worries relate to ritual, the institution of the representative, and embodiment.

In the previous section, we have seen that the NT conceptualizes Christ's bearing burdens by recalling the Temple cultus enacted on Yom Kippur. We noted how narratively (in Mark) and systematically (in Hebrews and 1 Peter) the forgiveness Christ enacts is inseparable from temple-related functions and rituals. Christ is the greater and better site of God's conveying of healing, Christ is the greater and more perfect high priest, Christ is the greater and more perfect vehicle for offloading sin. The life, ministry, and cross of Christ explain the continuity with, fulfillment of, and the cessation of the temple rituals. But if the mindreading model is correct, divine forgiveness on the cross is enacted independently of ritual and temple. If a single synchronic scan of all human psyches suffices to load iniquity onto Christ's mind, the OT atonement-rituals and the NT arguments that Christ concludes them by fulfilling them are at best redundant, at worst perplexing obstructions for understanding divine forgiveness. And yet the NT writers we considered seem to think that these are important and even preeminent for grasping Christ's forgiveness and its exemplary, motivational role for believers.

A second worry pertains to the Hebraic institution of the substitutionary representative. In Chapter 2 I argued that the cultic and religious life of Israel is rife with transfer and symbolic representatives. The scapegoat, the priest, the prophet, and the Suffering Servant are representatives in Israel in a double sense: in some sense they symbolize God to the people, and in another, they represent the people to God. Furthermore, the sin and guilt of one individual can transfer to the collective, such as in the case of Achan. Vice versa, collective sin and corporate guilt can be transferred symbolically to a single consecrated representative of that group, such as when an undefiled Ezekiel is commanded to bear the sins of Israel for 390 days representing 390 years of Israel's faithlessness. The institution of the symbolic representative challenges the necessity of the mind-reading model. If the total guilt of a collective—Israel or the world—can be borne out through the symbolic suffering of a representative individual, there is no need for a one-to-one mimetic representation of every human evil in Christ's mind. All that is needed is that Christ be a fitting, innocent, representative individual and that his suffering stand symbolically for the sin of the collective—Israel's and the world's.

I have suggested so far that, biblically, the mindreading model is neither necessary nor sufficient for conceptualizing God bearing away human sin in Christ. The final worry is that the mindreading model downplays or unduly redescribes the embodiment of God by relying on an overly-noetic model of the atonement. The burden of sin is rendered as stains on the human psyche, and Christ's bearing of sin is rendered as a single mindreading event that uploads simulacra of human evil onto Christ's mind. My intuition is that the embodied action and the healing touch of Christ convey irreducible experiential and mental contents that cannot be captured reductively through mindreading.[57] Though philosophical analyses of touch are in infancy, some note that the tactile sense uniquely brings into awareness things external to the body and features of the body itself.[58] Others have argued that touch is phenomenologically foundational for co-presence: when the tactile sense is intact, the perceiver shares into the world of the perceived object, but when the tactile is lost, proprioception and kinesthesia along with it, there is no meaningful sense in which there is anything to be perceived.[59] Extending this observation, it is easy to see how, from caressing an infant, to holding the hand of a beloved, to wiping off the tears of a distraught friend, the sense of touch reveals irreducibly singular ways of being present to persons, of allowing other bodies to imprint upon one's self, and of co-valuing with other persons a shared perceptual and axiological world.

I have suggested that Christological forgiveness is modeled on healing, and that the healing work of Christ paradigmatically takes place by touch, by physical contact. Imagine that the divine presence is distributed throughout Jesus's body analogous to the way the consciousness of an octopus is distributed and suffused

---

[57] As an alternative to both representationalism and simulationism in the philosophy of mind, one might consider *Enactivism* (cf. Gallagher 2019). According to Gallagher, Enactivism can be characterized by the *4Es*: *Embodiment:* mental contents involve more than the brain, including a more general involvement of bodily structures and processes; *Embeddedness:* mentality functions only in a related external environment; *Enactment:* mentality involves not only neural processes, but also things an organism *does*; *Extendedness:* mentality is extended into the organism's environment.

[58] Cf. Merleau-Ponty 1968; Field 2001; and Ratcliffe 2008.   [59] Cf. Ratcliffe 2013.

throughout its entire body, rather than on the model of a captain running a ship. If what I said above about touch is compelling, then by the hand and body of Christ, God is present to humanity in epistemically direct, unmediated, and intimate ways, ways that singularly bring into attunement God and human self-awareness. Not by mindreading or declaration alone, but by touching and being touched, Christ conveys the full, immediate, intimacy of God's presence to the afflicted in a mutually shared environment, a divine intimacy which they recognize as a healing of their tissues. Inverting Levitical causation, the life properties that flow from Christ are transferred to and incorporated into the sick, while the human diseases get absorbed and extinguished into Christ's divine life.

If Christological forgiveness is modeled on physical healing, the gestures of Christ's hand and body convey a qualitatively distinctive aspect of divine forgiveness, irreducible to either mindreading or declaration. Christ's touch not only inoculates humans from disease, but aims to incorporate *a divine moral healing* into human nature. Consider some Christ-gestures leading up to his death on the cross. Jesus shares a last meal with the betrayer, and accepts Judas's performative kiss while continuing to refer to him as a friend. A priestly guard intends to arrest him, while one of Jesus's zealous companions promptly unsheathes the sword and cuts off his ear. "No more of this," Jesus says, then touches and heals the man's ear. These words and gestures target both Jesus's afflicted assailant and Jesus's companions. They mark not only a denunciation of violence in self-defense, but also trace out a strategy for responding to injury and wrongdoing, one essentially aiming at healing the injurer. Or consider the vehement accusation, the ridicule, the mockery, the beating by crowds both Jewish and Roman. Jesus takes in all this abuse, although he has twelve legions of angels at his disposal. He not only forsakes retaliation, but famously prays for the spiritual restoration of his assailants. Generally, then, these Christ-gestures reveal that bearing the burden of sin involves an intimate, reflexive, continued transfer of divine grace to afflicters in the hope of restoring them to spiritual health while he himself suffers bodily the consequences of their sins without blaming them. In his high priestly function, Christ lifts up the true identity of the offender into the very presence of God.[60]

We are now in position to systematically identify the four distinctive Rs of Christological forgiveness as bearing burdens: ritualism, universality through the representative, recapitulation, and radical embodiment. It is ritualistic, in the sense that it evokes and completes the scapegoating ritual of Yom Kippur. It is representative in at least two ways. First, as the ultimate representative of God, Christ bears the sins of the entire mankind by absorbing paradigmatic sins of humans who are representatives of the collective to which they belong. By absorbing Peter's denial, Judas's betrayal, and the crowd's fickleness, Jesus bears

---

[60] Refer back to the semantic resonances of *nasa awon* in Chapter 2, especially the gestures of the high priest in Exodus 28:15–29.

the collective denial, betrayal, and fickleness of Israel. And if contained in Israel's paradigmatic sins lies seedlike the world's entire rebellion, then thereby God absorbs it all through Christ's work.[61]

In a different way, Christ is a representative of Israel who recapitulates in his individual life key historical episodes of their collective betrayal, but undoes their failure through faithfulness to God. Christ is the first truly healed exemplar of humanity who keeps faith with God where others fail. When he rejects the devil's offer of immediate satisfaction, along with the temptation for political and religious power, Jesus effectively undoes Israel's betrayal at Sinai. When he repeatedly heals and feeds the needy crowds in the wilderness, Christ effectively undoes and heals Israel's historical mistrust in Yahweh's care, precisely in places that symbolically evoke historical distrust due to scarcity. When he drinks the cup in Gethsemane and lowers himself below his proper ontological status, Christ undoes Adam's desire to elevate himself above his status. In other words, whenever he goes to the site of an original disaster, Christ absorbs the collective sin by an obverse symbolic action that keeps faithfulness with God. And through these subversive reenactments of Israel's history, Christ incorporates healing into human nature. He is the first human that did it, and by contact with him, by union with him, we also can be morally healed to keep faithfulness with God and become conduits for transferring grace and forgiveness to others.

The representative and recapitulationist nature of Christ's gestures reinforce the importance of *realization through touch*, through embodied contact. The key point conveyed is that of organic union. Jesus is not merely a paradigm, a model of morally correct action. And Jesus is not merely a perfect retainer or refractor of human sin. Think about the Samaritan woman who comes in contact with Jesus at the well. Jesus decontaminates humans from their spiritual condition, and simultaneously "contaminates" those he touches with the good news, transforming their humanity, and healing them in order to carry out their human projects.[62]

---

[61] Consider a modern analogy. In the movie *Arrival*, "Abbott" and "Costello" are two Heptapod representatives of an alien species that travel to earth to impart a kind of understanding that would save humanity from annihilation. Some soldiers at the makeshift military camp that surveys the alien ship form a plot to detonate an explosive inside the ship. They succeed and Abbott is killed, but not before the two aliens have passed on their saving knowledge. Abbott's death can be interpreted as a kind of representative suffering, one that symbolically absorbs the xenophobic dispositions of the entire human race. Not *every* Heptapod dies as a result of one human detonating a device. And one Heptapod dies not as a result of *all humans* detonating their home-rigged devices. One representative savior dies as a result of a general enough disposition that typifies the entire human race. So, Abbott's death is representative in this sense. And it is also salvific. The Heptapods are omniscient. Abbott willingly absorbs the blow and the radical consequences of a representative human aggression because through that same process, namely Abbott's death, the aliens are able to impart to another representative of the same human race, Louise, the necessary cognitive tools to save humanity.

[62] Here's an analogy. A field of pure female-only poppy seeds comes in contact with a single male seed. Pretty soon the entire crop is blended. (I owe this organic reference to the fantastic show *Narcos: Mexico Season 1*.)

Union with Christ

The second main theological implication I want to start fleshing out is that of participating in Christ's forgivingness. As I will explain later in Chapter 5, I conceive of the human virtue of forgivingness as a quasi-Aristotelian syndrome of dispositions: affective, cognitive, motivational, explanatory, and justificatory. It is Aristotelian, because, as I will argue later, bearing burdens does involve finetuning of one's sensibilities through habituation to various forgiveness-enhancing conditions. But it is only *quasi*-Aristotelian because finetuning our forgiving dispositions depends in central ways upon being unified with the forgiving/healing work of Christ. We need serious assistance from beyond our powers, habits, and attitudes. In this sense, the forgiving character of Christ at once incorporates, justifies, motivates, and guides any of our paltry efforts at bearing burdens.

How, precisely, are we unified with Christ's forgiveness? How are we united to the God who is healing creation through Christ? I'd like to suggest two distinctively Christian answers: (a) *perspective-sharing*: the victim takes on God's point of view of herself as victim, of the offense, and of the offender; and (b) *incorporation*: the victim's imagination and practical identity is already incorporated through narrative immersion into the forgiving work of Christ.

The perspective-sharing view is proposed by Marilyn McCord Adams. Adams convincingly argues that a Christian model of forgiveness goes beyond civil or forensic models of performing forgiveness, because it entails a commitment to trying to forgive from the heart, which flows from a cultivated intimacy with God. Through prayer, the victim invites God to share into her perspective of being wronged, candidly laying out before God the pain, the humiliation, and even honest feelings of retribution and vindictiveness. But in intimacy with God, the victim also learns to see things from God's perspective, by sharing into God's own vision of herself as victim, of the offense, and of the offender:

> Usually, the victim's attempt to enter God's point of view will involve shifting from a one-dimensional picture of the offender qua offender to a more complex characterization, which recognizes him/her (i) as a person with problems, (ii) in response to which s/he has deployed inefficient adaptational strategies, (iii) resulting in behavior harmful to himself/herself and others. The victim will also acquire deeper insight into how God sees him/herself, sometimes (but not always) as a person with similar problems and comparable faults.[63]

In short, when the victim sees the offender in light of God's love, she releases him into God's power to heal, redeem, and reform. This double perspective-sharing has a triple effect for the victim, according to Adams: she deepens her sense of

---

[63] Adams 1991: 296.

being loved and inherently valued by God; she learns to relinquish her inappropriate projections of own self-importance; and she is freed to enter into God's love for the offender, to re-appreciate the infinite worth conferred upon the latter by such divine love.

While I resonate deeply with Adams's double perspective-sharing, I'd like to propose a strategy compatible with it, one that, in some sense, underlies it. I call this *double-incorporation*. Double-incorporation can coherently explain how one can share in the double perspective-sharing with God. By immersion in God's gracious narratives as related through Scripture readings, especially the Christ-narratives, liturgies, hymns, poetry, even nonsacred literature that evokes these, our broad ethical sensibility and imagination is *already* activated, transformed, or augmented so that our practical self is more disposed to acquire and entrench forgivingness than it would be otherwise. Through narrative immersion, the believer incorporates into her agency the forgiving character of Christ. On the other hand, whenever the believer acts from curative forgivingness, she *really* continues the work of Christ in her own personal biography. Through forgiving gestures, her agency is incorporated into that new humanity inaugurated by Christ, and participates in the new eschatological order of healing creation. Through acts and words of forgiveness, one's own life narrative is incorporated into and continues God's grand story of healing the world.

In the latter part of Chapter 5, I expound on three kinds of grace-narrative immersion: immersion in God's meta-narrative, a kind of attentiveness to unexpected, transcendent beauty, and a cultivated friendship with Christ. The idea is that by such steady immersion something happens to our background dispositions so that we become more inclined than we would be otherwise to acquire and internalize Christlike curative forgivingness. More precisely, through narrative immersion, believers develop a sensibility, a meta-disposition, to internalize a syndrome of dispositions associated with bearing burdens such as: the disposition to suffer with nobility the consequences of offenses; relinquishing the castigation of the offender; offering gestures of grace, and opportunities for the reform and redemption of the offender; and a disposition to perceive oneself and the offender as potential continuants of God's story of healing creation, both incorporated into Christ's new humanity.

I want to suggest a possible conceptual framework for understanding incorporation by narrative immersion. To do this, I invoke two concepts: that of *nested intentionality* and that of *practical vehicle externalism*. Famously, Alasdair MacIntyre argues that human intentions and motivations are intelligible in larger narrative structures that organize and direct them. "Deprive children of stories and you leave them unscripted, anxious stutterers in their actions as in their words," MacIntyre says.[64] This is not just a witticism about the development of

---

[64] MacIntyre 1984: 216.

moral vocabularies in children, but a more general thesis about the contours of practical reasoning and agency. The stories we tell ourselves bring coherence to the events we live through, provide emotional resolution, reveal self-understanding, connect us to our values and virtues, and attach us to particular communities and traditions. An agent "is not essentially, but becomes through his history, a teller of stories that aspire to truth." And consequently, practical rationality resides neither in fashioning agency *ex nihilo*, nor in merely following abstract, timeless principles. It must be sensitive to representing oneself on the map of this complexly structured dramatic-narrative terrain. "I can only answer the question 'What am I to do?' if I can answer the prior question 'Of what story or stories do I find myself a part?'"[65]

I may tell myself many stories. *I am a sanguine type and a recent immigrant from the Eastern European bloc who bootstrapped himself out of poverty. I am a resident alien in a country torn apart by racial injustice, in whose past lies holocausts of Original Americans and enslaved Africans. I am an intellectual and despite all my rage against injustice, sometimes I feel trapped like a beast in a cage.* For Christians, however, Christ's story has normative and explanatory priority. This means that among all my other self-explanatory stories, I valorize the story of Christ in a way that uniquely and paradigmatically explains, structures, and motivates my life's purpose and history. Immersion into the life of Christ structures my agency in a way that at least interrogates the adequacy of my sanguine, bootstrapping, or activist self-narratives, and positively, makes me countenance questions such as these: "which of the attitudes, gestures, and actions open to me best continue Christ's healing work in the world?" or "how is the story of Christ (to whom I belong) best continued through me and my actions?"

I'd like to explore a related sense in which our agency can be said to incorporate the mind of Christ. MacIntyre holds that the content of intentional and motivational states depends essentially on historical (external) practices and institutions.[66] But we can pursue a more ambitious thesis, namely, that *practical-thought structures, processes, and capacities themselves* are partially, but essentially, located externally to our minds in historical imaginaries and social narratives. To explain what I mean here, I borrow some seminal ideas from Mark Rowlands's account of vehicle externalism in philosophy of mind.[67]

According to Rowlands, in contradistinction from *content externalism, vehicle externalism* claims not only that mental contents are individuated by items in the external environment, but also are the *cognitive vehicles* (mental architecture and

---

[65] Ibid.

[66] Though there are many ways to express content externalism, an intuitive one is that the individuation of some mental contents depends on items that exist outside the heads of the subjects of those mental states.

[67] Cf. Rowlands 2003.

processes) responsible for mental operations. Rowlands sums up this framework in four main theses:

1. The world is an external store of information relevant to cognitive processes such as perceiving, remembering, reasoning and so on.
2. A process such as perceiving is essentially hybrid—it straddles both internal and external forms of information processing.
3. The external processes involve manipulation, exploitation, and transformation of environmental structures that carry information relevant to accomplishing the perceptual task at hand.
4. At least some of the internal processes are ones concerned with supplying the cognizing organism with the ability to use appropriately relevant structures in its environment.[68]

How might an analogous framework be developed for human intention and action? I want to stress the "analogous" aspect, because I am trying to explicate another sense in which agency is essentially informed and formed by narrative immersion. If Rowlands's vehicle externalism is correct, then if intentional processes depend on cognitive ones, perhaps it is more likely than not that a relevant version of practical vehicle externalism is also true. But neither the motivation for nor the truth of the practical framework has to depend on the theoretical framework. Consider then the practical analogue of vehicle externalism:

1. The social world (setting) is an external store of codified information (narratives) relevant to intentional processes such as valuing, deciding, practical reasoning, emoting, etc.
2. A process such as practical reasoning is essentially hybrid—it straddles both internal and external forms of intentional processes.
3. The external processes involve information that manipulates, challenges, and transforms the agent's existing stock of (external) historical narratives relevant to the piece of practical reasoning at hand.
4. At least some of the internal intentional processes are ones concerned with supplying the agent with the ability to use the relevant external processes in their historical setting.

On this practical externalist framework, immersion in the story of Christ provides the subject not only with unique mental contents, but also with unique and irreducible practical vehicles and processes for valuing, intending, deciding, and feeling. The work of Christ, including his work of curative forgiveness is

---

[68] Ibid. 189.

already there outside of our brains, encoded in Gospel stories, hymns, other historical and fictional narratives, poems, symbols, and a variety of liturgical practices. When the believer immerses herself in the work of Christ, then, she enters this richly textured narrative environment saturated with practical tools that are causally effective in challenging and augmenting her current sensibility, imagination, self-understanding, and capacities for decision-making. For instance, when she immerses herself in the Christ-wilderness narrative, she does not only pick up from Christ skills of resisting the allure of political, social, and religious power, but learns to feel rightly about such power. When she imaginatively follows Christ in the wilderness again, she does not acquire magical skills of multiplying bread and fishes. But she does feel surging in her guts a trust in the radical goodness of God in the face of moral horrors, and this trust reaffirms her fundamental identity to heal and beautify the world. And when she follows Christ to the cross, she learns affectively that the primal causal power of changing the world resides in tucking away the sword, in praying for assailants and unfaithful friends alike, and in blessing even the persecutor.

Two concluding notes. The first, is to underscore that grace-narratives and especially the Christ-centered grace-narratives have a kind of irreducible causal power to change and transform our imagination and sensibility. This thought resides on two assumptions. I simply assume that imagination and emotional sensibility underlie much of our processes of practical reasoning, including value systems, practical self-understanding, and decision policies. I also assume that the imagination is particularly responsive to story. The Christian rituals of baptism, Eucharist, or foot washing are all in their own ways compressed embodied narratives that present and represent that causal power of Christ's life incorporated in believers, power that transforms human nature. For this reason, I have favored and will continue to prioritize methodologically advancing the argument through story-telling.

The second concluding thought is that the syndrome of dispositions associated with Christlike forgiveness is not to be applied mechanically and unreflectively. I have claimed that curative forgivingness, as Jesus enacts it, involves the disposition to suffer the consequences of the offense. I also suggested that part of absorbing the consequence of an offense involves a muting of retaliatory motives, relinquishing blaming, and re-learning to see the offender as a continued recipient of God's grace. Clearly the Scriptures exhort us to forgive others as Christ has forgiven us. Does this mean that believers must simply put up with oppressors? For instance, should Christian women in abusive marriages continue to absorb the violence of their husbands? I have a lot more to say about this in Chapters 4, 5, and especially 6, but here I want to briefly forecast that I do not think this implication follows.

Curative forgivingness refers to a virtue, to a character trait, which is to be explicated as engraining a syndrome of dispositions. Developing Christ-like forgivingness does not imply a rigid duty to forgive every single offense in every single circumstance. For Christians there *is* a duty to develop a Christ-like character, which entails developing the imagination and sensibility, as we have seen, the meta-commitment to suffer the consequence of injury without blaming the assailant, while embodying continued grace toward him. But we do not respond slavishly or mechanically to such meta-commitments. A Christ-incorporated imagination may dispose a person to perform any number of gracious gestures toward an abusive spouse while still not offering forgiveness. In some circumstances, it may not be wise or safe or conducive toward moral health. In other circumstances, a Christ-incorporated imagination may dispose the former to declare the latter forgiven, but either leave the toxic relationship or draw sharper boundaries around its most noxious aspects.

At the same time, curative forgivingness will tend to transform the perception of the offender from someone who is deserving of my moral censure to someone continually worthy of grace and of healing. Entrenching this disposition would seem to require that a wife not see her spouse *only* as a violent jerk. He may also be regarded as a good soccer player, a decent father, clever card player, someone who needs counseling, and someone who is still capable of relevant moral goodness and transformation. Again, it may be permissible and even morally required for her to leave an abusive marriage out of concerns of prudence or wellbeing, but not out of spite or retaliation.

Suppose an individual has her imagination formed by stories of Christ's gracious healing and forgiveness. Are there *any* circumstances that could require her to curb, suppress, or mute the disposition to curatively forgive? Imagine a situation involving an unrepentant offender, one unrelated to her except through his violence, one whose character makes her even doubt there's such a thing as a common humanity. Consider Jean Améry who testifies to a particular horror he experienced at Auschwitz:

> The monster, who is not chained by his conscience to his deed, sees it [the torture] from his viewpoint only as an objectification of his will, not as a moral event. The Flemish SS-man Wajs, who – inspired by his German masters – beat me on the head with a shovel handle whenever I didn't work fast enough, felt the tool to be an extension of his hand and the blows to be emanations of his psycho-physical dynamics. Only I possessed and still possess, the moral truth of the blows that even today roar in my skull, and for that reason I am more entitled to judge, not only more than the culprit, but also more than society – which thinks only about its continued existence.[69]

---

[69] Améry 1980: 70.

Améry might be suggesting here that some crimes are so monstrous and the conceptions under which they are committed so dehumanizing that the perpetrators have de facto opted out of a shared human morality. It would seem that there is no healing for them. They are like the demons Jesus expelled in Mark 5. In such cases, it would seem necessary for the victim to resent and to condemn. This attitude would not only be a psychological necessity for the victim, but also a matter of the moral compulsion to witness to truth. Améry articulates the precise contents of such resentments:

> SS-man Wajs from Antwerp, a repeated murderer and an especially adroit torturer, paid with his life. What more can my foul thirst for revenge demand? But if I have searched my mind properly, it is not a matter of revenge, nor one of atonement. The experience of persecution was, at the very bottom, that of extreme *loneliness*. At stake for me is the release from the abandonment that has persisted from that time until today. When SS-man Wajs stood before the firing squad, he experienced the moral truth of his crimes. At that moment, he was with me – and I was no longer alone with the shovel handle. I would like to believe that at the instant of his execution he wanted exactly as much as I to turn back time, to undo what had been done. When they led him to the place of execution, the antiman had once again become a fellow man. If everything had taken place only between SS-man Wajs and me, and if an entire inverted pyramid of SS men, SS helpers, officials, Kapos, and medal-bedecked generals had not weighed on me, I would have died calmly and appeased along with my fellow man with the Death's Head insignia. At least that is the way it seems to me now.
>
> But Wajs from Antwerp was only one of a multitude. The inverted pyramid is still driving me with its point into the ground.[70]

I suspect one immersed in Christ's forgiving narrative will have a split reaction. She will notice Améry's attempt to humanize his torturer. She will be moved by his desperate, detailed attempt to find some modicum of grace, perhaps a bit of that common humanity with Wajs from Antwerp. At the same time, she will also be inclined to resonate with his desire to hang on to his resentments. Améry concludes this section by arguing that even the desire for "scant" conciliation "can only be either insanity and indifference to life or the masochistic conversion of a suppressed *genuine* demand for revenge." What of the commitment to absorb the consequences of the offense here? Should a person whose imagination is Christ-formed give up her resentments in these kinds of circumstances?

I have a number of reactions to this. I certainly think that in light of his own history, stories, rituals, and other external vehicles of practical reason, Jean Améry

---

[70] Ibid. 70–1.

is justified to hang on to *his* resentments, and does not need anyone's advice or approval. A Christ-like forgiver may even see in Améry's resentments a righteous protest against personal and systemic injustices. A Christ-like forgiver should eternally denounce the inverted pyramids, the entire social contexts, and the cultivated malice that turned Wajs into the torturer he became. Further, a Christ-like forgiver may not be able to imagine a way that grace could be extended to Wajs and other Capos.

At the same time, because of the way her imagination is formed, a Christ-like forgiver will also be incapable of imagining the intrinsic goodness of an enduring, cultivated ill-will toward Wajs and the Capos. And so, if she were to ever be placed in circumstances analogous to those of Améry, she might be impelled to give expression to the demands of justice and simultaneously to the demands of Christ's mercy, to keep both commitments in tension. In Chapter 6, I propose a model of practical agency that makes such seemingly opposite attitudes not only coherent but also mutually supportive. This commitment to live with tension is justified and ennobled by a radical trust in the goodness of God. In the Christ-like forgiver, the demands for justice and her resentments will be in some sense conditioned by her Christic imagination. There will be protests, there will be calls for revenge perhaps in public, perhaps in private. But these gestures and words will essentially be refracted through mercy, and so they would essentially also sound like lament and mourning. Whatever her resentments, a Christ-like forgiver would also mourn the condition of an offender who is twice removed from his Flemish Antwerp: first the man lost his Flemish identity in the inverted German death pyramid, and second his human agency as his hand becomes a "shovel," just a natural object, just a piece of nature. Whether intentionally or reflexively, her imagination would continually be disposed to humanize her attacker. Even when the wound is deep and wide, even when she cannot and should not lose her resentments, she would hope that she can at least *add* to all her angers also her laments. And then, she might hope that mourning would, in time, disband resentment. And then, perhaps she might also hope that God will show goodness to her and her assailant in ways that go beyond what she can now imagine.

4

Divine Forgiveness and Justice for All

"Steadfast love and faithfulness will meet;
righteousness and peace will kiss each other."
Psalm 85:10

In Chapters 2 and 3 I argued that the biblical imagination places gracious forgivingness at the center of God's agency. The idea that God is the quintessential and ultimate sin-bearing agent underlies the liturgy and theology of ancient Israel, satisfies deep intuitions about moral goodness, motivates the cultic and religious function of the representative, and finds a uniquely fruitful expression in Christ.

What about the theological and normative priority of divine justice? If God is perfectly holy, any sin ruptures the fabric of creaturely goodness and impugns the majesty of God's character. Thus, perfect justice requires that God be angry with sinners, and respond with harsh treatment proportionate to the gravity of the rupture and offense. If God exercises gracious forgivingness toward unwavering sinners, the normative fissures and the assault on God's holiness remain outstanding. At first blush, divine forgivingness seems in tension with the demands of God's perfect holiness and justice.

This chapter recovers a biblical conception of divine justice that communicates the wrongness of sin while also aiming essentially at restoration. I begin by clarifying some of the conceptual and theological roots of divine retributivism. In the second section I contend briefly against an extreme example, while the third section deals in depth with a more moderate and plausible version of divine retributivism. I uncover the latter's theological, rabbinical, and philosophical genealogy. I suggest that each of these strands is actually discretionary in light of the biblical evidence. The fourth section articulates an alternative to divine retributivism, namely, the communicative-restorative framework. Finally, I argue that there is a coherent and compelling narrative arc, running from the creation stories through the Law and the Prophets all the way to Jesus, that corroborates the communicative-restorative understanding of divine justice.

Conceptual Preliminaries

The idea of retributive justice evokes at least three common normative intuitions. First, a serious offense requires or calls out for a proportionate punishment.

Gracious Forgiveness: A Theological Retrieval. Cristian F. Mihut, Oxford University Press. © Cristian F. Mihut 2023.
DOI: 10.1093/oso/9780192873729.003.0004

Second, the punishment is intrinsically good if it is intentionally administered by a legitimate authority. Third, the punishment is unjustified if visited upon the innocent or inflicted disproportionately upon the guilty.[1] Retribution looks backward to the seriousness of the normative breach and aims to address it by inflicting a proportionate pain in the offender. Consequently, divine retributive justice entails that God, as the ultimate moral legislator, fittingly visits intentional and proportionate harm upon sinners *because* of their sin.

At first glance, the Judeo-Christian tradition seems to support and even enrich this conceptual picture. As creator of the universe, God's authority to dispense punishment is unquestionable. Furthermore, if sin is transgression against the order God imprinted on the cosmos, any moral lapse or wrongdoing seems to demand divine punishment.[2] In some quarters, it is not only our transgressions or tendencies to transgress that require punishment. Human nature itself is corrupt or corruptible at its very core. We are bad to the bone. Through and through, we are proper objects of God's wrath.

Consider how this idea gets fleshed out in the Reformed tradition. Question 10 of Lord's Day 4 in the *Heidelberg Catechism* asks whether God will allow disobedience and apostasy to go unpunished. The answer is unequivocal. God is both "terribly displeased" with sin and he will punish sinfulness with a just judgment "both now and eternally." Question 11 attempts to mollify this seemingly harsh stance: "But is God also not merciful?" The retort underscores not only the priority of divine justice, but also of a particularly punitive aspect of it. Transgressive contexts demand the exercise of punishment: "God is indeed merciful, but He is also just. His justice requires that sin committed against the most high majesty of God also be punished with the most severe, that is, with everlasting, punishment of body and soul."[3] Two assumptions here may appear puzzling, particularly to those who understand sin as a disease that needs curing more than as an offense requiring prosecution and penalty.

The first is that severe punishment is not only permissible but required by God's justice. The second is that an essential aspect of God's moral being can only

---

[1] See a thorough conceptual map of "retributive justice" in Walen 2014.

[2] Some could worry that I conflate two conceptually distinct domains: *holiness* and *morality*. As Leviticus insists, any number of morally neutral things (involuntary bodily emissions, sowing different seeds in the same ground, eating shellfish) can separate one from God. That being said, it is not illegitimate to take *moral transgression* as the paradigmatic target of God's forgiveness for at least two reasons. First, the narrative arc of Scripture places at the heart of God's law the love of neighbor. From Moses to Isaiah to Jesus, the first tablet of the law is increasingly unpacked through the second tablet. Isaiah goes so far as to say that, in the context of an unjust society, God hates purification rituals and worship. In his ministry, Jesus also tackles ways in which the category of "the holy" has been used to marginalize and exclude people. Second, some thinkers deem it appropriate to conceptualize moral wrongdoing, theologically, as a kind of pollution. Concretely, see Stump 2020 and Rea 2019 for discussions of moral wrongdoing as a stain on the soul. In short, the concept of sin can be defined paradigmatically by reference to moral transgression, and there is precedent in the literature for treating wrongdoing and sinning interchangeably.

[3] Christian Reformed Church 1987: 864.

be expressed through punishment. It is as if retribution reveals the vastness of divine majesty in a way that mercy could not. Forgoing punishment of the unrepentant would in some way diminish God's maximal moral greatness, and therefore God would cease to be God.

My Reformed interlocutor does not find these two assumptions perplexing. The Catechism prioritizes divine justice over mercy, she would say, because human depravity—"disobedience and apostasy"—is such a clear and totalizing reality. Generally, an account of divine moral psychology must be importantly responsive to philosophical anthropology, she would add. The stronger our doctrine of sin, the stronger the justification for divine retributivism.[4] The deeper the sin saturates human nature, the higher the moral demand for divine punishment. But this presupposition is doubtful for two main reasons.

First, my interlocutor simply assumes that a "strong doctrine of sin" is at home largely inside a forensic framework. But as we have already seen in Chapters 2 and 3, central curative and cultic contexts of the Bible do not always emphasize the legal concepts of sin. Sin sometimes is disease, burden, pollution, or alienation. Sometimes rebellion is a symptom of an underlying sickness. And sometimes even when sin is explicitly viewed as entrenched rebellion, the cessation of God's punitive acts is explained by divine actions or attitudes that transcend the forensic framework. A major narrative development in the post-exilic Psalms and Prophets is that due to a loving attunement to Israel's wounds, God recasts former offenders as present sufferers, thus relenting from prosecution. God suspends punishment for reasons inherent in a medicinal framework. Furthermore, as we noted in Chapter 3, the Incarnation is God's ultimate response to sin. God takes on human flesh in order to heal human nature from the inside, and from anything that would separate it from the divine.

Second, even if human nature were sin-saturated to the core, and even if transgressing God's law was a more fundamental conception of sin than disease, pollution, or alienation, it would still not follow that God's primary response to sin must be retribution. God's considered response to rebellion may be patience, kindness, or an infinite mercy. God may possess an infinite disposition for promoting reformist or rehabilitating strategies that combat or contain the violations of the moral law. Alternatively, God may have a disposition toward infinite sadness, were it foreseeable that all these other strategies end up in failure. Whether we go with Irenaeus or with Augustine in matters of philosophical anthropology and hamartiology, merely influences but need not fix our conception of divine retributivism.

Allow me to illustrate. Susie Irene thinks that the first sin was pedagogically necessary for Adam's maturation, but it neither warped Adam to the core, nor was

---

[4] I am particularly thankful to David DeJong for pressing this objection.

it transmitted like a bad gene to his children. Susie construes her own sins as instances of missing the mark, instructive failures that a good teacher can use to help her make moral progress. But Susie also holds that God *must* punish failing humans, because punishment communicates a unique moral disapproval, without which moral progress is impossible.

By contrast, consider Kelvin Augustinus, who holds that ever since Eve desired the fruit, all humans are walking disasters, bad to the bone, inherently broken pieces of rational nature. Sinning is constitutive of who or what we are. But Kelvin also thinks it is not rational to punish broken pieces of nature, especially if they are unlikely to reform through harsh treatment. And if divine punishment resembles pointless or vindictive human punitive practices, then, Kelvin thinks, it is also morally unsavory.

Susie shows that the Irenaean way of treating original sin as a kind of immaturity is compatible with divine punishment. And Kelvin shows that the Augustinian conception of sin as total corruption does not require a retributive God. Whether or the extent to which sinfulness is enmeshed in human nature does not *automatically* settle the issue regarding the retributive nature of divine justice. The answer depends on other complicated empirical, quasi-empirical, conceptual, and theological questions such as these: Is punishment more or less likely to foster moral growth (or to curb moral regress) in offenders, victims, and larger communities? Is punishment uniquely fitting to communicate divine disapproval of sinful behavior? What counts as divine punishment, and how is it different from projective error, that is, from mistakenly attributing to God fashionable human punitive practices?

At any rate, classical Reformed Christianity has not been alone in placing a high premium on divine retributive justice. As we have seen in Chapter 2, when systematizing the biblical intuitions about God's character, Michael L. Morgan makes a point strikingly similar to the Heidelberg Catechism:

> The biblical God is a lawgiver. Sin is transgression of divine law: it is disobedience to divine command and an affront to God, an act of rebellion. The normative response of God to sin is anger and retribution. The biblical God is a just God, and this justice is a feature of divine life and cosmic order that is canonized in the book of Deuteronomy and expressed extensively throughout the Bible.[5]

Unlike the Protestant Reformers, the Jewish tradition is not keen on making sin intrinsic to human nature. Like them, however, it sees divine mercy as a mere amelioration of retributive justice. Recall Morgan's characterization of divine forgiveness as a surplus left over after divine justice has done most of the heavy

---

[5] Morgan 2012: 139.

lifting. Because anger and retribution are lead actors while forgiveness and mercy play a secondary, supportive role in God's motivational profile, I refer to this view as *tempered retribution*. In a moment, I will return to evaluate it.

We are thus presented with a deep tension between two divergent biblical frameworks for understanding divine agency, the healing and the retributive. If a loving sin-bearing defines God's self-understanding with respect to belligerent Israel, if Christ is the utmost expression of undeserved divine grace toward the entire world, then mercy and curative forgivingness are center stage and retribution is eclipsed. But this does not mean that divine justice is jettisoned. Not at all. The healing framework requires a robust conception of justice, though it rethinks the concept of retribution.

A robust, punishment-reframing conception of justice involves the following: (i) God's condemnation of or taking a serious stance against sin; (ii) God's condemnation of sin being expressed through a host of non-retributive, censoring behaviors—God can rebuke, be silent, withhold or remove his presence, or show wrath toward sinful persons if these divine gestures are conducive toward some good or to the restoration of persons and relationships; (iii) divine censoring gestures cannot be a payback for sin; they must be in some sense oriented toward the good of the sinner—restoration, moral knowledge, or arresting one from descending into a deeper alienation from God, self, and others. Divine hard treatment is associated with or embedded in divine intentions to heal the wrongdoer or to prevent his moral gangrene from spreading. Clearly, this conception of divine justice allows pain as conducive to ultimate restoration, thus driving a wedge between punishment and retribution.

This chapter then extends the argument from Chapters 2 and 3. It interrogates the biblical, theological, and philosophical assumptions buttressing the centrality of divine retribution. It argues positively that sin-bearing forgivingness is consistent with a conception of divine justice that condemns wrongdoing while aiming to heal victim and victimizer. And it shows how, by restoring victims and offenders, God magnifies God's majesty and remains faithful to Godself.

Anger Gone Wild

The *tempered retribution* view of divine justice is distinct from a more extreme cousin. This radical cousin says that, for the most part, divine power and wrath run the gamut unobstructed by mercy or compassion. An angry, punitive God features mightily in the sermons of "fire-and-brimstone" preachers, and impresses the imaginations of church-camp teenagers.[6] But even elevated minds indulge it.

---

[6] Consider Mark Driscoll, an infamous Evangelical preacher, proclaiming the "good news" that God hates who we are in his notorious sermon "Jesus Sweats Blood." A quick YouTube search reveals an obsession with God's wrath in this and other sermons.

Jonathan Edwards's famous "Sinners in the Hands of an Angry God," expresses the view that the inhabitants of Hell are constantly and eternally the objects of God's un-arrested wrath. Speaking to a congregation whose actions evidenced an unconverted state, Edwards paints vivid pictures of what awaits them, should they remain unrepentant:

> Consider this, you that are here present, that yet remain in an unregenerate State. That God will execute the fierceness of his Anger, implies that he will inflict Wrath without any Pity: when God beholds the ineffable Extremity of your Case and sees your Torment to be so vastly disproportion'd to your Strength, and sees how your poor Soul is crushed and sinks down, as it were into an infinite Gloom, he will have no Compassion upon you, he will not forbear the Executions of his Wrath, or in the least lighten his Hand; there shall be no Moderation or Mercy, nor will God then at all stay his rough Wind; he will have no Regard to your Welfare, nor be at all careful lest you should suffer too much, in any other Sense than only that you shall not suffer beyond what strict Justice requires: nothing shall be with-held, because it's so hard for you to bear.[7]

This picture of the divine character seems strikingly at odds with the primacy of *hesed* we find in the grace-formula. Edwards makes it clear that this is no incidental wrath. The merciless torment inveighed upon "the wretched sinners" is a carefully choreographed bloodbath playing eternally before the powers of the universe, angelic and human, rebellious and submissive, so they may behold "the infinite Weight and Power of his Indignation." Evocative of the muscle-show of medieval monarchs in conquered territories, Edwards pictures a god who treads upon sinners with lavish contempt, their blood staining his raiment, ostensibly to flaunt his omnipotent glory before the cosmos.

Additionally, according to Edwards, God sees the unrepentant-but-not-yet-damned pretty much in the same light as the damned-for-good, that is, through the chilling glow of wrath, disgust, and contempt. Though hyperbolic and deliberately rhetorical, Edwards's images speak volumes:

> The God that holds you over the Pit of Hell, much as one holds a Spider, or some loathsome Insect, over the Fire, abhors you, and is dreadfully provoked; his Wrath towards you burns like Fire; he looks upon you as worthy of nothing else, but to be cast into the Fire; he is of purer Eyes than to bear to have you in his Sight; you are ten thousand Times so abominable in his Eyes as the most hateful venomous Serpent is in ours. You have offended him infinitely more than ever a stubborn Rebel did his Prince: and yet 'tis nothing but his Hand that holds you from falling into Fire every Moment...[8]

---

[7] Edwards 1741: 18.   [8] Ibid. 15.

Even if we abstract from the image of spiders dangling over blazes, the takeaway is obvious. In our unrepentant state God loathes us. The only reason God refrains momentarily from setting us aflame or from splotching his raiment with our blood is his arbitrary pleasure. It is not due to some intrinsic or relational feature we have. It is for the heck of it, simply because God can, because God delights in this particular use of divine power. Some see divine grace in this stay of execution. But is it really? This saving act looks to me fickle and arbitrary because it does not spring from stable divine dispositions and is not informed by sensible considerations. In a great subversion of the grace-formula, stylized as the mighty whirlwind and the great flood of God, *wrath* is the most entrenched disposition of the divine character, the lead player. Grace, if that is the name, is a mere dangling thread.

Due to its thinness and arbitrariness, *this* divine grace is hardly praiseworthy, and may even appear hideous. In Edwards's sermon, we are already over-determined to be damned and loathsome. The devil and his cohorts hate and would devour us were it not for God's arbitrary pleasure. Our loathsome inner natures suffice by themselves to rush us diving into the flames. Ours is a damned and loathsome world, inside and out. Instead of magnifying grace to the over-determined wretched beings, God *adds* his power and crushing wrath to the chorus. The arbitrariness and thinness of *this* grace, foregrounding the cosmic pervasiveness of aversion to these poor, self-destructive creatures, does not reveal an honorable moral character. This is desire for honor gone wild, and cosmic power turned pathological.

Tempered Retribution

The *anger gone wild* view of divine justice is a nonstarter. Perhaps effective only rhetorically today, this picture is, at best, biblically incomplete and philosophically and experientially flawed. Thankfully, we have at hand a more plausible alternative. The *tempered retribution* view sees divine justice as central. It agrees with the grammar of forgiveness we developed in previous chapters in the following respect. There is genuine interaction between divine positive and negative affections, between mercy and retributive anger, between divine forgivingness and divine justice. In addition, it exhibits impressive rabbinic, philosophical, theological, and experiential credentials. I proceed to add to its characterization and then move to evaluate some of its central assumptions.

In Chapter 2, I sketched the grammar of gracious forgivingness revealed by the network characterization inherent in the grace-formula. A proponent of tempered retribution can also appeal to a kind of network characterization that has a different starting point. The attribute of divine justice expresses quintessentially God's normative commitments, since divine majesty and the normative order are impugned by human transgression. Divine just actions and certain divine reactive emotions such as anger and indignation must thus be taken to reveal a coherent agency. In the very center we find God's integrity to Godself. Integrity expresses itself in the divine commitment to preserve divine honor or to restore it if lost. And this means that God must endorse his anger toward transgressions and must execute judgment. Mercy and forgiveness do get a hearing as mitigators of retribution. But they are essentially derivative from God's honor and justice.[9] Forgiveness and mercy must fit in a universe ordered and managed by divine legislation, for this legislation essentially expresses God's majesty.

The normative and motivational priority of divine justice over forgiveness seems supported by significant parts of the rabbinic tradition. Some of the sages look to divine justice as the ultimate and determinative attribute in the divine psychology. In this, they remain intensely aware of God's compassion. The power of repentance, they suppose, holds particular sway over God's mercy. But these rabbis, having hitched mercy—in the sense of clemency—to the horse of forensic justice, do not confer on divine compassion the power to *overturn* God's just judgments: "[The] Lord's compassion only diminishes the severity of the sentence, but does not annul it or replace it."[10]

The rabbinic tradition, however, does not speak in a single voice about this. In his masterful summary, Ephraime E. Urbach reveals the subtleties, ingenuity, and even inconsistencies embedded in the tradition. On Urbach's telling, some sages hold that divine justice is *rooted in* the attribute of compassion. Others argue that God is so responsive to virtuous human actions that the attribute of justice can literally *transform* into that of divine compassion. Others still see the two attributes as expressions of the same underlying divine disposition, while others argue that the two distinct and irreducible divine powers must remain equal in stature and motivational influence.

Surprisingly, some rabbis even argue that divine compassionate grace essentially upstages and subverts the demands of justice. According to Urbach, they assume that God's attributes could acquire causal powers, even person-like agency of persuasion and deliberation, independent of God's own being. This questionable thesis is not relevant to my point. I can gloss it as the claim that among all efficacious divine attitudes, only some are defining of God's moral identity. Perhaps the sages, as contemporary action theorists routinely do, recognized a distinction between actions motivated by a person's deepest self, and those motivated by more superficial concerns. One interesting rabbinic development is that God *identifies* Godself with the attribute of compassion, while justice becomes an advisor pushed toward the outskirts of divine agency:

---

[9] Cf. Psalm 130:4 and Sarah Coakley's "On the Fearfulness of Forgiveness: Psalm 130.4 and Its Theological Implications" presented at Tantur Ecumenical Institute, Jerusalem, May 23–26, 2004.
[10] Urbach 1975: 449.

In the Haggada that we have cited, and in similar stories, the Attribute of Justice strives to maintain its position unimpaired. Its aim is to prevent the scales from being unjustly inclined towards mercy, and the Lord answers its arguments. But in the course of the debate the struggle changes its aspects. From being a contest between two attributes it becomes a struggle between the Attribute of Justice and the Almighty, who becomes identified with the Attribute of Compassion.[11]

Urbach traces a second interesting evolution in the thinking of the sages. If the earlier tradition argued for the equality of the divine attributes, the latter sources seem interested in elevating the causal powers of justice. But *elevation in power* does not mean *centrality in God's heart*. Paradoxically, by growing in strength, justice becomes externalized from God's deepest self:

> The possibility of such an interchange in the sources – the Attribute of Justice transmuted into angels – provides proof of the growing power of the Attribute of Justice, but paradoxically, its potential activity became at the same time contracted and a limit was set to it. When it clashes with the cardinal belief in the power of repentance, the Lord conceals His actions from it and its significance is consequently annulled.[12]

Even as justice gains executive strength, it becomes increasingly removed from the divine motivational core, from the innermost divine counsel. Powerful in its effects but expandable with respect to guidance, justice is bypassed entirely when God responds to repentance. Compassion by contrast is God's most trusted advisor, a wise yet discreet confidant. It seems, then, that the rabbinic tradition does not provide decisive evidence for the priority of divine justice over forgiveness. And if Urbach's developmental insights indicate a *progressive* rabbinic elucidation of divine agency, the tradition certainly contains the seeds for subverting the normative and theological priority of divine justice over grace.

What about the philosophical and theological evidence? As I see things, the clearest philosophical picture motivating the tempered retribution view is that of the high-minded, noble person. As Aristotle suggests, the noble-minded individual has a properly elevated view of her own character, being attuned to the appropriate degree of honor, esteem, and admiration due to her. When others harm or insult her, they effectively disrespect her noble character, such defamations requiring a just response. A first appropriate response is anger. In her anger, the magnanimous individual remains virtuous. The response must be timely, reasonable, and proportionate to the offense. Irritability would show an excessive disposition toward anger, so the virtuous person tempers it with meekness or

---

[11] Ibid. 460.   [12] Ibid. 461.

gentleness. But significantly, the disposition toward meekness, which for Aristotle results in forgiving actions, leans toward deficiency in virtue, since it signals a blamable lack of anger:

> But the deficiency, whether it is a certain slowness to anger or whatsoever it may be, is blamed. For those who do not get angry at things one ought to get angry at seem to be foolish, as do those who do not get angry as one ought, or when or at whom one ought, for they seem not to perceive it and not to be pained, since they do not get angry and are not apt to defend themselves. For holding back when one is being foully insulted, and overlooking it when it happens to those close to one, is slavish.[13]

For Aristotle then, the high-minded individual has a heightened sensitivity to injurious harms or insults, a proper anger that does not degenerate into irritability, hot-headedness, or bitterness. If by defending honor, anger has a self-regarding, quasi-perceptual dimension, it also has an other-regarding, outgoing dimension. In its desiderative mode, Aristotelian anger is retributive, since it involves a desire for revenge, a desire to see the offender suffer for slights or injustices committed.[14] Here then is the picture we inherit from Aristotle: The magnanimous individual responds to transgression essentially by defending her own honor, the nobility of her character. Her anger is the chief disposition summoned up for this task, and anger is constituted by a trained sensitivity to detect undeserved injuries and offenses, and by the vengeful desire to strike back at offenders. Gentleness and meekness become salient only if anger oversteps its bounds.

I suspect that this Aristotelian conception of ideal agency implicitly or explicitly informs a preponderance of the classical theological theorizing about God's just character. Additionally, it seems to me that Anselmian theology, in particular, has performed at least two significant transmutations upon this Aristotelian conception. The first is that God's honor is seen as infinite. In the Aristotelian paradigm, a noble person responds to injury with a rational desire for finite retribution. In the Anselmian perspective, if God's honor is slighted, since God is infinite, it is rational and good for God to demand infinite retribution from the offender. To show that this is not just some arcane historical matter, consider a statement from a contemporary defender of this assumption:

> I have shown that the greatness of the one against whom an offence occurs need not determine the degree of the wrongdoer's guilt if, and only if, the one against whom the wrong is committed is within a comparable or commensurate

---

[13] Aristotle 2002: 72.
[14] Cf. *Rhet.* 1378a31–3; *DA* 403a31; and *EN* 1126a21–2 in Aristotle 1984.

ontological kind, such as 'non-divine'...However, in the case of a sin against God, this principle does not obtain, simply because God is not of the same ontological kind, and does have an infinite dignity and worth, which if offended carry infinite demerit.[15]

The second Anselmian transformation makes any transgression against the moral law a de facto insult against God's moral character, a violation of his honor. If God is *the* moral lawgiver, *any* transgression defames God's very being. The same modern theologian expressing support for the first assumption, articulates the rationale for the second:

> If every sin is a transgression of divine law, then every sin is a sin against God, the author of that law. For, on this version of Augustinianism, the moral law of God is an expression of the character of God. And to impugn God's character is to impugn God himself. Hence, on this particular understanding of Christian theology, all sin is against God, even where it is not intentionally against God, just as my jaywalking in the street is an action against the law of the land, even if I am blissfully unaware that jaywalking is an offense.[16]

Putting these pieces together we get the following Anselmian expansion of Aristotle. *Any* sin assails God's honor, requiring thus an infinite punishment. Repentance is merely a finite act, and, as such, insufficient to satisfy an infinite offense. Only an infinite subject can rectify God's impugned honor and meet the infinite demands of the law; or else, finite offenders for an infinite extension of time. The priority of divine justice thus vindicated, divine compassion can at most only mollify, redirect (from finite to infinite beings), or delay punishment.

The Anselmian expansion of Aristotle rests on three fundamental assumptions:

(*A1*) God's moral being is essentially constituted by God's valuing his infinite honor.

(*A2*) Any violation of the moral law constitutes an infringement against God's honor.

(*A3*) God necessarily desires infinite retribution for any infringement against God's honor.

How should we respond? We could easily challenge (*A1*). The language of divine majesty and honor, we might say, is based in "triumphalist, monarchical, and patriarchal" models of God.[17] Surely, in a pre-ecological, pre-technological, and pre-nuclear age, these metaphors might have been fruitful for organizing the faith

---

[15] Crisp 2003: 45.   [16] Ibid. 43.   [17] McFague 1988: xi.

and practices of believers. But these pictures have run their course. We need to develop experientially more credible models of God, based perhaps in the biblical metaphors of mother, lover, and friend. However exciting this strategy may be, I will not develop it here.

Instead, I grant assumptions (*A1*) and (*A2*), but question the adequacy of (*A3*). I grant that God wants to magnify his infinite honor in the world, and that, when properly understood, violations of God's law amount to impugning God's character. But, as we shall see, the biblically-sensitive glosses of (*A1*) and (*A2*) threaten to undermine the plausibility of (*A3*). Paradigmatic biblical stories understand the demand of God's honor without requiring that snubbed divine majesty entail the desire for retribution, much less infinite punishment. The divine lawgiver is a healer and restorer, concerned to redress the harm done to the victim, to repair the personhood of the offender, and to bring the two into relational harmony. Hard treatment is subservient to the goals of repair and restoration. What's more, punishment is often muted, subverted, or drops out precisely where the retributivist should find it center stage. But that is not to say that divine justice drops out. God is essentially committed to putting the world to rights, and one sees in the resurrection of Jesus the culmination of a story-line according to which God vindicates the victim while also working to restore the offender.

As we have seen in Chapter 3, by Christ's wounds we are healed. Christ's sin-bearing work *heals and expands* human nature by incorporating it into God's radical, gracious forgivingness. But human nature is also healed in a different sense through the Resurrection. In it we see divine justice, because God decisively recognizes, prioritizes, and vindicates the stance of the blameless victim. In the Resurrection, we also see divine justice as relational and restorative; we see God inaugurating a new, eschatological way of life where former enemies are brought together in a community of sharing and shalom, a way of life that obviates the need for punishment.[18]

Communicative-Restorative Justice

I have given some conceptual, theological, and biblical reasons for why retribution does not find an easy fit at the center of God's character. In this section I describe a justice framework that makes sense of divine wrath and of hard treatment as reprobative communications teleologically embedded in a larger work of restoration. Because it is a hybrid framework, I call it communicative-restorative justice. In the following section I will look at some biblical episodes that motivate, justify,

---

[18] Consider the way Paul uses the Resurrection to articulate a beautiful vision for both *personal* and *communitarian* transformation (Colossians 3:1–4 and 10–11).

and illustrate this conception of God's justice: in the Eden story, the Torah, the Prophets, and Christ's cleansing of the Temple.

From the get-go, I want to underscore two focal points of contrast between the communicative-restorative framework and the retributivist picture. First, the Anselmian picture focuses on the ontological distance, a distance strongly suggestive of a normative gap between the divine and the human, between the infinite and the finite, a gap that is essentially understood in forensic terms: finite, fallible creatures essentially have no moral standing before the judge of the universe. The communicative-restorative framework, by contrast, locates the divine-human normative gap in a different place: God's desire for intimacy with people is so profound and consistent that God's *hesed* far transcends what humans can imagine and internalize. God loves sinners with an unimaginable generosity, and it is only through union with God that humans can transcend their own limits to a reliable love of neighbor and enemy.

This observation leads to a second point of contrast. On the Anselmian picture, divine justice seems motivated by a kind of self-referentiality. It seems primarily concerned to maintain the integrity and the purity of God's moral being. Justice seems chiefly alert to violations of an abstract moral law which is the codified expression of God's inner life. In the communicative-restorative framework, divine justice is essentially relational, and divine integrity is essentially other-regarding. God's integrity involves protecting from oppression the integrity of those vulnerable and marginalized. As Psalm 8 puts it, God establishes strength from the mouths of nursing infants. That is to say, God's honor is measured by how the most defenseless of creatures are treated. To the extent that divine anger refracts through or reflects the pain of the defenseless, it communicates God's stance against evil and injustice. God's anger expresses the commitment to heal both victim and victimizer, thus supporting and intensifying divine mercy. Symptoms of God's concern to restore the shalom of others, divine justice, anger, and majesty are fully compatible with divine forgivingness.

In legal theory there are two main alternatives to retributivist theories of punishment: communicative/expressive views and restorative justice views. Let me take each view in turn. According to the former, punishment is an illocutionary act whereby a proper authority expresses symbolically to the offender a moral condemnation of the offense.[19] The purpose of this symbolic communication is pedagogical or reformatory—the proper authority intends to educate the offender about the badness of the act, or to induce the latter to repent, make atonement, or undergo relevant transformation.

A general limitation of expressive accounts is that the intended education or reformation of offenders could be accomplished through non-punitive means.

---

[19] Cf. Feinberg 1965; Holmgren 2012; Duff 2003; and Murphy 2014: ch. 6.

All other things being equal, it seems preferable to educate or reform offenders while avoiding causing pain or constricting their free agency. Theologically, communicative reprobation makes sense, because if there were inherent moral goods for the offender (and others) that could only come through specific hard treatments, God would certainly know about them. Still, I propose widening the concept of theological communicative reprobation beyond the narrow focus on the offender. I would like to consider the possibility that God's anger communicates at once to multiple audiences—it speaks to offenders about the wrongness of their offenses urging reformation, and it speaks to the victims (and other interested third parties) that their injury has been acknowledged, and that the offender has been called out to answer for his action and character. Consider, *Expanded Communicative Divine Punishment*:

> *ECDP*: Divine wrath or hard treatment of offenders expresses God's moral condemnation of the offense. Through symbolic gestures, God communicates to victims (and their larger communities) that their injury/pain is acknowledged and that the injurers are being called out to account for the caused pain, and to deserving offenders that their offenses are sinful and wrong, so that they might repent, atone for their sins, and reform their characters.[20]

There are obvious benefits to *ECDP*. Contrasting pure retributivism, the punitive act here does not have the morally dubious status of backward-looking payback; it addresses the full-fledged moral agency of both victims and offenders; and expresses the gravity of the offense. Still, an essential component of biblical justice seems missing or neglected even in *ECDP*. *Biblical justice is essentially embedded in a teleological, shalom-seeking perspective, since divine justice and condemnation ultimately aim at repairing the harm by drawing offender and victim in a communal way of living constitutive of mutual wellbeing.* Biblically, divine justice seeks creaturely restoration and relational flourishing. The lion shall lie down with the lamb, says Isaiah, poetically. Jeremiah advises Hebrew exiles in Babylon to seek the welfare of the very city that enslaved them and to pray for it, "for in its welfare you will find your welfare" (Jeremiah 29:7). Paul rhapsodizes about God's new society where walls of ethnic, economic, religious, and gender hostility have been broken down through the cross and resurrection of Christ. And the book of Revelation ends with the kings of the earth bringing their honor and glory through the gates of the New Jerusalem, though only four chapters earlier the same kings of the earth were described as committing fornication with the whore of Babylon. The narrative arc of biblical justice tends toward the healing of both victims and

---

[20] For another formulation see Jordan Wessling, "How Does a Loving God Punish? On the Unification of Divine Love & Wrath." Presented at the Center for Philosophy of Religion, University of Notre Dame, September 7, 2012.

offenders, toward a transformation of both in their respective environments that makes it possible for them to share in a life of mutual thriving.

To articulate deeper a shalom-seeking teleology we can help ourselves to concepts inherent in the restorative justice movement. There are different understandings of restorative justice, but common to all is playing down the concept of punishment—whether retributive or communicative—while shifting the focus on repairing the harm done by the offense and addressing the underlying causes of the harm.[21] As Howard Zehr, a figurehead of the restorative justice framework, puts it:

> Retributive theory believes that pain will vindicate, but in practice that is often counterproductive for both victim and offender. Restorative justice theory, on the other hand, argues that what truly vindicates is acknowledgment of victims' harms and needs, combined with an active effort to encourage offenders to take responsibility, make right the wrongs, and address the causes of their behavior. By addressing this need for vindication in a positive way, restorative justice has the potential to affirm both victim and offender and to help them transform their lives.[22]

In restorative frameworks, confronting the harm is a multifaceted affair engaging at once offender, victim, and the larger community. It involves aiming to repair the agency of the victim by elevating her moral and epistemic status through practices of acknowledging the harm by the community, truth commissions, or mediating third parties,[23] by issuing standing invitations to offenders to do the same, and by practices through which the community makes compensations to victims.[24] It involves encouraging offenders to take responsibility for and to confront the underlying causes of injury, harm, and offense, regardless of what they are—personality traits, past trauma, socio-economic conditions, dysfunctional peers

---

[21] Consider this helpful summary by Van Ness and Strong "There are multiple conceptions of restorative justice. For some, its essence lies in encounters, the restorative processes in which the parties may find healing. For others, it is a view of justice that insists that the harm caused by crime be repaired to the extent possible. For still others, it is a way of living that transforms relationships with others and with the physical and social environment" (Van Ness and Strong 2010: 58).

[22] Zehr 2002: 59.

[23] This point receives anecdotal support from the victims who told their victimization stories during the TRC hearings in South Africa, and commissioners overseeing the Human Rights Violations hearings. "Referring to the psychological value of testifying, one witness said: 'When the officer tortured me at that time in John Vorster Square, he laughed at me: "You can scream your head off, nobody will ever hear you!" He was wrong. Today there are people who will hear me.' Commissioner Mary Burton agrees that giving public testimony had been healing for many survivors: 'The right to be heard and acknowledged, with respect and empathy, did contribute to a process of healing in many cases'" (Graybill and Lanegran 2004: 6).

[24] The victims of the Sierra Leone genocide insisted in their TRC hearings that the commission seriously include the recommendation that compensations would be made to them through access to medical care, adequate housing, and free education for their children (Schabas 2003).

and family, etc.[25] The hope here is that this confrontation with the truth of caused harm and addressing its underlying springs will be constitutive of the offender's agency repair. The framework also typically involves aiming to ultimately return and reintegrate both victim and offender to proper functioning in their respective communities. Finally, as the framework has been used in countries torn apart by cycles of ethnic violence, confronting the harm aims at long-lasting healing by creating a climate where offenders and victims become stakeholders in the reconciliation process.

Applying these restoration concepts to a theological shalom-seeking justice framework is instinctive and legitimate, since at least some of these have been inspired by a Christian theology of forgiveness and reconciliation. I want to suggest that we think of God as playing the role of a mediating third party between offender and victim, analogous to the Truth and Reconciliation Committees. And so:

Divine Restorative Justice (DRJ): (i) God prioritizes the epistemic and moral stance of the victims by recognizing the harm done to them, by publicly echoing the truth of the harm, and by aiming to recompense the victims; (ii) God encourages offenders to take responsibility for their actions even as God works to ultimately heal the underlying causes of the harmful action in the offender; (iii) so that both offender and victim would be enabled through further divine assistance to be integrated into a larger healed community of shalom, and by their own healed agencies to stand against future recycling of harm, violence, or trauma.

Conceptually, *ECDP* is consistent with *DRJ*. Furthermore, there are obvious ways *ECDP* can be naturally embedded in *DRJ*. For instance, victims can recognize in God's anger with offenders God's resonance with the truth of that harm or a way for God to publicly endorse and validate the standpoint of the victim (expression of *DRJ (i)*). Additionally, victims could see in God's wrath a way to encourage offenders to take responsibility for harms or offenses, or to address their fundamental causes (expression of *DRJ (ii)*). *DRJ* adds that the ultimate goal of victim-recognition and offender-accountability is a kind of repair of both agencies and their integration into a well-functioning social environment. Perhaps this divine

---

[25] Obviously, I do not present these as mutually exclusive options. For instance, plausibly, the perpetrators of the Rwandan genocide are responsible for the shape of their own characters, but also that, at least in some cases, these characters are shaped by suffered trauma and past cycles of violence: "Attention must also be given to the wounds perpetrators have suffered. Often perpetrators have endured victimization or other traumatic experiences as part of prior cycles of violence. Their unhealed wounds have contributed to their actions. Sometimes past trauma has been fixed and maintained in collective memory, continually shaping the group's outlook and behavior. In addition, however, perpetrators of violence, and especially of genocide, can be deeply wounded by their own horrible actions" (Staub et al. 2003: 288).

telos can in some way even circle back and intensify divine wrath. A good parent can be fittingly angry with her child when the child fails, through her own actions or omissions, to actualize her potentials. God may also experience an anger wrought out of loving disappointment with all God's children who have shaped their agency to perpetually refuse repair, renewal, or community. If rational creatures can resist eternally the overtures of infinite love, hell might be the state that elicits a non-retributive anger in God, anger that is at the same time an expression of the deepest love for the estranged creature forever missing out on her truest good.[26]

Communicative-Restorative Justice throughout the Scriptures

The previous section introduced *DRJ* as an alternative framework to that of retribution for conceptualizing divine justice. This section turns to key biblical episodes where this understanding of divine justice is on display. I show how at key theological junctures, the divine justice in Eden, at Sinai, in the Babylonian and Assyrian exiles, and in Jesus's cleansing of the Temple—*can* be interpreted as supporting the communicative-restorative framework and compellingly so.

Eden

We meet God, the legislator, in the very first scenes of Genesis. Unlike the gods of their neighbors, the God of the Hebrews decrees with attention to the purposes and interests of mankind and other vulnerable entities. In the Babylonian cosmogony, creation stems from the gods' discord and humankind is the upshot of divine indolence—the gods need servants. In Genesis 1, by contrast, God's commands are teleological, intelligently oriented toward the thriving of mankind. God's legislative agency is other-centered, anthropocentric, domesticating gradually the primeval chaos into an environment increasingly more fit and fully equipped for human flourishing.[27]

When Genesis 2 zooms in on Eden, a Mediterranean garden, God's loving attention to the vulnerable is intensified. Instead of generically creating, like a master potter, God now fashions humans out of humus. Instead of legislating from afar, God breathes his breath into a clump of dust.[28] Portrayed successively

---

[26] Cf. Lewis 2009: Chapter 8.   [27] See this point argued compellingly in Walton 2009.

[28] With characteristic insight and economy Robert Alter remarks: "In this more vividly anthropomorphic account, God, now called *YHWH 'Elohim* instead of *'Elohim* as in the first version, does not summon things into being from a lofty distance through the mere agency of divine speech, but works as a craftsman, fashioning (*yatsar* instead of *bar'a*, 'create'), blowing life breath into nostrils, building a woman from a rib" (Alter 1996: 7, footnote 4).

as gardener, sculptor, therapist, anesthesiologist, surgeon, and matchmaker, the legislator God is resourceful, intimately caring, and generous to a fault. In sharing divine speech with humanity, the Lord God expresses at once the divine call to further legislate—to create through speech as in the naming of the animals—but also to be intimately present to the vulnerable. Taking dominion of nature is expressed through tilling/cultivating but also through watching over (*shamar*) the ground. In short, humanity is invited to mirror God's legislative concern and intimate care, to bring order from chaos, to use both the power of speech and power of touch for the wellbeing of others.

Had the original creation gone well, God's majesty would have been extended throughout the earth by the word and work of God's viceroy. But all things do not go well. In grasping for the forbidden fruit, humanity rebels against divine legislation in a very specific way. As some commentators note, that original grasp emblemizes humanity's apparent refusal to be a part of nature, our tendency to take ourselves as overlords instead of stewards of the land, and our refusal to see ourselves as dependent upon the ground—that vulnerable entity that needs tending and watching over.[29] We may plausibly say that while humanity defies God's command, nature generally, the fertile land or the ground more concretely, are the direct victims of humanity's disobedience. Rebellion against God victimizes the vulnerable nature, since the ecological beauty and thriving of the original creation have been corrupted *through* the action of God's viceroy. This theme is also evident in the intimate connection between the voice of the first human victim and the murder-polluted ground from which Abel's blood cries out to God.[30]

In light of this, the divine curses and gestures from Genesis 3 can be seen in a communicative-restorative framework. God publicly decries the harm that has befallen the ground/nature/creation due to the human's choice, signaling an identification with the vulnerable. By exiling humanity from Eden, God communicates the value of the vulnerable fertile land, while simultaneously issuing to the human a call to redress, to change course, to engage with the earth and nature in more godlike ways, by propelling it toward flourishing. We, however, know how the story goes on. Cain spills Abel's blood onto the ground, further polluting the fields he was called to watch over. Instead of turning the whole ground into an Eden teeming with abundant life, by the time of Noah, blood-spilling violence is so rampant that the entire ground is corrupted before the face of the Lord (Genesis 6:10–12). And so, the flood can be interpreted as God's attempt to heal, restore, and reset nature in the face of noxious human exertions. God stands with the victim over against the offender.

How does God's justice work to restore the offender? In Eden, God covers the shame of the original pair, while east of Eden God protects the murderer from

---

[29] Cf., e.g., Richter 2020 and Hiebert 1996.   [30] See Genesis 4:10–11.

retaliation. Through Noah, God makes provision for a new habitable space, where humanity and nature could be reconciled again. Biblically, restorative justice works like forgiveness. It is accomplished through an exemplar, a representative of a group. And so, Noah the representative of humanity will receive into his ark representatives of the animals, pair by pair. And, after the flood, Noah will try his hand at tilling the ground again. And much after the flood, an innocent human victim will walk out from the ground, signaling not only that God's Spirit resonates with the groanings of the entire creation, but also that the entire creation/nature itself through the paradigmatic and programmatic resurrection of the body "will be set free from its slavery to corruption" (Romans 8:21).

Exodus and Sinai

The Exodus story and the Law provides further justification for the aptness of the communicative-restorative framework. In the key episodes of the Exodus deliverance, God is attuned to the experiences of vulnerable victims, elevating their moral and epistemic status, God holds the offender to account through gestures meant to induce their repentance, moral healing, and transformation, and God aims to bring together offender and victim in communities of shalom. In its intent, the Mosaic Law essentially aims to do the same. I will take up each of these claims in turn.First, in the Exodus deliverance story, as in content of the Mosaic Law, God is attuned to the experiences of vulnerable victims, elevating their moral and epistemic status, and publicly reverberating the truth of the harm they endure. Consider God's self-revelation to Moses as a deity particularly attuned to the pain of the oppressed. In the prologue to the deliverance, God punctuates his conversation with Moses—the exiled stutterer—with explicit assurances that he has heard the groaning, observed the misery, and noticed the suffering of his people (Exodus 2:6–8a).

Additionally, God's attunement to the oppressed has a long history, universal scope, and moral bite. God's particular attention to Moses and his nation of slaves is mediated by the Lord's availability to Abraham, Isaac, and Jacob, all nomads and castaways, all rescued in the moment of dire need. But God's attunement to the oppressed is not rooted in a simple tribal or ethnic allegiance. Embedded in the history of God's presence to Abraham lies the story of God's compassion for Hagar. Exiled from her own Egyptian home, a slave to this Hebrew nomad and twice cast-away by him, Hagar also receives assurance that God has heard her groaning, observed her misery, and taken notice of her suffering. Yahweh's ostensible response to enslaved Hebrews in Egypt is modeled on God's ostensible response to this enslaved Egyptian. God has been present to hear the cries of Moses's family throughout their history, but also the cries of those oppressed *by* Moses's family.

The Torah codifies in legal precept what Exodus expresses in narrative: Yahweh is distinctly a God who has utmost concern for the fate of the vulnerable.[31] If freeing the Hebrews from under Pharaoh's thumb reveals a God whose mercy springs into action to free and elevate the vulnerable against oppression, the Law makes normative *within* Israel similar commitments. The Law aims to form the sensibilities of the redeemed community, by prescribing explicit policies of protecting their own vulnerable as direct ramifications of cultivating Godlike justice. In his careful exposition of the context and content of each of the Ten Commandments, Stassen argues that their cumulative case is to express that the Lord God cares about justice for the vulnerable, and that loyalty to this God implies doing the same:

> The ten commandments are unified by their heading—the character of the LORD as the one who sees the misery, hears the cries, knows the suffering of the powerless, the vulnerable, the victims of violations of their basic human rights, and calls us into covenant to protect them. The Ten Commandments are about faithfulness to the LORD who is the mighty and awesome compassionate deliverer of the weak and vulnerable.[32]

The normative lessons of Exodus together with the telos of the Law compel us to see an internal connection between God's moral identity and pursuing the well-being of the most vulnerable. Depriving the vulnerable of justice or shalom insults God's very being. Harming the vulnerable impugns God's honor. God not only makes legal and economic provisions in the Law for Israel's orphans, widows, poor, and resident aliens, God defines God's own identity, power, and awesomeness by the radical nature of his love for them.[33]

The *Deuteronomist* also remembers the Law as a particular expression of God's redemptive justice that motivates Israel's restorative action on behalf of the vulnerable.[34] And he is not alone. The Psalms and the Prophets consistently bear witness to the same conception of the divine judge, as "father to the fatherless," and "defender of the widows," as the one who executes justice on behalf of the humble.[35]

Second, the Exodus story and the Law show that out of concern for the vulnerable, God holds *offenders* to account through gestures meant to induce their repentance, moral healing, and transformation. In these key biblical episodes, God's anger with oppressors can be understood as a kind of reverberation

---

[31] For a detailed analysis of "The Vulnerability Principle," the idea that the Torah codifies multilayer protection for the most vulnerable, see Goldstein 2006.

[32] Stassen 2008: 370.   [33] See for instance Deuteronomy 10:17–19.

[34] See Deuteronomy 5:13–15; 23:8; 24:17–18; and 24:20–2.

[35] See Isaiah 1:16–17; Isaiah 58:6–10; Micah 6:6–8; Psalm 82; Psalm 76:7–9; Psalm 75; Psalm 74:18–23; Psalm 68:1–10; Psalm 146.

of God's empathy for the oppressed. In his wrath, God echoes the pain and anger of the abused. God's vexation with Pharaoh represents a first-order divine response to and a projection of the pain and anger experienced by Israel in captivity. Even God's wrath against freshly freed Israel at Sinai, the anger in the face of idolatry, can be understood as God's rebounding the pain of the original captives back onto their current, liberated selves. God might be expressing something like this: *When you, liberated people, engage in idolatry, when you enact the desire to turn back to Egypt, you are effectively endorsing the behavior of your own oppressors, unwittingly embracing national amnesia; you deafen yourselves to your own slavery cries, you forget the history of your own oppression, you lose your own identity.* God's anger with Israel on account of their original sin communicates not just another disavowal of oppression, but also rebuffs the insidious consequences and vestiges of oppression that simmer just beneath the surface in the psychology of the oppressed.

On the one hand, divine wrath communicates to victims, offenders, and third parties a reverberation of the pain of the oppressed. On the other hand, God's anger and hard treatment are expressive of goods in and for the life of the offenders, not in the least the realization that by harming others they misuse and corrupt their God-given power. Start with Cain. God exiles Cain, sentencing him as a perpetual nomad on the ground that he had corrupted through violence, putting distance between Cain's own fertile garden and himself. But this divine gesture can be seen to express at least three value-laden communications. By reverberating and amplifying the voice of Abel's blood screaming from the ground, God resonates with and identifies with the victim. By exiling him, God can be seen to awaken Cain to the enormity of his action. It is good for Cain to find out that elevating himself through violence over the vulnerable Abel means acting on a beastly, not a human, let alone a godlike, impulse. Finally, by protecting him in exile, when Cain himself has now become vulnerable and powerless, God communicates something else. Certainly, an aspect of God's action is pedagogical. God models for Cain how to protect the vulnerable, even when they give offense. God's sign of protection provides not only a saving grace, but also a reminder seared on Cain's skin that he ought to be his brother's keeper. That was Cain's call. And that remains his destiny, no matter how beastly the impulses crowding at the door.

Modeled on God's engagement with Cain, the hard actions against Pharaoh can also be seen as communicative gestures oriented toward Pharaoh's good. From one point of view, the plagues against Egypt can be seen as a contest between Yahweh and the pantheon of Egyptian gods. If Pharaoh represents Egypt's incorrigibly oppressive spiritual powerbrokers, they are caught in an absurd war of attrition against the Creator God.[36] On another level, however, the plagues

---

[36] See Sarna 1986: chapter IV (pp. 63–80).

reveal God's continued contending with a split and conflicted human individual. Only after Pharaoh effectively hardens his own heart five times does God proceed to solidify his decisions. Against this personal backdrop, the ten strikes can be seen as communicative gestures, as signs that God has not given up on Pharaoh (or Egypt), that God desires to curb and arrest his descent into rebellion.

In the end, God allows Pharaoh to have his own way. By hardening his heart, God solidifies in the monarch his deepest desire, but only after contending vigorously for his rehabilitation.[37] Despite God's sounding ten alarm bells, Pharaoh remains a rebel to the end. He deliberately turns toward chaotic forces and powers that by definition lie outside of the presence of God. God systematically tries to thwart Pharaoh's retreat into godlessness. By repeatedly spurning God's calls, Pharaoh succeeds in placing himself at the outskirts of God's providential care, in a territory haunted by the angel of death and the flood of the Red Sea, a poetic invocation of the primeval chaos. Even if he never turns toward God, *it is good* for Pharaoh and for Egypt to come to the terrible moral knowledge that personal and political hubris is self-destructive. When Egypt insists on oppressing the vulnerable, she succeeds only in wrecking her economy, devasting her own fauna and vegetation, endangering her national future, and undoing creation.[38]

Third, I claim that the Exodus narrative and the Law begin to hint that God's communicative actions, both in their resonance with vulnerable victims and in arresting the moral descent of offenders, are ordered toward the restoration of both in communities of shalom. We see this in at least three ways. To begin with, the story tells us that when the children of Israel departed Egypt, also "a mixed multitude went up with them, along with sheep and oxen, an exceedingly heavy (amount of) livestock."[39] The narrative not only mentions that Egyptians, former oppressors, are being incorporated into Yahweh's people, but it emphasizes that their joining the Hebrews is as fully-committed (*heavy*) as is the hardening of Pharaoh's heart.

Additionally, as we have seen, the Law codifies a specific set of programmatic instructions so that the communities Israel will create in Canaan will be decidedly anti-oppressive. Striking even for modern ears is the refrain that a distinguishing mark of Yahweh's chosen people is legislation safeguarding and even ensuring the thriving of foreigners living in Israel. For Israel, the lesson of Egypt should be this: create future communities of shalom where no one is in a position of being exploited. And tellingly, the motivation is this: Israel is in a uniquely privileged and intimate relationship with Yahweh, thus called to embody in their own communities a specific vision of God's justice. Furthermore, there are glimpses

---

[37] See Stump 1988.

[38] As a commentator puts it: "[the] image of Egypt at the conclusion of his plague-exodus narrative is of a land with no people, no animals, no vegetation ... A land in which creation was undone" (Zevit 1976: 210)

[39] Exodus 12:38 (Everett Fox translation).

even during the time of the monarchy that God's intentions for Israel's enemies and oppressors is a kind of restoration and healing that avoids any further retribution.[40]

Finally, there is a longer-range programmatic commitment. It becomes clear that Israelites in positions of political, religious, and cultural power are *particularly* called to protect the vulnerable. When, in fact, the justice of Israel's own vulnerable is perverted, it is indeed Israel's leaders who bear the brunt of the divine condemnation. The monarchy is terminated, priests lose their jobs as the Temple lies in ruins, prophets wail in sackcloth and ashes, the merchants are bankrupt, and Israel's youngest and brightest learn about Marduk in Babylon. But then again, in the aftermath of the two Exiles, God will, through the institution of the representative, symbolically resurrect the nation. The shoot from Jesse's stump will be the cause for the restoration of Israel's fortunes. In the gathering of the twelve disciples, Jesus the Messiah programmatically restores the twelve tribes of Israel. Symbolically unraveling Pharaoh's oppression and hardened heart, Jesus is a king who serves and has compassion. He ushers in God's new Exodus jubilee, bringing good news to the poor, pardoning prisoners, giving sight to the blind, and setting the burdened and battered free. And so, the church is built upon the cornerstone of a Pharaoh-inverted ruler, a gentle and humble priestly-king, whose power resides not in horses and chariots, but in healing and forgiveness. Through this earthly restored Israel, God will bring justice to the whole world. The church is God's new cosmopolitan community constituted by Hebrews, Samaritans, Romans, Scythians, and Egyptians and founded on pillars of mutual submission, other-love, and forgiveness.

The Prophets

The prophets continue and intensify the theme of divine justice at the heart of the Exodus and Law narratives. To be in an exclusive, covenantal relationship with Yahweh is to belong to shalom communities—contradicting the Egyptian oppression—organized around fairness and mercy for the marginalized and the vulnerable. Consider the courtroom setting in early Isaiah. God opens a legal case against the leaders and elders of Israel for plundering the needy and "grinding the faces of the poor."[41] Along the same lines, prophet Amos proclaims that God's punishment will not relent against Israel because:

---

[40] Consider the rather humorous story from 2 Kings 6:8–23. King Aram is an insistent and recalcitrant enemy of Israel, committed to trap and destroy Israel's army. God delivers Aram's army into the hands of the Israelites through the prayers of Elisha. The prophet advises the king to throw a party for the captured enemy instead of massacring them. Following the banquet, the Arameans are sent back home. They never raid again.

[41] Isaiah 3:15.

They sell the righteous for silver,
and the needy for a pair of sandals –
they who trample the head of the poor
into the dust of the earth, and push the afflicted out of the way

...

They lay themselves down beside every altar
on garments taken in pledge
and in the house of their God they drink
wine bought with fines they imposed.

(Amos 2:6–8)

Apparently during the monarchy, a new social elite had risen in Israel that made it easy for some to amass wealth and land—as Isaiah says "adding field to field"—thus creating the conditions for the exploitation of the land and the oppression of the vulnerable through expropriations and debt-slavery. Furthermore, the court systems increasingly privileged the elites, blinding them to and insulating them from injustices carried out against the poor, the widow, the orphan, the sick, and the foreigner. Even religious life had become a parody, where on the Sabbath the rich were rejuvenated while planning to expand their wealth by taking advantage of the powerless.[42]

To put it mildly, God does not approve. Isaiah describes the day of the Lord as a day of reckoning where a prosecuting Yahweh goes on a rampage against Zion's wealthy women, stripping them clean of the precious jewels that elevated their economic and social standing, and against Zion's elite young men, stripping them clean of their military might, that is, of their self-regarding political power.[43] Similarly, in gloomy imagery reminiscent of the plagues, prophet Amos has God doom the Northern Kingdom. God vows to demolishing the very institutions—religious, economic, and political—the entire social order that had oppressed the poor.[44] In other words, when Israel reverts to oppressive habits and social arrangements, she symbolically channels the brutal powers of Egypt, forgetting her very identity and her God. God's ire in the Hebrew prophets is thus an expression of deepest love and other-concern. Prophetic condemnations do not communicate a simple, generic repudiation of sin. They communicate God's intense love for the vulnerable; any violation against them is noted and accounted for. They also communicate God's intense love for the offender. When economic, political, or religious power turns the privileged away from their intended purpose as "brother-keepers," when through the exercise of their own power they become more "beastly" than "human," then stripping power away is a saving grace *in* and *for* the offender.

[42] See Amos 8:5–6.   [43] See Isaiah 3:18–26.   [44] See Amos 8:9–14.

Importantly, divine condemnation in the Prophets reverberates with the pain of the *globally* oppressed, while signaling that the good even for non-Hebrew offenders involves recognition and repudiation of their arrogance and of their corruptive, polluting power.[45] As significantly as in the Creation and Exodus narratives, divine condemnation in the Prophets is teleologically ordered toward the ultimate restoration of offenders and victims in communities of thriving. For instance, in the book of Isaiah, the healing of the land, the restoration of just institutions that ensure wellbeing for the oppressed, and the return of God's righteous presence in Zion are all interconnected. Loosening the bonds of debt-slavery, sharing one's economic wealth with the needy, and practicing hospitality to the vulnerable are at once concrete expressions of God's justice and a sign that God has returned to live again in the midst of the once-alienated nation.[46] Furthermore, beyond his vision of national restoration, Isaiah also sees God setting in motion a process of healing the nations, even former oppressors like Egypt and Assyria.[47]

Isaiah sees at the center of this global-restoration movement a Hebrew temple with a cosmic reach, a new kind of king, and new institutions informed by practices of unlearning violence and learning creation-stewardship.[48] Israel's institutions are healed—the monarchy, the temple, the economy, and the prophecy—but in such a way that they include and become attractive institutions to the entire world. The nations flock to the mountain on which God resides, a divine-like figure becomes the monarch-judge of the "many nations." The nations not only unlearn the art of warfare, but by beating swords into plows and spears into pruning hooks, they symbolically embark on a journey back to Eden. It is as if we are seeing a movie in reverse from the flood story to the creation story. Repudiating and rising out of the sewer of global violence, the entire humanity ascends back toward that garden on top of the primordial mountain, to live in harmony with God, the earth, and one another.

Jesus and the Attack on the Temple

The framework of communicative-restorative justice finds its ultimate justification in the person and work of Jesus. I cannot deal with the immense scope of Jesus's subverting retribution through his teaching and action. It bears mentioning that center stage in his teachings we find the theme we have seen throughout this section: an intimate link between radical monotheism and social justice, between the first and the second tablet of the Mosaic Law. Jesus dials up the connection

---

[45] For a small but representative selection speaking of God's global justice against global oppressing powers see Isaiah 10:12; 14:3–8; Ch. 15; 17:1–7; Ch. 18; 19:1–16; and Ch. 23. For condemnation of Assyria's power to victimize the ground see Isaiah 24:5–6.

[46] Cf. Isaiah 58:1–12 and esp. Isaiah 58:10–12.   [47] See Isaiah 19:18–25.

[48] See Isaiah 2:1–4.

between piety toward the one true God and justice, putting his own subversive twists on it. Like a classical Hebrew prophet, Jesus associates the irruption and diffusion of God's reign on earth with the restoration and thriving of the meek, the poor, the persecuted, and those who hunger and thirst for justice (*dikaiosune*).[49] Jesus also understands himself as the one who inaugurates this new Exodus and the Year of Jubilee. Put simply, Jesus contends that practicing true justice consists in radical love of the vulnerable neighbor.[50] Jesus famously repudiates the reciprocity code, and reframes *who* is one's neighbor: the Roman soldier—the oppressor, the good Samaritan—the ethnic other, Zacchaeus—the native collaborator with the oppressor.[51] Additionally, through his teaching and actions, Jesus elevates the status of shunned, neglected, or marginalized people (children, widows, prostitutes, lepers, prisoners, the blind), relating to them as individuals fully worthy of God's love and care.

Instead of residing on these well-known themes, I want to focus on a single, contrarian episode: Jesus's cleansing the Jerusalem Temple. Regardless of whether we read it in the Synoptics or in John, at first blush we might see in the whip and the overturned tables an expression of a retributive divine character. And if we *are* temples of the living God, isn't God just to use hard action and pain to purify us or to drive us to repentance?

Consistent with the refrain from this entire section, Jesus's cleansing of the Temple coheres better with the communicative-restorative framework than with retributivism. Jesus enacts not an assault on people as such, but on the oppressive cultural, political, and economic policies and institutions that had become interwoven with temple worship. The net result of these unholy alliances was to alienate Israel's vulnerable people from the divine presence instead of bringing them into communion with God. Evident in his denouncing of the Scribes and Pharisees, Jesus stands against *any* power, be it ideological, economic, or religious that hinders or makes harder the access to God. And so, the whip that drives away the money-changers and the hand that overturns the tables communicate three things at once.

First, these gestures show a kind of solidarity with those excluded from worship—the ritually impure, the economically heavy-laden, and others—solidarity meant to remove the obstacles lying in their path of union with God. Of course, if, as I argue in Chapter 3, Jesus is the replacement for the Temple—a more perfect organic Temple—then all those excluded by predatory religion can find healing in him. This performative action then is a symbolic demonstration of this fundamental truth that Jesus had already been enacting throughout Galilee even before setting his face toward Jerusalem.

---

[49] Cf. Matthew 5:1–11 and Luke 6:20–49.   [50] Cf. Leviticus 19 and Mark 12:30–1.
[51] Cf. Matthew 5:38–48 and Wolterstorff 2011.

Second, these gestures call out to the powerbrokers to dignify the marginalized, for by doing this, the religious and other leaders (the oppressors) would be healed of their own illusions, and would recapture the original vision and function of their temple-related vocation and work. In a remarkable juxtaposition, Matthew tells us that the blind and the lame come to Jesus in the cleansed temple to be healed, even as the chastened merchants, priests, and teachers of the law stand by, watching indignant.[52] Jesus demonstrates to the powerbrokers that true power lies in opening wide the gate to all, especially to the most vulnerable, so they may be made whole and healed.

Finally, Jesus's actions are ultimately a propaedeutic to the realization of that Eucharistic community, a newly reconstituted temple, where former enemies and those excluded and marginalized are brought together inside a peaceable community and inside communion with God through a sharing of the body and blood of Jesus.[53]

Conclusion

I do not mean to suggest that there is no divine retributivism in the Bible. As the Appendix shows, that thinking is alive and well, even in a post-exilic text such as Lamentations. But I will show there that such retributivist thinking is in conflict with other theological commitments of the prophet. That being said, the biblical arc I highlighted in the previous section gives us sufficient warrant to deprioritize retribution in favor of communicative-restoration. We do not have to read into the divine motivational profile the intention to punish transgressors for violations of the moral law. Instead, the key biblical episodes we examined make available an understanding of God that is more pained than offended by sins, since God cares about the harm inflicted on the vulnerable, since God cares that those entrusted with capacities and offices of power and responsibility live up to the dignity of their nature and offices, and since God ultimately cares for relational healing. When, for any number of reasons, offenders do not really resonate with God's fundamental concerns, God can at once bear the sin of the transgressor and sound the clarion for her reformation, God can fully love the

---

[52] Matthew 21:12–17.

[53] It is of course expected that the Gospel writers would see in Jesus—organic temple—the new intense locus of God's abiding presence with humanity, since they write with knowledge of the destruction of the Jerusalem temple. But what is striking is that Paul himself sees the church, the body of Christ, in this way as well, and that he sees union with Christ through the eucharist as a way of forging new kinds of non-oppressive social bonds. Cf. 1 Corinthians 11:17–23; 1 Corinthians 3:16–17; and Ephesians 2:19–22.

sinner and also be fully angry with him, and God can forgive and execute justice without retribution.[54]

The blessed marriage of divine forgivingness with the communicative-restorative conception of justice has the consequence of preserving an important insight in Aristotle's characterization of the magnanimous individual. God is sensitized to all sorts of considerations that would violate divine majesty, but God's honor is essentially tied to the fate of the vulnerable, those at risk due to their lack of power, and those who endanger themselves through unfitting exercise of power. God travels widely along the paths of human concerns, attuned to the voices of Hagar and Abraham, of Abel and Cain, of Pharaoh and the Hebrew slaves, of Jonah and the Assyrians. And as we have already seen, God travels even deeper into the human wilderness through Jesus Christ of Nazareth. Through him, God essentially enters into the human experience of vulnerability. I argued in Chapter 3 that God expresses forgivingness most clearly through the life and work of Jesus Christ. Jesus expresses most vividly God's commitment to remove our transgressions from us, and God's commitment to absorb into his own being the ramifications of our sin. And so, God's honor is expressed just as much through forgivingness as through justice.

[54] I don't mean to suggest that God's responses to offender are bifurcated, only justice and forgiveness. There is a NT context that, at first blush, seems tailor-fit to evoke divine anger. In Luke 19, in the scene preceding cleansing the Temple, Jesus sees Jerusalem from afar, the city that has consistently rejected the Messiah and will change, within the span of a week, from acclaiming him as king to executing him in a row with common criminals. The context clues us in that this is a reiteration of the prophetic trope in which daughter Zion has been unfaithful, consistently rejecting Yahweh's overtures. But unlike some prophetic literature where God burns with wrath and actively punishes Jerusalem for its unfaithfulness, here Jesus weeps over the city. Luke knowingly recasts the prophetic understanding of divine pathos. Divine anger is recalibrated as divine lament.

5

Curative Forgivingness

"As many of you as were baptized into Christ have clothed yourself with Christ."

Galatians 3:27

In Chapter 3, I argued that Jesus radicalizes and deepens the Hebraic understanding of sin-bearing divine forgiveness. More precisely, God's forgiveness through Jesus is tied to fulfilling temple-related rituals, and is effectuated through a representative who recapitulates redemptively previous scripts of alienation from God, and who brings the most intimate healing presence of Yahweh through touch. The life properties that flow from Christ are transferred to and incorporated into blighted and burdened humans, while their moral and physical sickness gets absorbed and extinguished into Christ's divine life.

What carries God's forgiveness into the future is no longer a set of rituals tied to a specific location, but the person of Jesus Christ. He not only fulfills the old temple functions, he not only embodies the paradigmatic scripts of God's forgiveness, but he also stretches and expands human capacities in new directions—he shows mercy and grace to offenders when others would demand retribution, and he trusts in God's goodness when others would despair of injustice. Christ-like forgivingness begins by incorporating one's imagination and agency into the forgiving work of Christ through narrative immersion. That's how we become disposed to stretch and expand our capacities grace-ward. In Chapter 3, I explained the ready availability of the forgiving work of Christ as encoded in stories, hymns, and poetry. This chapter advances the argument by proposing a two-tiered account of curative forgivingness. The first level develops a basic Aristotelian intuition that sees virtue as a syndrome of dispositions, a sensibility, responding to all sorts of salient interpersonal conditions. The second level involves a conception of one's whole life as embedded into the life of God that justifies and motivates accepting personal suffering and forbearing with offenders.

The first section introduces a general map about the understanding of virtue, and locates forgivingness in it. The second section evaluates a view according to which forgivingness is properly exercised only in response to offender-repentance, or similar such gestures that aim at making amends. I argue against this reductive understanding of the virtue. The third section articulates a two-level account of curative forgivingness. I follow Robert C. Roberts when I see in forgivingness a sensibility attuned to various blame-reducing, beneficence-maintaining

Gracious Forgiveness: A Theological Retrieval. Cristian F. Mihut, Oxford University Press. © Cristian F. Mihut 2023. DOI: 10.1093/oso/9780192873729.003.0005

conditions. But I go beyond him, showing that curative forgivingness involves the conception of one's life as a trusting participation in a transcendently good God that cauterizes and contains our individual suffering. I then give three examples of such participation: appropriation of a teleological meta-narrative, participation in grace as an aesthetic phenomenon, and developing a lifelong friendship with Christ.

Is Forgivingness a Virtue?

I simply assume the psychological reality of character traits. Though their ontological status remains contested in the literature, I am inclined to think that militant virtue skepticism dismisses or minimizes without much warrant features of our psychological, relational, political, and social life that make more sense if trait realism obtains.[1] Realism about character does not mean endorsing spooky properties or being committed to non-naturalist accounts of human persons. For instance, "virtue" or "character trait" may pick out perfectly natural (sets of) dispositions to perceive, feel, think, and act in specific circumstances.[2] It's easy to see how forgivingness could fit the bill of virtue. Forgiving individuals are persons who, in the aftermath of insult or injury, tend to be authentically and consistently gracious or non-retaliatory in word and deed toward their offenders. A plausible explanation is that their behavior springs from cognitive, conative, or affective habits at the center of who these people are, habits that bear the appropriate trait-designation.

Folksy identification of personal traits, however, can also go wrong. A person designated as forgiving may sadly succeed only to condone, excuse, or all-too-eagerly pardon her offenders. Natural discourse may still pick out real personal dispositions, but these could be mislabeled. Those unhappy with the vagueness or equivocation of folk-psychological identifications luckily have available other starting points. The classical Greek tradition viewed character traits as habituated, admirable moral excellences, rooted in practical reasoning and ultimately conducive to human flourishing. It is instructive to take a brief look at Plato, an exemplar in this tradition. Famously, Plato's characterization of moral virtue is rooted in intellectualism, puts a high premium on psychic integration and internalism, and presupposes a supersensible ontology. Consider book IV of *The Republic* where, having just completed the piecemeal discussion of the four cardinal virtues, Socrates gives his audience an account of the virtuous life:

> And in truth, justice is, it seems, something of this sort. Yet it is not concerned with someone's doing his job on the outside. On the contrary, it is concerned

---

[1] For character-skepticism Doris 2002. For responses to character-skepticism see Miller 2017.
[2] Cf. Flanagan 2009.

with what is inside; with himself, really, and the things that are his own. It means he does not allow elements in him each to do the job of some other, or the three sorts of elements in his soul to meddle with one another. Instead he regulates well what is really his own, rules himself, puts himself in order, becomes his own friend, and harmonizes the three elements together, just as if they were literally the three defining notes of an octave—lowest, highest, and middle—as well as any others that may be in between. He binds together all these and from having been many, becomes entirely one, temperate and harmonious. Then and only then should he turn to action... In all these areas, he considers and calls just and fine the action that preserves this inner harmony and helps achieve it, and wisdom the knowledge that oversees such action; and he considers and calls unjust any action that destroys this harmony, and ignorance the belief that oversees it.[3]

This Socratic characterization of virtue strings together some loosely associated commitments. One is *internalism*: only forces or capacities internal to the makeup of a person are relevant to a good, virtuous, and right human life. Relatedly, there is a strong emphasis on the *integration* and *harmonization* of various drives: virtue is a matter of internal organization, of keeping under wraps "naturally lower" forces, and allowing "naturally noble" capacities to surface to the top. Wisdom or practical reason is the capacity tasked with superintending the internal work of this organization and synchronization. As the ruling drive, practical reason analyzes, rank-orders, and integrates the motley crew of psychological attitudes or capacities into a coherent psychic whole. After three more chapters, Socrates finally discloses that psychic harmony is simply a reflection of an ontologically more fundamental reality, one not belonging to our physical world. To that supersensible realm only wisdom in its theoretical mode has access. And so, Plato has Socrates drive to the conclusion that only philosophers are the paradigms of moral virtue. They alone enjoy a view of the way things really are beyond appearances, because they have taken the trouble to integrate their drives and lives around that intellectual vision. Integration around intellection yields virtue *and* bliss.

Plato's universe does not seem to comport well with our modern intuitions about moral excellence. Some astrophysicists or academic philosophers may very well be paradigms of moral virtue, but we rightfully chuckle at the suggestion that their goodness is essentially rooted in their theoretical insight. On the flipside, a great aunt with an eighth-grade education might be wiser and kinder than anyone else we know. More to our present concerns, Plato's virtue theory seems particularly ill-suited to capture some of the central features of forgivingness.

Becoming a forgiving person presumably requires habituating forms of attention that go beyond forces *internal* to our own psyche—relevant moral features of

[3] Plato 2004: 132.

our assailants, the motivational profiles of forgiving exemplars in our communities, and other pertinent considerations of our broader normative worlds. Even the deepest reflection on our current drives and capacities can only take the victim so far. And so, if developing forgivingness is more like learning a craft than accessing a priori knowledge, we need help from outside of ourselves to develop relevant forgiving dispositions. Consequently, strong internalism is far from enough to take us there. Worries arise also for strong psychic integration. It is hard to see a sufficient causal link between volitional integration and growth in forgiveness. People can be wholeheartedly bitter toward or uncompromisingly angry with their offenders. And so, forgivingness may require at times unsettling capacities and dispositions that victims have been hitherto integrating beautifully under the banner of revenge, retribution, or *lex talionis*.

Finally, engraining forgivingness entails neither the ascent of the soul toward nonphysical, fixed realities nor does it have to directly contribute to a happy human life. A habitual forgiver, in the sense I wish to develop, tolerates a fair bit of inner conflict between the demands of strict justice and those of mercy. If she regards Jesus Christ as a paradigmatic forgiver, she accepts a fair bit of suffering in her life by absorbing offenses, and is disposed to sacrifice personal happiness in favor of a life intended to heal and show grace to others.[4]

Though Platonic virtue ethics may fail, we need not despair. The rejection of internalism, strong integrationism, or robust intellectualism is consistent with another ancient Greek option. My own predilections fall in a broadly Aristotelian camp. I understand a person's character as constituted by stable and enduring traits rooted in distinctive cognitive, affective, or conative dispositions. These traits play various functional roles connected to understanding, explaining, predicting, evaluating, and modeling an individual's behavior. Additionally, in a person of moral character, these traits are responsive to various considerations that lay normative claims upon her life, their differentiated saliency determining distinct courses of action in specific situations. Aristotle articulates this intuition in the famous doctrine of the mean. The courageous person likely does not respond in all the circumstances in which the rash or the overconfident do, but she may act decisively in some of the cases where most of the cowardly refrain

---

[4] I do *not* mean to throw doubt on the notion that following Christ is constitutive of an objectively meaningful human life. I *do* mean to suggest that a good life is not reducible to Platonic, Aristotelian, or Millian happiness. The way I see it, forgivingness involves a kind of availability to others and openness to suffering that is incompatible with standard eudaimonistic ethics. Both Jesus and Paul emphasize that Christian discipleship entails an orientation toward the cross, which I take to mean, at the very least, pursuing a kind of life that is open to tragedy. Jesus says some pretty demanding stuff: "And whoever does not pick up his cross and follow me is not worthy of me" and so does Paul: "Jews ask for signs, and Greeks look for wisdom, but we preach Christ crucified, which is a scandal to Jews and foolishness to Gentiles." And so, at *the motivational level*, a virtuous follower of Christ cultivates a healthy distrust of things constitutive of "Greek" eudaimonia, and a healthy commitment to purposive suffering.

from acting. In the courageous person deliberation is so finely tuned to her own life-circumstances that she strikes the right balance between acting rashly and being paralyzed by fear. Similarly, the forgiving person engrains a trait that is importantly distinct from the dispositions to condone, to forget, to make excuses, or to reflexively issue pardons.

Common in the current literature is also the assumption that full moral virtues must exhibit cross-situational consistency. This implies that the moral agent instantiates the trait in salient circumstances spanning a wide range of action-domains, even when, or precisely when, the situations are not favorable to the relevant trait-behavior. For instance, Tony Soprano fails to possess the full virtue of kindness, since the trait seems restricted to the domain of family relations. For as much as Tony lavishes affection on Meadow his daughter, he seems incapable of beneficence or mercy toward former associates or competitors.

If cross-situational consistency, diachronic stability, explanatory power, and finetuning to salient circumstances are necessary features of virtue, we also find some *common* conditions of its instantiation. A virtue *might* be signaled by any of the following four characteristic markers. First, virtue-possessors typically become increasingly skilled at recognizing the appropriate conditions for the instantiation of the virtue. The courageous person becomes increasingly more aware of situations that demand her courageous interventions, and the forgiving individual becomes increasingly more skilled at recognizing situations that demand forgiving action. Relatedly, virtue-possessors typically become increasingly less resistant to the motivational pulls of the trait. The virtuous tend to perform more actions of the relevant kind than they would have performed in the absence of the virtue. The courageous person tends to perform more courageous acts, and the forgiving person more acts of forgiveness. Additionally, the virtuous person commonly begins *to see herself as embodying the specific virtue*, that is, the trait becomes a self-reflexive mode, a lens through which the person interprets her life and her connection to the lives of others. The courageous person sees herself as courageous. Similarly, provided that she has a healthy self-assessment overall, the forgiving individual also understands that she is forgiving.[5] Finally, perhaps less commonly, the virtuous person does not only see herself as virtuous, but also grows to embrace that trait as a way of life, as a part of one's identity, may even come to love the possession and exercise of the virtue.

---

[5] The relationship between the virtue and the self-awareness of the virtue is complex. Some people are courageous but don't think of themselves as such, in part due to the shame they feel about the fears they overcome. That's alright. Being truly courageous is compatible with understanding yourself as less courageous than one could be. Virtue comes in degrees, and so does the self-conception about the relevant virtue. Sometimes thinking oneself courageous entrenches deeper the virtue, and sometimes thinking ourselves insufficient does the same. My point here is rather minimal. To the extent that a virtuous person is self-aware, and to the extent to which she grows in internalizing a specific virtue, she will also experience a more-or-less accurate awareness of that growth.

These four common virtue-identifiers, together with the diachronic stability of virtue, may very well be explained by the phenomenon of trait entrenchment. Acquiring and entrenching a trait involves a profound forming or reshaping of agency, perhaps a publicly noticeable personal transformation by habituating interlinked and enduring emotional, volitional, and perceptual dispositions. Rosalind Hursthouse explains:

> One important fact about people's virtues and vices is that, once acquired, they are strongly entrenched, precisely because they involve so much more than mere tendencies to act in certain ways. A change in such character traits is a profound change, one that goes, as we say, 'all the way down'. Such a change can happen slowly, but on the rare occasions when it happens suddenly, the change calls for special explanations—religious conversion, an experience in the person's whole outlook in life, brain damage, drugs. It is certainly not a change that one can decide to bring about oneself overnight, as one might decide to break the habit of a lifetime and cease to have coffee for breakfast.[6]

According to Hursthouse, a trait may be so strongly entrenched that it becomes a valuable, inherent mode of understanding one's practical identity, a reflexive mode of the agent. The trait can no longer be neutralized or dislodged at will. Analogous to Harry Frankfurt's understanding of love as a volitional necessity, strongly entrenched traits fix the boundaries of agency, they are practically necessary. The person of entrenched courage doesn't desire to be un-courageous, is no longer susceptible to the temptations of rashness or of cowardliness, and cannot imagine wanting to be so tempted. It is conceivable for strong trait entrenchment to occur instantaneously, through sudden conversions, fortuitous epiphanies, a rush of mystical or ecstatic experiences, and the like. More likely, however, a character trait is strongly entrenched gradually, with time, as a result of various factors: rituals, habits, the presence of moral exemplars, the existence of a special relationship, the presence of relevant and valuable personal or social scripts, and so on. Hence the allure of motivational/normative externalism. I will develop this idea later on, but for now I note that part of the explanation for why entrenched traits could permeate all the way down into the nitty gritty of our psychic structures is that they are anchored in stable features of the social and normative worlds outside the confines of our brains.

Let me conclude this brief conceptual sketch by illustrating how some of these trait-conditions come to life in an illuminating recent account of forgivingness. According to Robert C. Roberts, forgivingness is the settled disposition to reduce moral anger "without abandoning correct judgment about the severity of the

---

[6] Hursthouse 1999: 12.

offense and the culpability of the offender."[7] Specifically, the forgiving individual becomes disposed to overcome the affective construal of the offender as "bad, alien, guilty, worthy of suffering, unwelcome, offensive, an enemy, etc."[8]

Note how Roberts's conception fills in a non-intellectualist, Aristotelian connection between practical reason and forgivingness. Wisdom sensitizes and attunes forgivingness to respond appropriately to fitting circumstances. Forgivingness for him involves ingrained patterns of thinking, judging, feeling, and perceiving that avoid at once the extremes of condoning the wrongdoing and of judgmentalism toward wrongdoers. In the forgiving person, judgmentalism or the punitive affective construal of offenders is not overcome haphazardly or arbitrarily, but intelligibly, "on the basis of considerations of a certain type or types which promote a benevolent perception of the offender."[9] As Roberts sees it, entrenching forgivingness consists both in developing a more refined "sensitivity" to all those anger-reducing and/or to all those benevolence-enhancing considerations. And whereas the *target* of practical reason relevant to forgivingness is primarily the offender, interestingly, there are multiple intentional *objects* for wisdom's exercise in different contexts pertaining to him.

Roberts develops a plausible case that forgivingness is responsive to five different types of circumstances. As I have just mentioned, the target of the intelligent application of the virtue is the offender, and yet practical wisdom finetunes our sensibility to several general types of conditions. These are: (a) the repentance of or some reparative sign made by the offender; (b) the moral commonality with the offender; (c) the suffering of the offender; (d) the existence of excusing circumstances; and (e) a relationship with the offender. Though there can be overlap between these conditions, it is also clear that there will be specific instances of each type in which the wise person will see sufficient reasons to act forgivingly, even in the absence of the others.

Rosie and Carla have been good friends for a long time. Suppose Rosie voted for a political candidate whose policies she knew would jeopardize Carla's wellbeing, social standing, and employment. Rosie also knew her friend would find her political choice morally repugnant, so she hid the truth from Carla. Carla finds out about Rosie's decisions, takes issue with Rosie's symbolic devaluation of her, but is hurt most by Rosie's deception. There is no excuse or moral justification for this, Carla thinks, and Rosie has made yet no signs of reparation. But now suppose that as a result of a nasty divorce, Rosie begins to experience crippling anxiety and acute loneliness. Moved by compassion for her friend in her new circumstances, Carla sees in Rosie not so much a confused, political adversary but a person in need of grace, stable relationships, and acceptance. So, after she explains to Rosie how the deception was wrong and hurtful to her, Carla offers Rosie forgiveness.

---

[7] Roberts 1995: 293.   [8] Ibid.   [9] Ibid.

Regardless of Rosie's responses, it is conceivable on Roberts's analysis, that Carla's action springs from forgivingness. In this case, it is a combination of conditions (c) and (e) that activates the virtue, even in the absence of conditions (a), (b), and (d).

As the example illustrates, Roberts's conception of forgivingness is teleologically oriented toward the perception of the offender as one with whom I may be reconciled. This is not the only way to begin constructing a broadly Aristotelian account of forgivingness. Some may begin by prioritizing the victim's own self-perception in relation to the offender.[10] Carla may perhaps acquire forgivingness by repudiating the construal of her own agency as an angry, hurt person, and by endorsing herself as one who embraces with equanimity her friends, even when they betray. Although I resonate with Roberts's idea that forgivingness *targets* the offender, the curative aspects of theological forgivingness have a number of *other* intentional objects. Curative forgivingness emerges from a dynamic interplay between self-attention, offender-perception, community, and our perception of God in Christ. As I flesh it out, forgivingness has at least four central intentional objects—Christ, the offender, the affected community, and the self. In the third section I suggest that the cognitive level of the two-tiered framework accounts well for the intentional objects of curative forgivingness. In the next section, I deal with an important objection that aims to limit the scope of forgivingness.

Is Repentance a Necessary Condition of Forgivingness?

According to a popular perspective, it is morally dubious to offer forgiveness absent the repentance of the offender. If the act of forgiving is to be a salutary response to wrongdoing, unless the wrongdoer in some way repudiates his act, the victim has *no moral* reasons to act. Revisit Rosie and Carla. Carla might undergo a psychic change with respect to Rosie, she might come to see Rosie in a more benevolent light, but if Rosie does not disown her betrayal, Carla's declaration of forgiveness is not forgiveness proper, but a simulacrum, or a morally dubious species of forgiveness. If this general argument is on the right track, and if the concept of moral virtue entails acting for the sake of morally salutary reasons, forgiving in the absence of the wrongdoer's repentance is never virtuous.

I want to disentangle two different strands of this argument. These are not exhaustive renditions, of course, but paying attention to each version reveals serious concerns the general argument sketched above would have to overcome. The first strand focuses on what strict justice demands from the wrongdoer. Consider Jerome Neu:

---

[10] Cf. Verbin 2010: ch. 4.

Forgiveness involves an interplay of attitudes. The forgiver foreswears resentment, but the evil-doer, to be morally deserving of that effort, must acknowledge
his wrong and repent or in some other way suitably distance himself from his
wrong and the message of disrespect so often tied to it. Only then does the
forgiver have the sort of moral reasons needed to make his or her act of
forgiveness the manifestation of a virtue.[11]

Neu's argument may be reconstructed as follows:

(P1):   The only reasons the forgiver has for acting out of forgivingness (the
virtue) are moral reasons.

(P2):   The only moral reasons relevant to acting from forgivingness are based or
preconditioned upon the offender's morally deserving forgiveness.

(P3):   The offender is not deserving of forgiveness unless she acknowledges the
wrong and suitably distances herself from the wrong.

Conclusion: Repentance is the only way to activate forgivingness.

I am prepared to grant (P3), but (P2) and (P1) are questionable. The third section
develops in more detail my rationale for rejecting (P1), but here I want to say a
little more about why (P2) is doubtful. In short, the moral desirability of forgiveness need not depend upon an ethic of desert. Even if all my reasons for forgiving
are rooted in moral duties, since *quid pro quo* or desert considerations are only a
subclass of these, the moral norms relevant to forgiveness can be independent of
desert-considerations or of moral trade-offs between me and my offender. We
could even grant that any hurt or insult accrues a kind of moral debt in the
offender toward the victim. Even so, it is not clear why the moral deservingness of
offenders should be *a* precondition, let the alone *the* baseline, in the deliberative
landscape of virtuous agents considering granting forgiveness. Virtuous victims
may possess all sorts of moral reasons for offering grace, independent of the
wrongdoer's just desert—commitments to God, to one's own self, commitments
internal to the nature of one's relationship with the offender, and even commitments to one's broader moral communities.

Suppose that by studying Scripture or my faith-tradition I learn that God
commands me to forgive others as God in Christ forgave me. Part of the
description of how God forgave me is this: *while I was still in my sins, Christ
showed me unmerited grace.*[12] On this basis, it is not unreasonable for me to form
the belief that my moral duty to God entails an aspirational learning to forgive

---

[11]   Neu 2011: 136.

[12]   That Christ is our moral exemplar with respect to forgiveness is a given. Cf. Ephesians 4:32. But
Paulinian theology also supports the claim that Christ's forgiveness entails showing grace to the yet
unrepentant. Cf. Romans 5:6–9. Striking is the claim that God reconciled sinners to himself while they

those who do not deserve it. Suppose you now show me a conceptual analysis according to which forgivingness entails showing grace only to the properly deserving. All other things being equal, it does not seem rational or virtuous for me to find such an analysis more compelling than the entailments of my duty to God.

An ethic of desert can also be superseded by normative considerations derived from goods inherent in relationships. Return to our example. It is not hard to imagine that Carla values inherently the friendship-bond she has co-created with Rosie; their joint efforts, their shared history of their other-regarding sacrifices, and the interplay of mutual affections and commitments give rise in Carla to a special, *prima facie* obligation to act in ways that continue the friendship. Special bonds such as friendship, parent-child, and marriage give rise to *prima facie* obligations to value not only *the relata*—the persons forging the bond—but also to value nurturing and deepening *the bond itself*.[13] Indeed, these types of special bonds give rise to moral obligations directed toward the bonds, and not only toward the persons attached through the bonds. For Carla, the friendship-bond may be so valuable that she finds in it decisive reasons to redeem her shared history with Rosie, though psychologically it would be easier for Carla to cut her losses and move on to find a more supportive friend. And so, for the sake of saving the relationship, Carla moves decisively to prioritize restoring trust in Rosie through gestures of grace beyond what Rosie strictly deserves. In this case, Carla moves toward forgiveness neither due to a duty to Rosie to sustain the friendship, nor due to a duty Carla has to herself. Instead, Carla is moved by the duty to value this third thing, this joint historical project she and Rosie have been fashioning. Valuing of these patterns of joint action gives her a new decisive reason to act graciously and forgivingly.

An ethic of desert can also be superseded by moral features inherent in the victim's own self-conception. Suppose Carla has organized her life around Aristotle's ideal of the magnanimous individual, or the ideal of the Stoic sage. Carla has internalized affective, cognitive, and agential practices according to which it is pathetic or petty to expect or demand repentance from her offenders. Such moral demands or expectations are simply beneath Carla, and the moral

---

were weak, enemies, helpless, unrighteous, in short—underserving. Now, reconciliation seems a stronger concept than forgiveness, since it entails it without being entailed by it. So, it is not irrational to form the belief that Christ *forgives* me *while* I am still a sinner.

[13] Some people talk as if their relationships take on a life of their own, in ways that are not reducible to the properties of the persons forging them. Something new emerges from the complex pattern of historical attachments and interactions between persons. Relationships have their own distinctive maturation conditions ("The two of us went on a father-son hiking trip to Colorado to invest in our relationship"). They seem to have distinctive causal powers emanating from distinctive patterns of interaction of the persons constituting them ("Your marriage inspires me to have hope in the possibility of a life-long monogamous relationship"). Relationships also seem to have distinctive causal powers to affect the self-conception of persons constituting them ("I would be an entirely different person were it not for our friendship").

demands generated by idealized versions of her own self propose to Carla that she forgive Rosie, regardless of Rosie's attitudes.

Additionally, desert-overriding moral reasons can be generated, as Robert C. Roberts argues, from a sensibility particularly finetuned to the common humanity we share with our assailants and offenders. Such finetuned sensibility was displayed for instance in the Sikh community's response in the Oak Creek mass shooting.[14] Another interesting class of moral reasons for offering forgiveness can be generated from taking a symbolic stance against evil and injustice. For example, in expressing forgiveness for Dylan Roof, some of the relatives of the Charleston-massacre victims took themselves to express a stern public denunciation of hatred and racism.[15] These last couple of paragraphs illustrate, then, that the moral norms relevant to forgiving others need not always involve the deservingness of offenders and are not always preconditioned upon it. Even if all moral reasons consistent with forgivingness are deontological, these duties need not depend on the moral duties our offenders have toward us. God, nature, relationships, the self, and other considerations can generate fitting duties to cultivate a generous forgiving disposition toward offenders.

If the first argument is grounded in an ethic of desert, the second proceeds from an ethic of communicative respect. Three basic premises support this argument. The first is that hostile emotions victims feel toward offenders—e.g., resentment or anger—are morally communicative events. Second, by tracking self-respect in the victim and respect for the victimizer, these hostile emotions communicate to victims, victimizers, and the larger community the inherent value of respect for persons. Third, offering forgiveness in the absence of wrongdoer-repentance essentially dials down or mutes the moral force of these salutary, pedagogical, person-affirming communications. Let us dig deeper.

The support for the first and second premise is rooted in recent work on the communicative function of punishment. The general idea is that punishment communicates at once at least three things: a reprobation, a direction back to morality, and a call to reform. Reprobation is met because harsh treatment expresses a strong moral disapproval of wrongdoing by the state or some other moral authority. State punishment for instance communicates a kind of communal solidarity with the victim. The punishment is also presumably intended to direct the offender's attention toward the moral and interpersonal norms he has

---

[14] See the moving tribute Raghvinder Singh pays to his father, who was one of the victims in the Oak Creek assault. He talks not only about how his father's belief in the oneness of all mankind was a source of freedom from hatred, but how that particular Sikh community chose to memorialize the attack: "Today, when people arrive at the gurudwara in Oak Creek, they find an unrepaired bullet hole in the lintel of the front door, and a plaque under it that reads, 'We are one.' My father often preached about our oneness with all of humanity" (Singh 2015).

[15] Consider especially the testimony of Bethane Middleton-Brown who lost a sister in the shooting, and whose "I have to forgive you" expressed a strong moral obligation to respond to the forces of evil with the strength of love. Cf. Gerson 2015.

violated. In doing this, it is argued, penitential pain ostensibly respects the autonomy of the offender, for it urges the wrongdoer to see himself as the real agent of wrongdoing, to come to terms with the offense, and repent of the crime. On the communicative view, harsh treatment is appropriate even if the offender is likely to harden rather than soften throughout the punitive process. What matters is the goal internal to the punitive process, the expressive, illocutionary function of penitential pain, not the actual but rather the intended outcome of the censure. Consider one contemporary statement of the communicative theory of punishment, *CP* below:

> *Communicative Punishment (CP)*: Punishment is an illocutionary act by which the state or some other authority expresses to the offender (perhaps also to the victim and the community) moral condemnation of the offense, and this communicative act "has a purpose, such as educating the offender about the wrongfulness of his act, or inducing him to repent, atone for wrong, and reform his moral personality."[16]

It is easy now to see the psychological application. If punishment administered by some external authority such as the state can educate and lead to the reformation of offenders, the hostile emotions expressed by victims could play an analogous role in interpersonal contexts. Consider *CAP* a psychological analogue of *CP*:

> *Communicative Attitudinal Punishment (CAP)*: The punitive reactive attitudes of the victim express a moral condemnation of the offense, and these communicative events aim reflexively at educating the offender (and others) about the wrongfulness of his ways, or at inducing him to repent, atone for wrong, and reform his moral personality.

CAP intends to capture an inherent moral function of attitudinal punishment. Interestingly, it's not the cognitive content of the judgment I make—"It was wrong for my friend to betray me"—that communicates the moral condemnation, but the distinctive emotion or emotional pattern attached to the thought. The affective dimension of moral condemnation is standardly identified as resentment or anger, though it should be clear that these sentiments belong to a broader class of reactive or punitive attitudes, we might call *hostile* to offenders. This broader class of offender-hostile attitudes include morally neutral emotions such as fear and apprehension, and morally questionable sentiments such as malice and contempt. According to *CAP*, a subclass of hostile emotions are morally appropriate communications, even though they share with malice and contempt the desire that the

---

[16] Holmgren 2012: 218.

offender should suffer (in some way). The key difference between morally salutary hostile emotions and the rest is that desire for offender-pain that enters the content of the broader attitude *essentially aims at communicating some inherent moral good*. Morally salutary offender-hostile emotions express that a boundary important to my personhood has been violated, they send off pedagogical or reformatory messages to my offender, and perhaps call out for the re-affirmation of my slighted personhood before the community.[17] Thus, they play an essential and irreducible moral role.

To sum up, according to *CAP* a victim's hostile emotions are interpersonal gestures that signal normative breaches between her and the offender, expressing, in various ways, respect for the agency of victim and victimizer alike. This is the first stage of the argument. But now, the argument continues, to soften or sideline these hostile attitudes, while the inherent pedagogical and reformatory goal of punishment has not been achieved, represents a blameworthy failure of grasping the moral law. Consequently, the softer attitudes associated with grace and forgiveness could not spring from a virtuous character. If a victim softens her punitive attitudes in the absence of the offender's serious sign of moral transformation, she implicitly communicates a culpable disregard for normative reality, a lack of self-respect, or an indifference to the offender's restoration, perhaps even an indifference toward the offender's own personhood.[18] Softening hostile attitudes is virtuous only if and to the degree to which there are public signs of offender-transformation. Unlike the first argument where the offender's amends are required as a kind of moral payback, here they are required to signal that a restorative change has been taking place in the agency of the offender. Acting from forgivingness is predicated here also on offenders having made atonement, but the justification is different. As rational agents, victims and offenders are creatures worthy of dignity and respect. But as insult or injury chips away at these moral qualities, making atonement is a necessary condition for restoring the moral worth of both parties.

While my final word on anger will have to wait until Chapter 6 where I deal with the anger of the marginalized and vulnerable, I make here three main responses to this argument. First, in the remainder of this section I articulate the worry that the moral use of hostile emotions is at once too weak and too

---

[17] Margaret Walker claims for instance that "[r]esentment at serious wrong…deserves morally appropriate responses from the wrongdoers and from the community that claims to embody the standards violated" (Walker 2006: 138).

[18] It's not only that the hostile emotions are essential to communicating respect for persons. Additionally, the *lack of such emotive expression distinctly signals disrespect*. Jeffrie Murphy claims "[a] person who does not resent moral injuries done to him … is almost necessarily a person lacking in self-respect" (Murphy 1998: 16). We could extend Murphy's point. Lack of anger or being overly-quick to relax anger could signal a culpable disrespect for the offender's agency. It signals that the offender is merely "a piece of nature," one with little agency or accountability for the normative breach. Or so the story goes.

strong. In the next section, while developing a positive account of grace-responsive curative forgivingness, I suggest that the reformation of the offender can be pursued independent of attitudinal hostility. Along the way, it will also become clear that a curative, grace-responsive forgivingness pursues goods for the offender independent of her reformation.[19]

Defenders of *CAP* see an internal connection between offender-hostile reactions and communicating respect for the dignity of persons. But the argument is overplayed in one respect and does not go far enough in another. *Pace* an entire philosophical tradition stretching from Aristotle, Aquinas, and Butler all the way to contemporary retributivists, I first want to register a modest skepticism about our abilities to track a clear and obvious distinction between moral and immoral forms of attitudinal hostility. In an argument remarkable for its honesty, Jeffrie Murphy, formerly a main defender of character retributivism—the view that people ought to be punished in direct proportion to their wickedness—argues that the desire to punish people, despite its purported claim to justice, relies on a dubious moral psychology. Many theoreticians of punishment proceed from the assumption that the chariot of retribution-seeking is pulled by the better angels of our nature—justice, temperance, and fairness. Unnerved by Nietzsche's suggestion that the labor may be performed by malice and spite, the irrational nags of the soul, Murphy confesses:

> I see in myself, alas, a person whose impulse to punish has been—at least in some cases—very powerful, and Nietzsche has caused me to mistrust myself and the abstract theories I have been inclined to use to rationalize that impulse. In this essay I share with you the nature of my mistrust.[20]

Murphy goes on to reflect that those concerned more generally with justifying other-regarding punitive attitudes are bedeviled by a distinctive motivational danger—beneath the claims about pursuit of justice lie the incentives of malice, hatred, and cruelty:

> Nietzsche does not, of course, give intellectual arguments against the claims of retributivism—arguments that could perhaps be met by counter-arguments. Rather, he offers a diagnosis of those who favor punishment on such grounds—speculating that, for all their high talk about justice and desert, they are actually driven by a variety of base and irrational passions—malice, spite, envy—passions for which Nietzsche uses the French *ressentiment*. At their best,

---

[19] In Mihut 2014, I suggest a Kantian answer to the problem of attitudinal hostility. Some of the language here reflects the language I used at that time to describe communicative attitudinal punishment.

[20] Murphy 2014: 22.

retributivists—with their scorekeeping cards and their tit for tat—have sensibilities of accountants: "their souls squint." At their worst, retributivists are
simply cruel.[21]

I bring up Murphy and his doubts about the moral psychology of retributivism,
because I worry that the moral psychology of *CAP* falls prey to analogous concerns.[22] Backstage, behind the publicly expressed, noble impulse to reform offenders through attitudinal hostility, we may find, on reflection, more tit-or-tat or
cruelty than we would like. Hostile attitudes, unlike deliberative actions, are
reflexive reactions to people or events. On the one hand, it is difficult to believe
that there is an *inherent* connection between an emotional reflex and a moral
purpose. How would an argument for this thesis even get off the ground?[23] On the
other hand, it may be held that the connection is *pragmatic*, hostile attitudes
tending to connect with moral purposes only when reflection—or wisdom or
rationality—gets in the mix. Whenever reason latches onto a hostile attitude, *the
pragmatist* may argue, it typically directs this blind drive toward the reformation
or rehabilitation of the offender. Two quick responses about this possibility. First,
note that on the *pragmatic* approach, the key motivational component that leads
to moral goodness is not attitudinal hostility but reflection. If reflection is the
essential ingredient that builds the bridge to goodness, and if attitudinal hostility is
merely a coincidental part of the total motivational package, then other less hostile
attitudes can also serve the same role and mixed in with reflection lead to salutary
purposes.

Second, suppose *the pragmatist* claims: "But the [reflection + hostility] motivational mix brings about unique moral goods, goods that could not come
about from the [reflection + non-hostility] mix." In retort, I would like to see
the empirical or conceptual evidence that bears this out. I doubt that it is
forthcoming.[24] But even if it was, Murphy's doubts return here with a vengeance.
A volition integrated around reflective anger has at least as much chance to bend

[21] Ibid.

[22] In conversation, Mike Rea noted another reason to agree with Murphy's doubts. Though good
people who wrong others often willingly accept consequences (self-imposed or other-imposed) for the
sake of their rehabilitation, few of them take a retributivist attitude toward their wrongdoings. It is rare
to find a rational person who thinks: "I just need to be punished retributively"; though many would
think, "I would willingly undertake suffering for the sake of rehabilitation."

[23] If our motivational profiles are just products of evolutionary forces, they are what Bernard
Williams refers to as "an ill-assorted bricolage of powers and instincts," hardly the kinds of things
that naturally and necessarily pursue intelligent and good purposes. And if our motivational profiles are
designed by God, it's even harder to imagine that the biblical God established a necessary connection
between our first, irrational reactions and moral goodness. According to the basic Christian story, the
human heart is desperately wicked and inclined toward evil as a result of the Fall.

[24] In fact, there's some good evidence to the contrary. Cf. Nussbaum 2018: 348–9, where she argues
that anger as a response to wrongdoing is almost always irrational and destructive and Pettigrove
2012a, where he argues that meekness has significant moral and epistemic advantages with respect to
anger (and other hostile attitudes).

toward goodness as toward badness. Do we have overwhelming evidence to believe in the unequivocal orientation of reason toward the good? That might well be another dogma. That is, reflection mixed with anger might very well *rationalize* the continuation and nurturing of hostile attitudes. The worry is not only that reflection transforms attitudinal hostility into virulent blame—by ruminating on the wrongdoing—but also that reflection would continue to perpetuate and advertise blame—and other insidious dispositions such as malice, contempt, and disgust—as more noble dispositions than they actually are.

This tendency toward rationalizing anger and blaming is not a negligible probability. It is empirically supported in at least two ways. Consider the well-documented phenomenon of *fundamental attribution error*. As a species, we seem predisposed to consistently underestimate situational forces while overestimating personal agency in the explanation of behavior. We seem inclined by nature to discount or downplay causally effective "criminogenic" factors—poverty, homelessness, prisons—while inflating or over-ascribing personal culpability in offenders. The desire to see offenders suffer seems, in part, rooted in a deep-seated cognitive bias. Additionally, recent psychological findings seem to confirm aspects of Nietzsche's motivational story. Apparently, whenever punishment is seen as deserved, its application is generally attended by a kind of smugness and pleasure. Carol Steiker, a reputable legal scholar at Harvard, records:

> Recently, psychologists and neurologists have demonstrated both the willingness of subjects, under experimental conditions, to punish rule-breakers, and the way in which the infliction or even the anticipation of such punishment seems to involve the reward center of the brain. Indeed, the greater the activation of the reward center, the greater the costs that the punisher was willing to incur in order to punish. All of this suggests that the line between appropriate retributive anger at wrongdoing and the baser emotions of pleasure in another's pain is fine, indeed.[25]

Suppose none of this is compelling. Suppose we continue to insist that there is a conceptual connection between resentment and moral rightness. And we persist in thinking that in practice we can purify our resentments of malice, by diligently associating them with salutary values: self-respect, communicating respect for the offenders, and resonance with community norms. Some could still worry that over-moralizing certain types of interpersonal resentments has a shadowy side. The more we over-moralize *individual* hostility, the more we tend to under-moralize types of angers directed toward *social institutions, structures,* and *historical practices.*

---

[25] Steiker 2008: 12.

Alice MacLachlan draws attention to the resentments of the most marginalized—populations of indigenous minorities, illegal immigrants, detainees, those suffering from mental illness, and others. Their angers, she argues, do not always have an articulable moral content, are socially devalued, and have the phenomenology of screaming out loud for recognition rather than communicating or demanding moral respect. As an example of the socially devalued, MacLachlan mentions people on welfare in highly stratified capitalist countries who are resentful at their beneficiaries. As an example of the first and third aspects of anger, she mentions the resentment of feminist writer Dorothy Allison who relates her experience of growing up in a violent, poor, incestual home in these words:

> It was hunger I felt then, raw and terrible, a shaking deep down inside me, as if my rage had used up everything I had ever eaten ... that dizzy desperate hunger edged with hatred and an aching lust to hurt somebody back. It was a hunger in the back of the throat, not the belly, an echoing emptiness that ached for the release of screaming.[26]

MacLachlan goes on to argue that resentment points in the direction of things we value, even when we cannot identify a *personal* culprit, or a *discrete* violation, or provide a *justificatory* story for it. An important upshot of MacLachlan's argument is that some of these social and political resentments could be seen as communicative actions against non-personal transgressors and aggregated historical violations. Another is that over-moralizing standard cases of interpersonal resentment obscures from view the ethical import of these latter angers that scream for accountability in no immediately-present individual wrongdoers, but in agents dispersed throughout corporate and structural forces. Her worries could be generalized. If our hostile feelings track real violations, and our moral judgments are biased in the direction of personifying, concretizing, and justifying evils, victims would be at least as apt to pin the bulk of causal responsibility on proximal individual offenders rather than on agents dispersed through structures, institutions, and corporate entities that are at least as causally responsible for harms.[27] And so even if we accept the moral import of hostile affections, we will reject the assumption that dignifying victims and offenders requires focusing animosity on proximal personal agency at the expense of agents perpetuating structural evil.

---

[26] Dorothy Allison quoted in MacLachlan 2010: 433.

[27] Some people may wonder about this. Think about the way the law treats corporations as persons, and so our tendency to personify corporations and institutions shows that we do tend to blame structures rather than persons. This observation is true as far as it goes. But I would emphasize that when the public blames structures or corporations, leaving aside the legal phenomenon of personifying, it also holds with equal vehemence people responsible for corporate failings. See for example the resignation of Volkswagen's CEO and of the Chief Engineer for Audi and Porsche in the aftermath of the company's failure of social and environmental responsibility.

Carla may feel anger toward Rosie for aligning herself with a political ideology that devalues Carla's dignity. But Carla's anger is a mere rarefication of the rage that burns against economic, legal, social, and historical forces that promote chauvinism and xenophobia while advertising them to ordinary folks under the guise of patriotism and decency. Dignifying persons in a manner consistent with forgivingness may very well require realigning our moral condemnations to spot, track, and hold accountable structural forces and the agents within them who are truly responsible for harms and insults in a way that decenters (at least part of) the blame off of proximal offenders.[28]

I have argued that affective hostility in the aftermath of insult or injury has a complicated structure. Its communicative content is not obviously or directly constitutive of or conducive to the kind of forgivingness that heals, humanizes, and dignifies the offender and the offended. Ostensibly, our publicly expressed resentments may demand the reformation of offenders; in actuality, malice and contempt desire to see "those monsters" suffer. Ostensibly, seemingly irrational rage demands release from pain; in actuality, the feeling is a compressed call for the reformation of dehumanizing institutions, or the undoing of an entire history of abuse. Entrenching curative forgivingness, on my view, entails a serious, careful, and finely-grained formation of our affective lives.

It involves taxonomizing and differentiating among various offender-hostile emotions—sadness, grief, depression, anger, resentment, contempt, malice, and disgust. It also involves learning to express these hostile emotions on various sliding scales. For instance, orientation toward the goal of relational healing may permit expressing contempt of the assailant *privately* to God in prayer, but *publicly* it allows only the expression of grief. As another example, to a mutual friend, Carla may express disappointment with Rosie's deceiving her, but when Carla extends forgiveness to Rosie face-to-face, she may also express frustration with her, in part because Rosie has not been a good friend. Curative forgivingness involves a teleological interrogation of hostile emotions. As I have shown, the interrogation implies recognizing the desire to hurt offenders as a skilled survivor that attaches seamlessly even to our noblest impulses. It implies additionally the recognition that our affective lives are not fatally fixed, that we can make progress toward the goal of peaceability. Honest expression of contempt for an enemy in prayer may give way to an expression of mere annoyance with him, followed by grieving for him, and finally leading to accepting him as a creature loved by God.

---

[28] Considering the interaction between rage against structures and anger with persons, Carla may come to this thought: "I forgive Rosie for symbolically devaluing me, because *its* deeper causes are structural and historical ones. While I continue to rage against these, I realize Rosie is not responsible for them. At most Rosie is responsible for a kind of epistemic carelessness or misplacement of her political trust. I am angry with her for these traits/actions. She just does not see or doesn't accept how her political commitments devalue people like me. The 'not seeing' and 'not accepting' is blamable. The devaluing is not."

Forgivingness, as we have seen, could also teach us to constantly de-focus our more insidious hostile emotions away from proximal offenders and refocus them on the agency dispersed through structural and historical forces.

All of the above notwithstanding, I need to clarify that while I do reject emotional hostility rooted in malice and disgust, I remain open to the possibility that non-malicious angers can be compatible with forgivingness. Looking ahead, Chapter 6 provides a qualified endorsement of the virtue of anger in the lives of historically oppressed people. Some types of anger with people can be compatible with a generous graciousness toward them, even while disgust—whether of an angry or non-angry flavor—can never be compatible with a forgiving disposition. Looking back, in Chapter 3 I discussed divine communicative retributivism. This section has dealt in part with *human* communicative attitudinal retributivism. There is a difference in kind between the two forms of communication. God's wrath as a symbolically communicative act is essentially devoid of malice and disgust. Additionally, it is essentially nested inside a restorative framework. The punishment God communicates to offenders is essentially oriented toward their own good. By contrast, human communicative retributivism is prone to infiltration by malice and other base emotions, and is not easily integrated in a psychological framework that seeks the good of the offender. Nevertheless, even aside from the angers of historically oppressed individuals, to the extent that attitudinal hostility approximates or echoes divine anger, it could, in principle, be justified.

Grace-Responsive, Curative Forgivingness

I'd like to propose that curative forgivingness involves a two-tiered syndrome of dispositions, an interaction between two psychological frameworks in the forgiver: (a) a skilled sensitivity to conditions that reduce the castigation of the offender and maintain (or at least do not reduce) concern for their continued good;[29] and (b) a conception of one's life as a whole—a perception and appreciation of a reality that frames one's life story—that justifies and motivates absorbing relational, psychological, and moral costs of the offense while keeping an honest, full, unedited view of the awfulness of the offense.

I want to emphasize several things about this characterization. First, understanding curative forgivingness in terms of a reproach-reducing, benevolence-maintaining sensitivity aims to fit the complex nature of a forgiver's moral psychology. It implies that a forgiver can continue to experience disappointment with, even anger toward her offender, as long as she begins to dial down

---

[29] This disposition is on a scale, depending on the nature, intensity, and enduringness of the offense, and of the nature of the relationship between the offended and offender.

demonizing the offender. The reduction of any single hostile emotion by itself does not signal reliably that forgivingness has taken root. Imagine that with the passing of time Carla's anger toward Rosie subsides, only to be replaced by contempt instead. "Dolts such as you voted for the rabble-rousers who through their self-serving policies make my life a living hell," Carla thinks to herself whenever she sees Rosie. Though seething anger has dissipated, cold contempt expresses a blame that is incompatible with a forgiving spirit. On the flipside, a forgiving Carla can fulminate against social forces and actors that promote misogyny and xenophobia, can express frustration with Rosie for being duped by them, but refuse to blame Rosie for the harm these forces cause her personally.

Second, I follow Robert C. Roberts in holding that at the first psychological level, curative forgivingness is directed toward the offender and involves a skilled sensibility to respond to her contrition, or to a common humanity with her, or to her misery and pain, or to the nature of a special love relationship, or to a hope in her restoration.

Third, this characterization makes good on the promise of explicating the biblical image of bearing burdens (*nasa awon*). I argued that by bearing Israel's burdens God expresses two interwoven commitments: the commitment to separate Israel from her sins and the commitment to absorb into God's own being the cumulative historical effect of Israel's transgression. Human forgivingness also gives voice to the commitment to imaginatively separate the offender from his offense. This intention becomes permanent and motivationally efficacious by habituating *both* the disposition to reduce castigation and the disposition to maintain concern for the offender's wellbeing (expressed above as (a)). What about the human analogue to the second divine sin-bearing commitment? How can human persons absorb the consequences of harms or insults?

In explicating the second level of curative forgivingness (b), I begin by noting that the larger moral-narrative framework of one's life, its shape and directionality, already largely fixes one's set of moral reflexes, desires, and dispositions. This important Aristotelian point is that the conception of one's whole life sets in play frameworks of salience for our desires and intentions.[30] Hurts and insults unfold in a psychological landscape embedded in a thoughtful life-plan or self-narrative that is *already* responsive to a rich and textured axiological reality. Therefore, a forgiving disposition is formed not only by a skilled sensibility that responds redemptively to the offender, but also by a long-range practical perception of the thread of one's own life.

It seems naïve to identify an essential element of forgivingness, be that forswearing resentment, or forgoing the right to retaliation, or separating the offender from the offense, without recognizing that these attitudes would be

---

[30] This point is made in different ways in MacIntyre 1984 and in McDowell 1979.

downstream from a fundamental perception of the shape of one's life. This idea allows me to circle back to the distinctively non-Aristotelian aspect of curative forgivingness: the axiological reality of the Christian forgiver, the prime matter explaining and motivating her life-plan and story, is the life and work of Christ. As we have seen, the axiological landscape of the curative forgiver is shaped by forgiveness rituals, grace symbols, and redemption stories that disrupt the flow of ordinary time, the cycles of retaliation, the rehashing of centuries of oppression, and the determinisms of "you get what you deserve." The curative forgiver perceives a reality where God has been continually at work in healing sin-disordered people and relationships. Indeed, she takes herself to be a continuant of that transcendent, gracious reality. When offended, the curative forgiver perceives herself and her offender (potentially) as continuants of God's story, both incorporated into a new humanity. When she brings this fundamental perception of her life to bear upon assessing the offense, herself, and the offender, she will be inclined to act toward the offender in ways not conditioned by the harm done, even while keeping that harm clear in view.

A curative forgiver condemns the harm against her, but is also the continuant and the representative of a cosmic story that terminates cycles of oppression, retaliation, and tit-for-tat mentality. The social furniture in the anteroom where she is crafting her life story is populated with tokens, symbols, and paradigms that help her do that. When she absorbs the costs of the offense, she takes intentional stances toward her offender that disrupt or supersede the natural, moral, or relational consequences of his wrongdoing. She will not pass the pain she herself experienced on to others, even on to her offenders. The buck will stop with her.

Recall the story of Esau and Jacob. It's been decades since Jacob tricked his older brother to steal the right and blessing of the first-born son, and since he ran for his life from Esau's wrath. Expecting the worst, the trickster Jacob sends ahead carefully choreographed gifts intended to soften Esau's heart and save his own life. Esau's heart, however, does not need softening. Esau has already moved past the natural desire for revenge. He has also moved past the desire to teach his brother a moral lesson, to remind him of his duties.[31] He seems genuinely surprised by Jacob's symbolic attempts to make restitution. Instead, Esau runs straight up to fall on his brother's neck and embrace him. Esau's attitude and action interrupt in surprising ways the causal and moral necessity that would otherwise unfold downstream of the wrongdoing. The reader of the story, along with Jacob, expects a natural revenge, or at least a moral lesson that would remind Jacob of his place in

---

[31] For a telling comparison, consider the way Joseph extracts a moral lesson from his brothers (cf. Genesis 43–5). Joseph withholds forgiveness for quite a while. Before offering it, he devises a number of tests to convince himself of the trustworthiness or transformation of his brothers. Never mind that in the process, he also ends up causing not only his brothers but also his father, Jacob, quite a bit of suffering.

the world. Instead, we get a gracious, generous, and gratuitous teleological suspension of the natural and of the ethical.

As readers we are and should be puzzled. What happened to Esau? What is *his* story? How is it that the once-avenger has turned into a hugger? We do not know, of course. As we shall see, the biblical text drops some interesting clues, but for the moment we must note not only Esau's transformed sensibility, but also consider the possibility that it is explained and justified by a grace-infused axiological perception.

In sum, I proposed a two-level framework characterization of curative forgivingness. The first is associated with our sensibility and tracks salient conditions for reducing blame of and maintaining goodwill toward the offender. The second involves a perception of one's life-thread as a participation in God's gracious restoration of the world. In what follows, I want to focus on three developments of this account. I will explicate and illustrate aspects of the axiological reality available to those inclined to embody curative forgivingness. I begin by placing curative forgivingness in an overall teleological framework. I continue by explicating the intimate connection between this virtue and the beauty expressed through gestures of grace. I conclude by highlighting yet another way of entrenching curative forgivingness, namely through friendship with Christ.

Curative Forgivingness and Cosmic Renewal

As suggested in Chapter 3, curative forgivingness functions quite well in a teleological framework. I do not have in mind the natural teleology of Aristotle, but instead the social teleology of Alasdair MacIntyre. A natural teleology would think of human excellences as innately or biologically ordered toward good ends. By contrast, in a social teleology, moral virtues are embedded in socially-constructed processes and contexts that aim at attaining or maintaining various goods. As MacIntyre claims:

> The virtues find their point and purpose not only in the sustaining of those relationships necessary if the variety of goods internal to practices are to be achieved and not only in sustaining the form of an individual life in which that individual may seek out his or her good as the good of his or her whole life, but also in sustaining those traditions which provide both practices and individual lives with their necessary historical context.[32]

For MacIntyre, virtuous human actions reveal a three-folded teleology. At one level, the virtues aim to maintain the integrity of one's own narrative—the

---

[32] MacIntyre 1984: 223.

intelligibility one ascribes to one's own life. The virtues also maintain goods internal to the social practices of which one's life is a constituting part, alongside of and in coordination with the lives of others. Finally, insofar as personal narratives and practices are embedded in larger historical traditions—moral, philosophical, or theological—the virtues also aim to maintain these larger diachronic entities.

I do not have the space here to engage deeply with MacIntyre's social teleology. To some, the matryoshka-doll-like inherent architectonic—virtues embedded in narratives embedded in practices embedded in traditions—may appear overly rigid and unnecessary. While I do not accept a rigid and comprehensive teleological architectonic, I am inclined to think that embodying curative forgivingness is likely to support robust self-explanatory scripts that give a unique direction and shape to various strands in a human life. In turn, when episodes of enacted forgiveness become part of our own remembrance, self-explanatory scripts of forgiveness are likely to become even more motivationally and epistemically efficacious. Personal memory and self-narration likely anchor the virtue closer to the center of one's practical identity. This is so especially when forgiving actions are seen as embedded in practices and rituals, and these in turn are seen as belonging to something like traditions or meta-narratives.

To begin with the latter, a generic Christian meta-narrative, consistent with any number of Christian traditions, one that renders more intelligible the virtue of curative forgiveness would go something like this: *From the first signs of creaturely brokenness and alienation, God has acted to renew and heal the cosmos. The decisive moment, the epicenter of God's healing the cosmos, is the life, ministry, death, and resurrection of Jesus Christ. Since the cosmos and the entire world history providentially move toward complete restoration and renewal, Christ followers in every generation are called to become the kinds of persons that creatively advance and participate in God's work of cosmic healing and restoration.* Suppose that from among all other meta-narratives Carla entertains, this one has a distinct normative pull, Carla understanding herself as a co-participant with God in the task of cosmic healing and renewal. All other things being equal, on this supposition, Carla would find it easier to disrupt motivational scripts that involve the desire to get back at Rosie, and would uphold intentions in which Rosie appears worthy of continued compassion and hope, than in situations where Carla prioritizes no particular tradition or is in the grip of a Social Darwinist or a Randian Objectivist meta-narrative. In other words, curative forgivingness flourishes better in some larger epistemic contexts than in others. The point I am making is straightforward. Some meta-narratives are better suited than others to sustain diachronic attitudes of hope, mercy, and grace toward wrongdoers. Some meta-narratives create more nurturing intentional-epistemic contexts than others in which forgivingness manifests itself and makes sense.

A related point regards social practices. Some communities, real or imagined, are better suited than others to manifest curative forgivingness. A community that has practiced over centuries a creative, non-violent resistance toward offenders and assailants is a more fertile ground for it than a community like the Westboro Baptist Church that specializes in inflammatory speech or demonizing its intellectual foes. Again, the point is fairly straightforward once we see the externalist dimension of instilling virtue. The depth, permanence, motivational force, and reliability of curative forgivingness depends not only on the meta-narratives available to forgivers, but also on the availability and creativity of social exemplars that embody the virtue in concrete communities.

Curative Forgivingness, Grace, and Beauty

I claimed that curative forgivingness manifests itself in larger social and epistemic landscapes, landscapes with features that exert a strong normative pull upon the forgiver to act restoratively and healingly toward oneself, the offender, and the affected community. One consequence of our stance so far is this: in forgivingness, the disposition to protest the evil done and the broken character from which it proceeds is buffered by and embedded in larger dispositions to seek and stand for the good of perpetrators. In important ways, curative forgivingness is predicated on the motivational and normative priority of *standing for the good of perpetrators*. In this section I want to explore some of the ways in which the intimate link between grace and forgiveness accomplishes this.

There is a close conceptual link between grace and forgiveness. Etymologically, forgiveness seems to suggest the idea of a preemptive goodness, a gift, a givenness offered in advance of the wrongdoer's atonement. Linguistically, forgiveness is associated with the idea of unmerited favor at the heart of grace. Glenn Pettigrove articulates the connection like this:

> Forgiveness is another common manifestation of grace. The favour that is shown when a wrongdoer is forgiven is seldom merited. It is because he has acted in a way that does not merit favourable treatment—in fact, in a way that would justify unfavourable treatment—that forgiveness is possible in the first place.[33]

Pettigrove seems to think that typical forgiving actions are species of gracious actions. But he also explores the connection between the virtue of grace and the virtue of forgiveness. For instance, in characterizing the virtue of grace, Pettigrove claims:

> The gracious person is identified by her "inclination and spontaneous readiness" to promote others' interests in the kind of ways that tend to evoke gratitude from them.[34]

---

[33] Pettigrove 2012b: 38.   [34] Ibid. 128.

And so, it appears that for Pettigrove the virtue of forgiveness involves analogous inclinations to advance the wrongdoer's good in ways that even he may recognize:

> For ... grace involves the inclination to promote another's joy, which in the case of forgiveness would seem to require keeping the one forgiven in view.[35]

It is hard to overstate the ethical, altruistic import of this point. If the inclination to advance the interests of the other has become spontaneous and second-nature, the gracious forgiver may reasonably act out of it, even when she keeps clearly in view the personal, relational, or psychological costs to herself. Recognizing some of the ways a gracious forgiver can prioritize seeking the good of the offender allows us to tie up some loose ends from the previous section. We confronted there the idea that the disposition to seek the restoration of the wrongdoer is virtuous only if it is rooted in attitudinal punishment or in the meritorious behavior of the wrongdoer. It is now easier to see that when forgivingness keeps the offender in a generous view, it advances the offender's good in ways that neither necessarily communicate punishment nor scrutinize offender-merit.

If we are concerned with the moral transformation of the wrongdoer, a gracious forgivingness can be activated by a finely-tuned hope that trusts—for good reasons—that the offender will make moral progress in the future and perhaps even come to repentance, though he has yet to embark on that road. Relatedly, a forgiving person may offer a gracious gesture in the hope that it may effectively *contribute* to the wrongdoer's moral transformation. As Pettigrove observes, invitational gestures of forgiveness "might enable the wrongdoer to see the significance of his actions and come to repent."[36] When we graciously behold the wrongdoer, moreover, there are ethical reasons to offer forgiveness even in the absence of hope in his moral transformation. For one, curative forgivingness responds to considerations of mercy. A finely-tuned compassion may respond to the present suffering or humiliation of the wrongdoer.[37] In Jesus's parable, a lavishly forgiving father runs, embraces, and immediately elevates to the status of son a filthy, emaciated, and dehumanized prodigal, who had become accustomed to thinking of himself as a hired-hand and companion of pigs. A finely-tuned compassion may also be sensitized to *the past* sufferings and humiliations of the wrongdoer, events in which the forgiver may come to see the seed of the current perpetrated insult or injury.[38] Forgivingness may also initiate a gracious action because it is finely-tuned to goods inherent in the relationship between the forgiver and the forgiven, such as the friendship bond between Carla and Rosie.

---

[35] Ibid. 148.   [36] Ibid. 148.
[37] Roberts 1995 and Pettigrove 2012b argue for similar conclusions.
[38] For an interesting argument to this effect see Calhoun 1992.

Finally, curative forgivingness may also be responsive to a kind of finely-tuned diachronic prudence. The forgiver extends the olive branch because she sees clearly that, in some circumstances, maintaining attitudinal hostility has little chance of advancing either her wellbeing or that of the wrongdoer, or has a better chance to make life more miserable for both.

And so, when forgivingness focuses graciously on the wrongdoer, it discovers a host of virtuous reasons for action. But it also can generate a host of salutary, self-regarding reasons, that we may conveniently label "magnanimity." In other words, through habits of gracious action, the curative forgiver becomes more and more magnanimous. This should not be taken as a strict causal claim. I don't mean to say that other-focused grace directly *causes* self-reflexive magnanimity or vice versa. Also, I don't mean this as practical or moral advice. It strikes me as a bit tacky, maybe even unvirtuous, to aim at gracious forgiveness for the purpose of becoming magnanimous, or vice versa. Rather, the relationship seems to me more indirect. The non-instrumental development of gracious habits solidifies both our altruism and our self-conception as magnanimous. Other-focused goodness and magnanimity supervene upon nurturing capacities responsible for gracious forgivingness. At the same time, finetuning and nurturing one's aggregate capacities for restorative justice, compassion, hope, attachment, and prudence makes it more likely that forgivingness will both discover reasons to prioritize the good of the offender and, at the same time, create in the forgiver an expansive, gracious magnanimity.

To illustrate this point, revisit that mysterious story of Esau and Jacob. This is a just-so scenario. Imagine that after the initial shock and anger, Esau starts reflecting on a possible nexus of reasons that may have moved Jacob to steal the blessing from their father, Isaac, and the right of the first-born son. At first, Esau had seen in his brother only a self-interested, manipulative deceiver. But now, the fog of rage having lifted, Esau considers the larger social forces and family dynamics. He can now see Rebekah's deceptive temperament and machinations, Isaac's blind patronage of arbitrary inheritance-transmission norms, and Jacob—the sapling trying to make his way out of the kitchen on the strength of his wits, in a context that values brawn more than brains. In Esau's compassionate re-visioning, Jacob now appears a clever but sad teenager caught in the power struggle between mom and dad, almost admirable in his youthful iconoclasm. Notice what has happened to Esau. Through a focused compassionate remembrance of the wrongdoer and through an apt understanding of the causal precursors of the wrongdoing, Esau has expanded his ability to absorb a host of harms and insults *without* blaming Jacob. Openness to mercifulness amplifies his capacity to contain the pain of betrayal. While he still acknowledges and decries the wrongs done to him, he will put up with Rebekah's preferentialism and Isaac's senility, he will suffer the prolonged absence of this younger brother, and he will absorb the loss of status and of inheritance without planning retaliation on any of the parties responsible.[39] Imagine that this script forms in Esau's chest: "If I ever see Jacob again, I'll run to him, embrace him, and show him he is reinstated as my beloved brother." By expanding compassion, Esau becomes not only better at focusing on Jacob's interests and more inclined to show visible signs of grace, but also more magnanimous, more adept at bearing away, more skillful at absorbing with grace the consequences of evils done against him.

I have focused so far largely on the ethical aspects of gracious forgivingness. In the remainder of this subsection, I want to argue that grace and forgiveness have an oft-neglected but important *aesthetic* dimension.[40] Gracious, curative forgivingness makes the world a better place by responding to *beauty*. Reliable gracious gestures are also *graceful*; they extend and deepen the beauty of and in the world. The beauty in gracious gestures can enhance the ethical value of the relevant actions, or orient us more reliably toward the ethical good, or reveal the inherent value of their own beauty. I begin by drawing on the work of John Casey, and then I show my point through an extended example of beautiful, gracious forgiveness.

In his magisterial study of pagan virtues, John Casey describes one connection between grace and beauty in the following way:

> Grace in a person is always a quality of expression. The movements of a ballet-dancer are graceful as part of an expressive whole. Without music, and without our sense of the pattern of the dance, and perhaps also of the drama, they lose nearly all their gracefulness. And a single gesture may have grace entirely because of its dramatic context, as when the Count kneels to ask pardon of his wife in *The Marriage of Figaro*.[41]

As the examples below will illustrate, some gestures of gracious forgiveness are exquisite, not only due to the dramatic context into which they are performed, but also because they proceed from a beautiful character. While the graceful movements of ballerinas reveal physical elegance, artistry, and beauty, forgiving gestures in fraught contexts are indicative of a surprising and admirable exquisiteness belonging to noble persons. Gestures of gracious forgiveness stand out because grace in ordinary life seems like an intrusion from a different, more beautiful reality, giving us glimpses of a more harmonious normative world. They transcend what we can typically imagine in the face of evil, they transcend the

---

[39] Imagine Esau looking back into the family history, with a compassionate refocusing of offenders and a desire to grasp the underlying forces at work. When he now looks at Rebekah and Isaac, he might see people trying to do the best they can in miserable circumstances. He imagines how it must have felt for a displaced, alien woman to pick up Sarah's manipulative mantle as a strategy for survival in a new place. He imagines what it would have been like to live with the memory that your father raised the knife to sacrifice you over to God.

[40] Earlier I deliberately used the term "axiological reality" because the values that form and shape the perception of our forgiving lives are not only ethical but also aesthetic.

[41] Casey 1990: 112.

psychological barriers hoisted up by fear and hurt, and they transcend our continued, conditioned fascination with merit, tit-for-tat, pedagogy, or retribution. Gracious forgivingness is, in a motivational and normative sense, beautifully transcendent. Casey quotes Marcel Proust who writes of the charm of Saint-Loup, one of the characters in *Remembrance of Things Past*:

> ... there were moments when my mind distinguished in Saint-Loup a personality more distinguished than his own, that of the 'nobleman', which like an indwelling spirit moved his limbs, ordered his gestures and his actions; then at such moments, although in his company, I was alone, as I should have been in front of a landscape of harmony of which I could understand. He was no more than an object the properties of which, in my musings I sought to explore.... In the moral and physical agility which gave so much grace to his kindness, in the ease with which he offered my grandmother his carriage and helped her into it, in the alacrity with which he sprang from the box when he was afraid I might be cold, to spread his own cloak over my shoulders, I sense not only the inherited likeness of the mighty hunters who had been for generations the ancestors of this young man .... I sensed in it above all the certainty or the illusion in the minds of those great lords of being, 'better than other people.'[42]

And here is Casey's commentary:

> The [Saint-Loup's] body is, as it were, owned and given meaning by a tradition of behavior and self-esteem. Saint-Loup's physical grace is redolent of a social role of which he is largely unconscious. He lives in his body in such a way that it is an emblem, whether he will or not, of something in the service of an ideal.[43]

In Casey's and Proust's view, Saint-Loup's temperamental and physical elegance represents the artistic embodiment of an entire noble tradition. His graceful actions reveal a body that naturally, harmoniously serves that beautiful ideal in ways that are attractive to the eye, morally admirable, and evocative of a better world. Speaking analogically, gracious forgivers also put their bodies in the service of a beautiful, almost transcendent normative ideal. When gestures of gracious forgiveness proceed from characters that seem to have been almost artistically shaped and possessed by a transcendent grace, they are attractive, admirable, and conducive to healing. Even if those forgiven never respond to the gesture of grace with repentance, restitution, or a movement toward reconciliation, the world still remains a more beautiful and better place with such gestures of forgiveness in it than without them. Let us consider one such beautiful gesture of gracious forgiveness.

---

[42] Ibid. 112–13.   [43] Ibid. 113.

The dramatic context: I have already foreshadowed some of this. Nevertheless, two narrative prequels will aid the reader to see the transcendent beauty of Esau's grace-gesture. In the first prequel we return to the scene of the betrayal. Jacob steals Esau's first-born blessing by trickery and pretense. Jacob takes on Esau's hunter persona, complete with hairy arms and hairy neck, while Isaac transfers over to the younger the blessing due the older with an embrace and a kiss. The second context immediately precedes Esau's reunion with his brother. Jacob had been devising stratagems to ingratiate himself to Esau in order to avoid what he expects to be retributive wrath. Jacob sends ahead herds and servants, but he stays behind by the Jabbok River to wrestle a mysterious person whom he later identifies as God or a manifestation of God. After the nightlong brutal combat, Jacob wrests a blessing from God, names the place Peniel—*the face of God*—and walks into the sunrise with a limp and a new name, *God-wrestler*, to meet his brother.

The gesture: "Then Esau ran to meet him and *embraced him, threw his arms* around *his neck,* and *kissed him.* And they both wept" (Genesis 33:4). Since the story had primed us for revenge, this sequence of gestures is as surprising as it is moving. But the offer of forgiveness is even more surprising (and moving) when, in light of the first dramatic context, we see that the sequence re-enacts the original betrayal, with a twist. The original sequence of actions is embedded in a new context, Esau's grace subverting Jacob's original noxious intention and replacing it with a salutary one. Jacob had betrayed Esau by making himself deceptively the recipient of a full-bodied embrace and a kiss. Esau forgives Jacob by making him anew, this time without any dissimulation, the recipient of a full-bodied embrace and a kiss. Consider the communicative power packed in that beautiful gesture. Esau seemingly brings to light the entire sequence of deception, but only to unsettle its original meaning and to replace it with new meanings of compassion, hope, and restitution.

Jacob is so moved by Esau's extraordinary and unexpected forgiveness that he is grasping for explanations. "*It's like I've seen the face of God,*" he says. Jacob, namely Israel, we remember, has just had a theophany—he bears fresh in his hip the sign of having wrestled with God in the mud. But the experience of receiving Esau's grace leaves a mark as deep as the experience of seeing God. Whether Jacob sees in Esau's face a continuation of that first God-experience, an intensification of it, or a deeper recalibration of his own understanding of God's character, here's something uncontroversial. Esau's gesture comes to Jacob from a different, more beautiful world, unexpected, unimaginable, unconditioned, attractive, and admirable. If in the divine embrace that dislocates his hip Jacob comes face-to-face with the crippling consequences of his own planning, devious, hard-nosed, calculative self, in Esau's embrace Jacob experiences a divine mercy that softens, restores, and aims to heal him morally and relationally.

We return to the mystery of Esau's transformation. The Genesis story tracks Jacob's development from a clever, young chef, overly-susceptible to Rebekah's machinations into a calculative and hardened God-wrestler whose life is made miserable by the deceptions of men even more hardened and calculative than himself. Perhaps we see a kind of poetic justice in Laban's midnight switcheroo, and in Simeon and Levi's genocidal treachery. But Esau we did not see coming. The wild-man from the beginning of the story has now become magnanimous in his love, the initial hunter has morphed into a hugger, his massive appetitive for food has been replaced by a focused compassion for his younger brother, and the carelessness with which he sold his birthright has been replaced by a careful disposition to restore the past and to advance even the interests of the betrayer.[44] Genesis is silent on the root-causes and process of Esau's transformation. And such a shocking transformation is ripe for speculation. We get one clue from Jacob. "... *It's like I've seen the face of God*." Perhaps it's not only that Jacob experiences Esau's forgiveness *as* the beauty and goodness of God. Perhaps, somehow, mysteriously and in ways we can only fill in imaginatively, Esau's dispositions have been themselves transformed by God's grace. Perhaps Esau has been putting his body in the service of the ideal of divine gracious forgiveness.

The other clue we get from Jesus. The parable of the prodigal son is modeled on the Esau and Jacob story, with the father playing the role of Esau. It is the father, lavish in generosity who runs to greet, embrace, and kiss the son who had run away with the family fortune. And it is the father who also goes out from the party to meet the older, hardhearted son. The point in Jesus's story is not hard to miss. God is lavishly generous at once to the prodigal and to the hardhearted. Jacob is at once a prodigal and a hard, calculative schemer. And Esau? Well, if the father embodies the lavish forgiveness and generosity of God, Esau does too. And it's plausible to suspect that Esau had a transformative encounter with such divine grace that not only disarmed him, but made him capable of gracing his archnemesis. The conception or perception of his life as graced and blessed by God might very well explain the transformation of Esau's sensibility.[45]

In conclusion, beyond some basic requirements of forgiveness, Esau's actions reveal much more. Given that he was the primary victim of Jacob's deception, Esau has the correct standing to offer forgiveness to his brother. But we see in his gestures not only the overcoming of resentment, or a forswearing of retaliation. We also see a more beautiful and ambitious forgiveness that responds to the condition of a brother's alienation while still remembering the wrongdoing. We see a welcome, a restoration of Jacob's identity as brother and as citizen of Canaan. And we suspect that Esau's response is in part justified and motivated by his own transformed conception of the goodness and grace present in his own life. Esau's gestures can be taken to spring from the two-tier framework of forgivingness and

---

[44] For evidence that Esau is cast as a "wild-man" type and that there's development in his character see Mobley 1997 and Bakhos 2006: ch. 1.

[45] Cf. Genesis 33:9.

they can be taken as an instance of double-agency. They are gestures incorporated into the agency of God, gestures through which God communicates continued blessing and protection to the prodigal. If through the Jabbok warrior's embrace God communicates the blessing of judgment in Jacob's life, through Esau's embrace God communicates unconditional forgiveness, grace, and restoration.

Finally, it must be said that even though in the story Esau never declares Jacob forgiven, the words would be redundant in this particular context. The sprint, the teary embrace, and the kiss already communicate full forgiveness and more. These gestures of curative forgivingness pack richer content than a propositional declaration could. Through the sense of touch Esau expresses an intimate and full forgiveness that outstrips a mere declaration. Had Jacob gotten a mere declaration of forgiveness at arm's length, he might have reason to doubt that full forgiveness is granted. But through Esau's gestures he receives the certainty of grace even without the explicit propositional content. In the midst of a violent, scheming, and loss-filled world, this gesture of gratuitous forgiveness communicates that reparation and restoration are possible. And though Jacob may not be ethically reformed through Esau's beautiful gesture, and though the relationship might not have been restored, the world with this gesture in it is, all things considered, a better world than one where Esau does not perform it.

Gestures such as Esau's arise from sensibilities attuned not only to the ethical (the good), but also to a kind of transcendent beauty. Curative forgivingness involves developing gracious responses finely attuned to oft-concealed realities of mercy, hope, and charity. In a world conditioned by revenge, retribution, and tit-for-tat stories, having a conception of one's life oriented toward these axiological realities is truly beautiful. Forgivers developing these capacities have a better chance to become at once more attuned to the grace in their own lives, more magnanimous, and more attentive to the good of the forgiven. They also open themselves up to becoming channels and vehicles of a rare but desirable beauty ideal. Through their gracious forgiving they make and co-make with God the world into a more beautiful, hopeful, and worthwhile place to live in. They enhance and extend the range of salutary human responses to evil. And while they somehow embody forgiveness artfully, they also become models for all of us. In the final subsection, I suggest another way that Christians can make themselves more reliable conduits of grace and forgiveness, one more way in which they incorporate their own agency into that of Christ's, namely through friendship with God.

What a Friend We Have in Jesus

In an insightful recent work, Michael Rea argues that faith offers victims distinctive resources that could redeem, defeat, or contribute to defeating traumatic events in their lives. Rea focuses on events that leave stains on the souls of victims through no fault of their own. Traumas caused by betrayals, assaults, or manipulations define or shape the explanatory narratives we tell ourselves about ourselves. Like vandals, these narratives tend to colonize our inner sanctum and "threaten to consume our sense of self."[46] But intimacy with God sets in motion different stories. Through baptism, Eucharist, and other church liturgies, or through immersion in Gospel stories, a believer has at her disposal a stock of self-defining scrips, narratives that *others*—God, Christ, the community of believers—tell her about her identity. Perhaps these scripts form something like a redemptive memory bank, an extended mind as it were, from which she can distinctly internalize that she is reborn of God, adopted of God, or friend of God. By accessing and internalizing these redemptive scripts, the subject can co-author a sense of self no longer in the grip of the old sin or trauma narratives. As Rea puts it:

> To the extent that these new narratives of our lives can be overall beautiful and good, and to the extent that they can play a role in making us into . . . who they say that we are, we would seem to have here a promising story about how the work of Christ and his solidarity with both victims and perpetrators might defeat, contribute to defeating, the evils—even the horrors—in which we have participated.[47]

I resonate with the idea that sin and trauma can function as colonizers of our inner being. That is an apt metaphor. And Rea fruitfully recognizes that the new self-descriptions won through the cross of Christ contribute to defeating those evils by launching counter-narratives that decolonize our mental space. But sin and trauma are not only colonizers of inner spaces. They *also* strain, sprain, fracture, and even break relationships *between* persons. And they *also* infect the social environment. That is the serious Levitical point to which we must return over and over again. To deal with the breakage and the infection wrought by sin and trauma, I want to expand Rea's suggestion. Believers are invited not only to reframe their personal narratives of brokenness in light of Christ's victory, but also to enter into Christ's own narratives of brokenness. Believers are invited to follow Christ where *his* relationships are strained or broken, where *his* social environment is infected by horrors or traumas. When we do that, we cultivate a reciprocal intimacy with God, a two-way friendship with God. On the one hand we appropriate the redemptive scripts won through Christ's victory over sin. On the other hand, we enter into a kind of attitudinal resonance with Christ's own reactions to traumas and with his self-understanding in the midst of horrors. That

---

[46] Rea 2019: 131.   [47] Ibid. 132.

is, we allow the self-explanatory scripts of a broken, abandoned, burdened Messiah to enter into dialogue with our own reactions to interpersonal evil.

Through friendship or narrative intimacy with the broken Christ of the Gospels, we have access to yet another set of scripts and self-descriptions that can reframe our own responses to sin, wrongdoing, or trauma: "the lamb of God who lifts up the sin of the world"; "the wounded healer"; "the one who declares forgiven the mockers and blasphemers"; "the hospitable parent who welcomes the prodigal and the dutiful"; "the friend who cooks breakfast for the one who publicly denied him"; and so on. Attending to the ways Christ responds to concrete sin-wrought breakage and infection in his own life, opens up in us the possibility of interpreting our own encounters with interpersonal evil (colonization, breakage, or infection) through the lenses of paradigmatic scenarios laid out by Christ. Christ's reactions to interpersonal evil become windows through which we gain fresh perspectives to stand-back from and reflect on our own de facto reactions. This does not imply a mechanical procedure that pairs up a specific Christ-appropriate pattern of emotional responses to any and all of our situations. What I am after is the cultivation of a kind of holistic attitudinal sensibility, one shaped by *abiding with* Christ's own sensibility—his responses to breakage and infection—which being in some ways alien from ours, is given friendly permission to access, interrogate, and reframe our de facto emotional responses to interpersonal evil.

Jesus, Grace, and Broken Relationships

Consider one example. How does Christ respond to strained or broken intimate relationships? In the Gospel of John, we read of Peter's public denial. Jesus's criminal proceedings are drawn out late into the cold night, meanwhile outside the courtroom, among the officials and servant-girls gathered by the fire, Peter disowns Christ as his friend and teacher three times. Surely not a moral horror, but bad enough to strain a friendship. The next time Jesus meets Peter is post-resurrection. Peter and the disciples come up empty-handed after a night of fishing. A man on the shore tells them to throw the nets on the other side of their boat. When they recognize the man as Jesus, they oblige. They reel in the motherload: 153 fish. Impetuous, Peter jumps into the water and swims to the shore, only to discover Jesus cooking some fish and bread on a charcoal fire. Jesus asks Peter three times whether he loves him, and upon hearing the affirmative three times, Jesus reinstates Peter as a shepherd to the flock.

The story beautifully illustrates how a victimized friend attends to the rehabilitation of the offender. From the early generous catch of fish, to his three-folded declaration about Peter, Jesus goes out of the way to reclaim and restore Peter's identity. Jesus's gestures help move Peter from a fisherman lost at sea to the purposive leader of a floundering community, and, more personally, a continuer of Jesus's own shepherding ministry. Peter is enfolded back into Jesus's purposes and identity. Peter's identity is not only re-set on the professional-ministry track, but also re-forged and re-embedded in an intimate relationship with Christ. Note the key, graciously forgiving gesture: Jesus cooking the fish—which the disciples did not catch—on the open fire. As others have noted, these symbols—the fire and the meal—are signs that speak volumes to Peter.[48] The fire recalls the truth of the betrayal. It was by the fire that Peter denied Christ, and Jesus does not pretend that the event did not happen. But while the injurious event is not forgotten, it is reframed by an invitation to a hearty breakfast. Jesus does not have to say: "I know you've betrayed me, but I want you back inside the fold, as a friend, intimate companion, and continuer of my ministry." The fire, the steaming fish, and the bread are already declaring this reality loud and clear. These forgiving gestures are issuing a gracious invitation to reconciliation. And while it can be argued that Peter also takes steps, or swimming strokes, toward repentance, forgiveness is already waiting for him on the shore.

The believer acquainted with this Christ of the Gospels gains empathetic access to a stock of gracious scripts like this one. One who follows this gracious Christ puts her body in the service of a gracious ideal of action. Friendship with Christ shapes a lifelong axiological outlook nurturing a sensibility that inverts and re-orients our natural responses to offenders: it tends to bless instead of curse, to invite inside instead of exile, to point to truth in rehabilitating instead of accusing ways. And so, friendship with Christ allows a Christ-formed sensibility to frame the details of our own experience of being hurt, denied, or betrayed by friends. The believer hears not only that she is beloved of God when her dearest friend abandons her. Through friendship with Christ, her imagination becomes *prima facie* primed and her sensibility *prima facie* inclined to look for opportunities to show hospitality and grace to the unfaithful friend, while at the same time, acknowledging the reality of the wound and inviting the friend to face it.

Jesus, Grace, and Polluted Environments

Consider another example. How does Jesus respond to horrors that threaten to colonize not only his mental reality, but also to infect the larger, social environment? We read about Jesus's trauma of losing his cousin John the Baptist to the despot Herod Antipas. It is apt to name this event a "trauma" or "horror," given the type of evil it is, and given its personal, political, and theological significance. John's beheading takes place at an opulent feast, the result of a chain of events that include a seductive dance by Salome, Herod's step-daughter, followed by his promise to offer her anything she wants. For all of Herod's ostensible opulence and power, he seems ironically more of a pawn in the intrigue between Herodias and Salome to have John executed. What begins as a sensually and culinarily

---

[48] Cf. Williams 1982: ch. 2.

stimulating celebration of Herod's birthday, ends with the grotesque spectacle of a severed head presented as food, on a platter. We also recall that John is not only Jesus's cousin; he is a prophet, an influential religious leader impacting the lives of many Judeans, and the precursor and inaugurator of Jesus's own ministry.

The severed head on a platter is an atrocity with personal, political, and theological entailments for Jesus. No wonder his first reaction is to withdraw to a place of solace. But when he takes note of the crowds following him, Jesus is moved by compassion to heal them and then to feed them in the wilderness. The three events—John's murder, the healing of the crowds, and the meal in the wilderness—are not merely causally or psychologically connected. Terence Cuneo insightfully connects the first and the last in the sequence. He argues that the feeding of the five thousand is a holy protest against the beheading. In the face of horror, Jesus does not avenge, does not rectify, does not lead a political revolution against Herod and Herodias, does not cynically retreat from the world, or rage against God. Jesus's action is more than an attempt to cope with grief and violence by doing a little bit of good. Rather, "by feeding the multitudes, Jesus thereby symbolically protests or stands against the evil by symbolically being for good."[49]

Building on Cuneo's insight, I want to make two brief observations. In social environments polluted by evil, symbolically being for the good expresses itself not only in Jesus's actions—the healings and the miraculous feeding—but also in the roles that Jesus adopts, in his self-understanding and self-presentation. And these—Jesus's actions and the roles—symbolically stand against the horrific actions *and* against the roles of the perpetrators. In the Gospels generally, and in this story in particular, set against the backdrop of Israel's wilderness experience, Jesus acts from his identity as Israel's healer and Israel's host. This is not the first time the nation recoiled against its spiritual leaders or threatened its prophets. This is not the first time the crowds wandered helpless or famished through the wilderness. But here, just as God had done at Marah and Elim, Jesus will heal. And here, just as God had done countless times in the wilderness, Jesus will feed the famished crowds. John's severed head represents a symbolic infiltration of evil in Jesus's personal, political, and theological spaces. In the face of personal, political, and theological evil, Jesus's actions flow from his deepest identity, his self-conception of a good human life—he heals and he hosts the crowds to a banquet of God's goodness.

At another level of description, Jesus's actions subvert the roles and actions of the violators. They declare a pointed and defiant "No" against the monstrosity, by affirming creation, persons, and the goodness of God. Consider the multiple

---

[49] Cuneo 2014b: 436.

symbolic subversions in the story. Herodias and Salome conspire to murder. Meanwhile, Jesus and the disciples confer about how to feed thousands. Herod orders a hideous beheading, a dismemberment. By contrast, Jesus heals broken tissues. Herod's banquet halls are desecrated through the breaking of a body, while the wilderness becomes the scene where the blessing, followed by the breaking of fish and bread brings consecration of desolate places and relief to desolate thousands. One story ends with disciples collecting a broken body, the other ends with disciples collecting the broken pieces of food left over after an abundant feast in an unlikely place. If Herod advances the script of Israel as a nation of prophet-slayers, Jesus not only bucks that trend, but sets the history of Israel on an entirely new trajectory.[50] Jesus, the paradigmatic Israelite, unravels the murderous script by healing, consecrating, and hosting afflicted multitudes to a restorative banquet.

To summarize, when Jesus is victimized by the tentacles of wicked political power, he symbolically stands for the good *and* for the beautiful. Through gracious actions that flow from his deepest identity as healer and host, Jesus confronts specific evils by alleviating the suffering of other victims *and* by pointing toward the beautiful restoration of broken things. Sometimes it is not possible to enhance our positive perception of our perpetrators. Sometimes the perpetrators are legion; sometimes their personal agencies are concealed and embedded in larger structural and historical entities. Sometimes *our* anger flares up against the penthouses where Herodiases plot, Salomes dance, and Herods slay prophets. But this does not necessitate giving way to despair, resignation, vengefulness, or violence. Friendship with Jesus involves, at least in part, being justified and motivated by the beautiful ideal that Jesus embodies. And that motivational ideal is a standing invitation to act out of *our* self-conception as healers, consecrators, and hosts to God's abundant goodness. Jesus's life calls out to us to act in ways that heal the eco-system infected by the evil that touches us personally—to act in solidarity with victims, to help nurture around us communities of goodness, beauty, and care, and to refuse the ugly action that keeps vengefulness or "eye-for-an-eye" alive.

Cuneo argues that the Eastern Orthodox church with its Eucharistic liturgies has recognized and re-enacted Jesus's beautiful protest against evil. The liturgies have kept alive for centuries this gracious ideal of action. They reveal an interesting dynamic between a first moment in which we admit our powerlessness in the face of evil and a second moment in which the bread is blessed, broken, shared, and eaten together in a communal, Eucharistic meal. The two liturgical moments, isomorphic to John's beheading and Jesus's feeding of the five thousand, are essentially related:

---

[50] Cf. Matthew 23:37 and Luke 13:34.

When assembled, the church addresses evil protesting its presence in the world by symbolically being for the good in the taking, blessing, breaking, and sharing the bread, just as Jesus did in the feeding of the five thousand.[51]

I have tried to show that friendship with Jesus involves a kind of aesthetic immersion in the Christological narratives that tracks Jesus's gracious responses to personal and political evil. But I do not want to suggest that being motivated by the gracious ideal that is Jesus essentially stays tethered only to ecclesial or liturgical contexts. Sensibilities formed in dialogue with Jesus and persons shaped by the gracious ideal that is Jesus, can, in any number of ways, break into our world, to continue that trajectory of healing, consecrating, and hosting inaugurated by the gestures and the self-conception of Jesus.

I return to the Nickel Mines Amish. Historically, the Amish have forged their communal identity around the pieces in Jesus's Sermon that dismantled the reciprocity code and hail love of the enemy. When George Roberts IV killed the Amish schoolgirls, this particular afflicted community embodied what was in their cultural DNA for centuries. Though openly admitting to grief and pain, a number of the family members who had lost their girls told reporters that they have forgiven the shooter. When asked how that is possible, they simply said "Through God's help." When I initially tracked that story, I was shocked by the immediate, almost reflexive Amish offer of forgiveness. But what happened next seemed even more confounding.

That week the Roberts family had a private funeral for their son. As they went to the gravesite, as many as thirty Amish people came out from around the sides to surround George's family like a crescent. They came to be near their neighbors in their time of loss and to form a protective wall from the snooping cameras and media attention. As the cordon tightened around the grieving parents, the mother, Terri Roberts remembers: "love just emanated from them."[52] This gesture—coming together as a group to show solidarity with the grieving parents of the murderer—seems like the exercise of the same capacities that allowed the Amish to forgive the shooter. The disposition to absorb the consequences of wrongdoing, when crystalized through the ideal that is Jesus, focuses attention to the manifold ways evil colonizes inward spaces, tears apart relationships, and desecrates commons spaces. In part due to their historically-cultivated, communal friendship with Jesus, these Amish people were able to attend to these dimensions of evil through the eyes of grace and mercy. Many people would have isolated themselves and their grief from the Roberts family, or even actively blamed them for raising a

---

[51] Cuneo 2014b: 442.

[52] Renee Montagne (host), "A Decade after Amish School Shooting, Gunman's Mother Talks of Forgiveness." *StoryCorps*, NPR, September 30, 2016. https://www.npr.org/transcripts/495905609. Last accessed August 23, 2022.

mass-murderer. Not so the Amish. They come to the tomb of the murderer. They stand in solidarity with other sufferers affected by the atrocity. They come close to form a community of care around *other* vulnerable folks. They come close to heal and consecrate their own social eco-system.

"Because of the response of forgiveness, we were able to heal," said Terri Roberts in an interview ten years after the events.[53] The Amish crescent at the graveyard moved Terri to get to know and care for the community that stood by her in the hour of her need. For years, Terri showed up every Thursday evening to the King family farm where she bathed, read to, and cared for Rosanna, one of the survivors her son's shooting left paralyzed for life. When Terri underwent treatment for stage four breast cancer, in turn, it was the Amish women who attended to her, another survivor cleaned her house, and a bus-full of Amish children came on Christmas Eve to sing her carols. These mutual, gracious gestures are all the more remarkable, given that the community continued to witness daily reminders of the lasting traumatic effects of the atrocity. Rosanna King will never be able to speak or move by herself, and she will continue to be gripped by seizures in the middle of the night. Aaron Esh Jr. will continue to wrestle with the guilt and self-blame for failing to protect the fallen girls. After a decade there are lost futures and gaping holes in the lives of many. And yet, despite the fact that trauma and pain of loss endures, it also remains true that those early gestures of Amish gracious forgiveness have blossomed over the years into lasting, beautiful bonds of friendship and mutual care.

---

[53]   Ibid.

6

Sing Rage

"Be angry but do not sin"
Ephesians 4:26

I have argued so far that curative forgivingness is a complex blame-reducing, goodness-maintaining, evil-absorbing disposition that also interacts with a conception of one's life as infused by divine grace. In the previous chapter we traced an explanation of how grace informs the trait of curative forgivingness. When grace indwells persons, their gestures and actions are put in the service of an ideal that express a way of life—e.g., the gracious way of Jesus of Nazareth—that is redolent of a whole tradition of healing forgiveness. Through gracious forgiving, persons enhance and extend the range of salutary human responses to evil, making the world a more beautiful, hopeful, and worthwhile place to live in. And *one* way some take themselves to participate in that reality of grace, and reflexively put their bodies in the service of that ideal, is through friendship with God.

The main question I want to take up in this chapter is this: Can we recommend curative forgivingness to people living under circumstances of oppression? Is gracious forgiving an apt response to wrongdoers whose actions express and perpetuate systemic oppression? Recent literature has focused on the aptness of anger as a distinct moral response to personal and systemic oppression, especially in the lives of women and ethnic minorities.[1] In previous chapters, I have noted that the emotion of anger, even of rage, against unjust systems and practices is compatible with embodying curative forgivingness toward individuals. I have also articulated the view that God's anger is compatible with and even entailed by divine love. Free of rationalization and malice, divine anger is apt and admirable. But some theorists insist that in some non-ideal circumstances, anger is *a human virtue*, an enduring and admirable character trait, directed not only toward unjust systems but also persons. Consider an example.

Macalester Bell recounts a daguerreotype of Frederick Douglass that reveals a particular aspect of his character:

What is most arresting about the image is the expression on Douglass' face: his countenance smolders with tightly controlled anger. Douglass quite deliberately

[1] Cf. Bell 2005; Bell 2006; Bell 2009; Callard 2018; and Srinivasan 2018.

Gracious Forgiveness: A Theological Retrieval. Cristian F. Mihut, Oxford University Press. © Cristian F. Mihut 2023.
DOI: 10.1093/oso/9780192873729.003.0006

presents himself as a strong, stern, and angry man. As I interpret it, the portrait has not captured a fleeting emotional state, but something more enduring about Douglass' character. The fact that this is a daguerreotype is significant: given the long exposures required by this process, those who sat for these portraits could exercise a level of control over their representation that would be impossible in a painted portrait or in the short exposures of many of today's photographs. So when we look into the eyes of the young, incandescently angry Douglass, it is not unreasonable to infer that we have before us an accurate representation of one aspect of Douglass' character, or at least one aspect of how he wished to be regarded.[2]

Bell goes on to argue that Douglass's anger, as an enduring aspect of his character, was responsible for his resistance against the abuses of Edward Covey the slave-breaker to whom Douglass was rented out when he was only sixteen. Douglass himself recalls it like this:

> This battle with Mr. Covey was the turning point in my career as a slave. It rekindled the few expiring embers of freedom, and revived within me as sense of my own manhood. It recalled the departed self-confidence, and inspired me again with a determination to be free. The gratification afforded by the triumph was a full compensation for whatever else might follow, even death itself. He only can understand the deep satisfaction which I experienced, who has himself repelled by force the bloody arm of slavery...My long-crushed spirit rose, cowardice departed, bold defiance took its place; and I now resolved that, however long I might remain a slave in form, the day had passed forever when I could be a slave in fact. I did not hesitate to let it be known of me, that the white man who expected to succeed in whipping, must also succeed in killing me. From this time I was never again what might be called fairly whipped, though I remained a slave four years afterwards. I had several fights, but was never whipped.[3]

Several features of this account stand out. First, Douglass experiences his anger not only as a protest against Covey, the white man who abuses him, but more generally, as a resistance and protest against slavery. Second, the anger and its causal consequent—resisting the whipping—activate and shore up other virtues in Douglass: courage, self-trust, and a renewed determination to fight for freedom. Third, the anger against this white man and against the system Covey represents, together with other excellences that anger props up in him, are so long-lived that they ground a new self, or at least a new self-understanding in Douglass. Anger

---

[2] Bell 2009: 166.   [3] Quoted in Bell 2009: 166.

and its fruit produce a "glorious resurrection" of this new self from the "tomb of slavery." Finally, even if not conducive to personal happiness, liberation from slavery, or the liberation of others, Douglass's anger seems admirable. Even if he were to die, unmarked by any public measure of success, Douglass's angry protest seems good. In this particular context of fighting for liberation and survival, anger seems to be its own reward.

Even in modern contexts, black anger may be instrumentally conducive to all sorts of goods: it educates white folks, it creates solidarity among different oppressed people-groups to resist oppression, and it clarifies one's perceptions of who are the enemies and who are the friends of justice.[4] But Douglass's anger goes beyond instrumentalism. It suggests that by resisting oppression, it not only stands against the bad, but also becomes constitutive of the good. This anger contributes to the construction of positive value by enhancing the capacities oppressed people have to resist their own oppression. This anger looks like a virtue because it provides a mode of self-expression and self-expansion of Douglass's agency that had been reduced or fragmented by individual and systemic badness. His anger seems partly constitutive of the very power oppressed people have to resist their own oppression.

Would we recommend to Douglass to develop curative forgivingness toward Covey? If our answer is an unqualified yes, at first blush it would appear our view has some troubling consequences. It implies recommending dispositions that diminish the power victims have to resist their oppression, by perpetuating both hermeneutical and affective injustice against them. Hermeneutical injustice occurs when the linguistic-conceptual tools available to systemically oppressed persons either fail to capture their experiences or delegitimize their standpoints as victims.[5] Affective injustice occurs when oppressed people are made to feel bad for their own rage against injustice, or when they experience a virulent inner conflict between pursuing their own wellbeing if they internalize the norms of the system that oppresses them, on the one hand, and justly raging against that system at enormous personal costs, on the other.[6] And so, if the linguistic-conceptual and motivational-normative tools necessary for cultivating gracious forgivingness contribute to the perpetuation of either hermeneutical or affective injustice against oppressed people, they are bad tools. It seems then that in contexts of oppression, the cultivation of anger or rage as an alternative to forgivingness would be

---

[4] Consider the interesting argument and observations in Lorde 2017.

[5] Cf. Fricker 2009: esp. ch. 7.

[6] Srinivasan puts it like this: "Affective injustice is a second-order injustice that is parasitic on first-order injustice, a sort of psychic tax that is often levied on victims of oppression. But it is not only a psychic tax. Like more familiar kinds of injustice, the wrongness of affective injustice does not lie primarily in the fact that it makes its victims feel bad. Its wrongness lies rather in the fact that it forces people, through no fault of their own, into profoundly difficult normative conflicts—an invidious choice between improving one's lot and justified rage" (Srinivasan 2018: 13–14).

motivationally and conceptually more salutary. This problem seems particularly acute in contexts and communities where the concept of forgiveness has been used historically to legitimize oppression and to gaslight the experiences of victims.[7]

Consider the following genealogy of anger and justification for its mitigation. In the beginning, anger was the prerogative of affluent, free men whose brute power overshadowed law or custom. When the rich, free, and powerful learned to control or check their anger, they acquired even more political, legal, or religious power. Restraining anger even more by ingraining dispositions of meekness, compassion, and forgiveness afforded these men the crown jewel—spiritual power. As Amia Srinivasan argues, this genealogy of anger reveals that the question about the exercise and limits of rage is directly and deeply connected to acquisition of power: the tribal leader's praiseworthy rage (Achilles) gives way to a legislator's check on anger (Seneca), and is radicalized in Christianity as the transformation of anger into meekness. But, as Srinivasan argues, the possessors of these attitudes and of the corresponding military, legislative, and religious power afforded them have always been *men*, at the exclusion of *women* and *slaves*:

> It was simply taken for granted that women and slaves had no business getting angry; the debate about anger was never about them. Christianity told the same men that they should be neither judge nor warrior, but instead forgiving and meek. Here women and slaves might have been the model, but they were only models; it was through a free choice to willfully transfigure oneself into a submissive lamb that Christianity offered its deepest power.[8]

If forgivingness turns out to be at home in this genealogy of anger-softening, it seems packaged together with a set of other normative and motivational tools that traditionally have disempowered women and nonwhites. By recommending forgivingness as a form of anger-replacement to these traditionally disenfranchised groups of people are we not denying them one really effective normative and motivational power they *could* wield? As Srinivasan continues:

> A recognition of anger's aptness might seem to threaten a return to the petulant and vengeful Achilles, a backwards slide into a form of life in which justice is not the business of the state, but the personal lot of each man. We tell ourselves that we have set anger aside, that we no longer have any need of it. Invoking the spectre of the raging Achilles, we condemn anger. But in so doing we neglect, as

---

[7] Cf. Panchuk 2018 for case studies and analysis of how religious language and practices can traumatize victims in religious contexts. Cf. Thomson 2001 for an example of how the concept of forgiveness can be used in non-religious contexts to prop-up tactical and performative policies of unity and reconciliation in post-genocide Rwanda.

[8] Srinivasan 2018: 142.

we have always neglected, those who were never allowed to be angry, the slaves and women who have the power of neither the state nor the sword.[9]

In what follows, I do four main things. First, I survey and clarify several ways in which anger can be taken to be virtuous. Second, I introduce an understanding of practical selfhood that aims to accommodate both a robust forgivingness and the virtue of anger for individuals living in seriously non-ideal circumstances. Third, I present and respond to the worry of anger-entrenchment. I conclude by suggesting a Christian meta-narrative that makes sense simultaneously of the virtues of anger and of forgivingness. On my view, anger is less likely to be a virtue in persons with immense power and privilege, and more likely to be a virtue in oppressed persons. So, at first blush, it would seem anger could not be a divine disposition. In response, I argue that divine anger is a sustained and deep divine affective pattern of echoing the pain and rage of oppressed people. The picture that emerges is this: the virtuousness of anger cannot be assessed piecemeal, in separation from larger psychological forces active in one's agency. These in turn depend on the larger meta-narratives constitutive of one's self-conception, and one of the stories available to those oppressed expresses God's own responses to systemic injustices. In short, the oppressed can cultivate virtuous anger and forgivingness by taking herself to continue God's cosmic battle against evil and injustice.

Virtuous Anger

Historically, many serious thinkers consider the emotion of anger to be incompatible with virtue. Anger is even seen as vicious for a number of reasons. Picking up on Aristotle's observation that it essentially involves the desire to harm perceived offenders, the Stoics argue that anger is both useless and morally wrong.[10] Others argue for its viciousness because, as Callard puts it, long-term anger is "unpleasant, unattractive, and exhausting."[11] Even assuming some forms of anger can be purified of malice, some have raised what has become known as the counterproductivity critique. For the sake of exposition, we may distinguish between the psychological, relational, and political counterproductivity of anger. Anger purportedly darkens our capacity to think rationally and clearly, therefore interfering with the pursuit of our long-term goals. Anger supposedly has the relational cost of alienating possible allies, such as when the rage of a black woman shocks a white woman away from making a common cause against sexism. And politically, anger may have the paradoxical effect of worsening the social,

[9] Ibid. 142–3.
[10] For a summary and evaluation of Seneca's views against anger see Nussbaum 1994: ch. 11.
[11] Callard 2018: 124.

cultural, and political conditions of angry protesters, as poignantly exemplified in this little vignette:

> Martin Luther King wrote of Malcom X that in "articulating the despair of the Negro without offering any positive, creative alternative" he has "done himself and our people a great disservice" for "[f]iery, demagogic oratory in the black ghettos can reap nothing but grief."[12]

On the other hand, galvanized by feminist and postcolonial reflection, a number of theorists have been quick to systematize against this tradition some of the psychological, moral, epistemic, and political benefits of the emotion of anger. For Douglass, prolonged anger constitutes an effective way to protest evil and restore a lost sense of self-dignity and freedom. For black people in the United States, anger may enhance the capacity to detect racism in ordinary contexts. While anger can heighten the victim's sensitivity to injustice, it can also have an additional epistemic benefit: it clarifies the normative status of oppressed individuals in their own community. Macalester Bell observes about the anger of women:

> Since women's anger is typically given uptake (i.e., taken seriously as anger) in a restricted range of circumstances, paying attention to how women's anger is received by others can provide knowledge about women's status in the moral community. In Frye's words, 'anger can be an instrument of cartography' which allows women to map out others' conception of their status.[13]

Finally, while anger sometimes makes things socially worse for protesters, at other times it can be an effective way to bring about social and political change. Malcom X observes that in some African countries the presence of anger in protesters tended to bring about swifter political change than in African countries without a felt presence of anger. The former countries experienced an accelerated march toward independence from colonialism.[14] For a different example, consider the anger of black women who helped spur a powerful AIDS activism, given that the HIV virus disproportionally affected black communities.[15]

To sum up, the evidence for the value of the emotion of anger appears to be split. In some contexts, anger is paralyzing. In other contexts, it is dignifying and freeing. In some circumstances, anger produces social change; in others it impedes

---

[12] Srinivasan 2018: 125.   [13] Bell 2009: 168.

[14] Malcom says: "Some areas of the African continent became independent faster than other areas. I noticed that in areas where independence had been gotten, someone got angry. And in the areas independence had not been achieved yet, no one was angry ... Usually when people are sad, they don't do anything. They just cry over their condition. But when they get angry, they bring about a change" (Malcom X 1994: 107).

[15] Cf. Harris 2018.

it. Some forms of anger stunt our sensibilities, others seem to open up our eyes to new epistemic and normative realities. Though it is hard to build a compelling instrumentalist case that shows the universal value of the emotion of anger in most situations, it seems equally difficult to construct a comprehensive instrumentalist case for devaluing anger.

At any rate, the foregoing discussion about the instrumental value of the emotion of anger is merely preparatory for considering anger as a virtue. We want to focus on inherently normative reasons to cultivate anger as an enduring motivational state of one's overall moral character. *Are there good intrinsic rather than instrumental reasons to nurture and engrain the trait of anger?* A virtue is an admirable, habituated, settled disposition of fitting cognitive, affective, and intentional response in specific circumstances. If anger is to be an admirable—read apt or virtuous—excellence, it must be the particular expression of a more general affective sensibility rightly fitting the circumstances, and this attunement obtains *only if* normative (as opposed to instrumentalist) reasons ground our affective responses to the world.[16]

I know of three accounts that aim to justify the inherent value of the trait of anger as an enduring character trait: *eventual-flourishing, appropriate attitude,* and *manifestation of care.* While each of these has its own benefits and costs, and while I have my own preferences, I don't have the space to launch a full-fledged evaluation here. Whatever the intramural debates, in the end, I aim to show two things. First, regardless of its grounding, the virtue of anger can be accommodated within a psychological profile that *also* instantiates forgivingness. And second, the compatibility between the virtue of anger and forgivingness does not depend on anger's normative grounding. Instead, it depends on how deep the trait of anger gets entrenched and engrained in an agent's character.

Eventual Flourishing

One way to justify the inherent value of the trait of anger is to argue that there is a kind of conceptual connection between it and flourishing. Lisa Tessman argues

---

[16] Clearly there is a difference between *an angry person* and *an aptly angry person.* On the one hand, the former description suggests a trait where anger is the person's habitual go-to response, whether apt or not. An aptly angry person may possess the trait even if she is very rarely angry. And so it seems that there will be little reason to cultivate the trait in the first case, and serious reason to cultivate it in the latter. On the other hand, the frequency or habitual expression of anger is not an automatic disqualifier for the presence of the virtue. In fact, the habitual presence and expression of anger in victims of systemic oppression may very well be a sign of the virtue. I am reminded of a quote often attributed to James Baldwin: "To be a Negro in this country and to be relatively conscious is to be in a rage almost all the time." While the habitual expression of anger is neither necessary nor sufficient for virtue, it is also neither necessary nor sufficient for the presence of its non-virtuous counterpart. An aptly angry person is wise, thus her anger habitually responds fittingly to circumstances. But it is still possible for the virtuously angry to manifest the virtue in inappropriate ways, due to other psychological pressures. Thanks to Mike Rea for pushing me to clarify this point.

that in oppressive circumstance some virtues either enable the bearer's survival or her resistance of oppression, even though they also seriously detract from her *present* personal flourishing. These traits are *burdened virtues*. Tessman goes on to argue that some burdened virtues *eventually* tend to be conducive to the overall flourishing of the bearer of virtue and to the general flourishing of others. According to her, oppositional anger, the anger that stands up against oppression is a burdened virtue. Oppositional anger fails the standard Aristotelian characterization of virtue, because in circumstances of oppression it is likely to be misdirected and excessive. Although it has high costs for its bearer, its presence in the agent must not be mollified or moderated:

> If tremendous anger is ultimately unhealthy or corrosive for its bearer, then the political resister with an angry disposition displays an example of what I have been calling a burdened virtue...if one chooses to be angered only in a measured way, then one must endure the degradation of oneself or of others on whose behalf one acts, but if one chooses to develop a fully angered/enraged disposition in response to the vast injustice one is fighting, then the anger can become consuming.[17]

The direction of explanation seems to be this. Unmitigated anger is at once necessary to protest one's humiliation *and* tends to bring about eventual salutary changes. So, eventual flourishing makes it necessary for the bearer to cultivate unmitigated anger now, even though she knows it wrecks her wellbeing in the present. Tessman concludes that the virtuously angry resister should experience regret for the negative consequences of her anger, whether befalling her or others. However, the function of regret is not to de-intensify her anger, but to add an evaluative layer to the agent's overall endorsement of her anger.

Two main worries about Tessman's account are relevant for our evaluation. From one direction, some have rightfully argued that the attitudinal mix of anger-regret is motivationally and normatively unstable.[18] If the felt regret is rational, it seems more likely that it will moderate one's anger, unless the agent also has a rational way to compartmentalize anger away from regret. But the more serious problem here seems to be normative. If protesters such as Douglass are really dignified through the exercise of undiminished anger, accompanying regret would seem to chip away at their freshly gained self-respect.

From another direction, some worry about the neo-Aristotelian connection. Of course, there are stock difficulties in specifying what the content of future flourishing would have to be. But some theorists argue that the justification for the virtue of anger should not be based *at all* in considerations pertaining to flourishing, present or future.[19] On their view, the normative fittingness of anger is

---

[17] Tessman 2005: 124–5.   [18] Cf. Bell 2006.
[19] Bell 2006; Bell 2009; and Srinivasan 2018.

rooted in its singular ability to uphold the victim's integrity and stand against humiliation and injustice.

Appropriate Attitude

A more promising approach is to regard anger as a particularly apt response to circumstances of humiliation and pain. On this view, the virtue of anger is justified neither by its utility nor by its conduciveness to human flourishing. Instead, anger is a virtue understood as "a kind of excellence in being for (or loving) the good and being against (or hating) the evil."[20] If degradations and humiliations are generally evil, then the trait that manifests a particular hatred of these kinds of evils will be virtuous. So, anger, as a singular mode of standing against humiliation and degradation, is virtuous.Anger is a singularly appropriate attitude of being (standing) against evil for two reasons: its unique affective-epistemological dimension and its unique expressive-supplicative dimension. Let's briefly take each in turn. Srinivasan argues that an essential aspect of anger is akin to a kind of aesthetic appreciation. When we get angry, we do not only come to know that an injustice has occurred, we also register affectively and aesthetically the full measure of the horror:

> I want to suggest that getting angry is a means of affectively registering or *appreciating* the injustice of the world, and that our capacity to get aptly angry is best compared with our capacity for aesthetic appreciation. Just as appreciating the beautiful or the sublime has a value distinct from the value of knowing that something is beautiful or sublime, there might well be a value to appreciating the injustice of the world through one's apt anger—a value that is distinct from that of simply knowing that the world is unjust.[21]

Anger, however, is more than an aesthetic phenomenon. It goes beyond an affective appreciation of the horrors of injustice; anger is also constituted by an expressive-supplicative disposition. "Anger is also a form of communication, a way of publicly marking moral disvalue, calling for the shared negative appreciation of others."[22] There's something intuitively plausible in Srinivasan's analysis. Apt anger does seem to require both an affective registering of injustices and the expressive call for the recognition of injustice and for publicly decrying its badness.

Still, I want to briefly mention two worries about this account. First, there may well be attitudes distinct from anger, that register affectively injustices at least as

---

[20] Bell 2009: 176.   [21] Srinivasan 2018: 132.   [22] Ibid.

well as anger in the same circumstances, and that express at least as forcefully solidarity with victims. For instance, non-angry disappointment, or non-angry censure or repudiation of perpetrators, or the non-angry commitment to eliminate the roots of suffered injustice may, in some circumstance, express more aptly the agent's self-respect and self-worth, as well as her respect for the dignity of the victimizers.

Second, the presence of virtuous anger as an apt mode of standing against badness can function within a sensibility *overall* diminished in its ability to stand for (or love) the good. More pointedly, sometimes the chronic anger that is especially apt at resisting injustice functions as an inhibitor of other dispositions that would otherwise enable the agent to love (stand for) the good. For instance, it may not be difficult to imagine that Douglass's apt rage against the cruelty of Edward Covey severely hampers his dispositions to see the good in aspects of Covey's humanity unconnected to his abhorrent trade, to empathize with Covey's own plight as a poverty-stricken white farmer, or even to orient Douglass himself toward his own good.

Anger as Caring

The final justification of virtuous anger I want to consider sees it as a particular expression of care. When I'm angry about an injustice, I give a hoot about it, and my anger involves an emotive-evaluative way of concerning myself with that wrong. Perhaps we can articulate a functional account of caring-anger that distinguishes it from caring-disappointment or caring-fear. Anger might publicly express care that wrong W has been committed against person P in the hope of making just amends for P or of ridding the world of wrongs of the type W. If something like this is on the right track, how do we distinguish between virtuous and vicious anger? An answer presents itself:

> When anger manifests moral concern, it reflects well on one's moral character. When anger manifests moral indifference or selfish concerns, it reflects poorly. Anger is virtuous or vicious by the underlying concerns that it manifests. So when anger manifests a concern for the wellbeing of others or for justice, it is virtuous. When someone's anger manifests a contempt or a concern to see the other harmed, it is vicious. As we have seen, anger can manifest a variety of concerns all at once... so it may be more accurate to say that anger is virtuous *to the extent* that it manifests morally important concerns.[23]

---

[23] Bommarito 2017: 13.

This approach appears fruitful at first blush, but it also needs further development. For one, the analysis would need to fill in the explicit content of moral concerns. We would want to know what are the moral concerns relevant to virtuous anger. If morally important concerns are either consequentialist, eudaimonistic, or deontic, the anger-as-caring account seems in principle reducible to the *instrumentalist*, *flourishing*, or *appropriate attitude* accounts we have encountered.

Additionally, recall the last problem we raised for the appropriate attitude account. We noted that ways of standing against evil can undermine ways of loving the good. Similarly, it might be argued that caring about humiliations can sometimes come into conflict with our ways of caring for the good. Interestingly, some have noted that concerns grounded by anger are *secondary* to the primary concerns rooted in our loving the good. Agnes Callard puts it like this:

> Anger, fear, sadness, disappointment, jealousy—these are signs of caring. Indeed they are ways of caring. But they are not the primary ways, since valuing proper involves feeling positive emotions, emotions that respond to the goodness of the good object.[24]

The consequence of this objection is that anger finds justification as a form of care, but it seems derivative and secondary. A positive form of concern for victims would have presumptive priority over anger. Even if this objection does not compel, there is a related hurdle. A virtuous person presumably cares about a number of things, his diachronic commitments expressing any number of distinct concerns. Of course, virtuous people living under oppression *should* give full articulation to their rage, they should care deeply about wrongs and injustices. But even for them, and perhaps especially for them, anger should not hold a totalizing sway over *other* concerns. And anger, by its very nature, tends to permeate and multiply.[25] We will return to this worry.

This section examined three justificatory accounts of the virtue of anger: *eventual flourishing*, *appropriate attitude*, and *caring*. While I am preferential to an appropriate attitude account of anger, making the case for that will take us too far off field. Instead, I will claim agnosticism about the grounding of the virtue of

---

[24] Callard 2018: 127.

[25] Cf. Pettigrove 2012a. In the second part of this article, Pettigrove presents a wealth of empirical evidence for the following theses: (a) anger alters the perception of risk; (b) when angry, people are more likely to attribute undesirable events to agential causes; (c) the more anger one experiences, the more blame one places on the perpetrator and vice versa; (d) when angry, people are less likely to trust others; (e) when angry, people are slower to associate positive traits than negative traits with members of the outsider group; (f) when angry, people tend to see themselves as exceptional, more competent, and wise, and less biased than others; (g) when angry, people are less likely to revise their plans or reconsider their judgments even when presented with evidence that under normal circumstances they would find compelling. The upshot is that anger alters our judgment and motivational structures not only in interpersonally transgressive contexts—when we've been wronged—but also in much wider, non-transgressive relational and political contexts.

anger, but remain a realist about the existence of such a trait. This discussion has proven helpful at least in clarifying some desiderata for a future theory that attempts to find the normative grounds for the virtue of anger. (D1) the theory must maintain the motivational efficacy of anger and not imply affective injustices against women and nonwhites; (D2) the theory must allow nurturing and developing diachronic dispositions that stand for the good, or express care for the good, and not only those that denounce the bad; (D3) the theory must do justice to the multivalent, pluriform nexus of concerns that persons have, perhaps especially those living under oppression.

Virtues and the Dramatic/Dialogical Self

Chapter 5 canvassed a conceptual framework within which we could make sense of forgivingness. Specifically, I referred to the social teleology of Alasdair MacIntyre. I claimed that entrenching curative forgivingness is likely to support robust self-explanatory scripts that give a unique direction and shape to various pursuits in life. In turn, when episodes of enacted forgiveness become part of our self-remembrance, against the backdrop of meta-narratives that see grace as a unique expression of strength, courage, and beauty, and when they are reinforced by gracious practices and rituals, then these self-explanatory scripts of forgiveness are likely to become even more motivationally and epistemically efficacious. They move forgivingness closer to center of one's practical identity.[26]

But now suppose we are compelled to also regard anger as a virtue. By the same MacIntyrian approach, we must accept the conclusion that the virtue of anger will support self-explanatory scripts perhaps of righteous indignation, and that these will further deepen the motivational and normative centrality of anger. This would be so, especially if my angry gestures are seen as embedded in social practices and rituals that stand against injustice, and when these, in turn, are seen as belonging to something like a tradition of protest.

It appears that I have argued for the value of self-interpretative scripts and meta-narratives of forgiveness, and for the value of self-interpretative narratives and related traditions of angry protests. Moral psychologists should intervene to demand the unification or integration of this poor self, split between the concerns of anger and those of forgiveness.[27] Several integration strategies may be offered at

---

[26] I don't mean to suggest that this process is one of automatic or linear growth. Sometimes the forgiver will remember their acts of forgiveness as a defeat, and that memory will threaten to alienate the virtue from the center of one's practical identity. But provided that her sensibility is formed by varied and explanatorily potent grace-affirming practices, rituals, and meta-narratives, the agent has at her disposal normative vehicles for mitigating and contextualizing failures of forgiveness.

[27] There are a number of self-integration accounts in the literature. For an example of synchronic integration see Frankfurt 1988: esp. ch. 12. For two examples of diachronic integration, see Bratman 1987 and MacIntyre 1984: esp. ch. 15.

this point.[28] (IS1): The integrated virtuous agent is the one who recognizes *when* there is a time for anger, and *when* a time for forgiveness. (IS2): The integrated virtuous agent is the one who loves the sinner but hates the sin. In our jargon, she nurtures preponderant dispositions to act graciously toward perpetrators of systemic injustice, while cultivating anger toward the injustices themselves. Or (IS3): The integrated virtuous agent is the one whose anger is directed at institutions or systems that perpetuate injustices and not at the individual actors within them.

In reply, (IS2) and (IS3) present poor strategies for agential integration generally, and are particularly bad for victims of systemic injustices. I do not have the space to unpack all the descriptive and phenomenological limitations of these strategies. A case could be made that anger is directed primarily at persons, and only secondarily at structures, events, or systems. A more significant problem is that both (IS2) and (IS3) obscure our intuitions about individual accountability. On the one hand, systemic injustices like the ones perpetrated within a racist justice system would not exist without racist policies embodied in, endorsed, or accepted by individual actors. If through her action or inaction an individual actor endorses or accepts unjust policies, she represents and reinforces the injustices of the system. On the other hand, severing the accountability link between a wrongdoing and the individual wrongdoer presents problems of its own. Some individuals *through their own deliberate actions or inactions* become more predisposed toward racist, chauvinist, or sexist actions. So, if the rage directed at a racist action is morally justified, it is all the more justified when directed toward the individual who through his own agency turns into a rather skilled racist.[29] Additionally, as I have indicated earlier, the suggestion that victims of systemic injustices attain psychological integration by a kind of affective re-education or re-focus away from individual offenders to systems or actions should reawaken our worries about hermeneutical and affective injustice.

What should we to say about (IS1)? The main problem here is vagueness and lack of explanatory power. Assume both apt anger and forgivingness are valuable. It is a given that the bearer of the virtue of anger will express it at the right time, and the bearer of forgivingness will declare her offender forgiven at the appropriate time, and in the right circumstances. But we want to understand *how* this happens. What specific circumstances call for the exercise of appropriate virtue? The self in which anger is a cardinal virtue becomes synchronically and diachronically attuned to injustices of wrongdoers and to ways of resisting them. The self that entrenches curative forgivingness is finely attuned to gracious, merciful,

---

[28] I am grateful to Mike Rea for suggesting in conversation some of these strategies. These are not exhaustive, but from my response one can concoct a more general recipe for critically evaluating other integrationist strategies.

[29] It seems possible to be a reluctant, accidental, or casual racist, sexist, or chauvinist. If these categories are possible, perhaps a case could be made that the wrongdoing could be seen more in the natural/causal biography of the wrongdoer than in his moral biography. Anger directed toward the wrongdoer may still be justified because presumably the individual had been inattentive or too complacent to cultivate anti-racist, anti-sexist, or anti-chauvinist dispositions.

charitable ways of construing the wrongdoer. Unless, implausibly, we switch valuations like perceivers undergoing a gestalt switch, we want to explain how these radically different ways of regarding offenders can be reconciled, especially in light of their diachronic stability. We want to explain the co-inherence of these virtues in the same person and in a way that does not compartmentalize them away in quasi or fully autonomous modules of one's practical reasoning.

In what follows, I sketch a model of diachronic agency that accommodates both apt anger and forgivingness, without fracturing the self, without imposing an overly-tidy psychological unity, and without diminishing the moral accountability of individual agency. Suppose virtues function as affective-evaluative ways of perceiving practical reality and of structuring one's diachronic intentions. Suppose further that the concept of narrative is helpful in explaining how the virtues support nested intentional actions over time. On the one hand, I'm angry with those who justify American police brutality against black men (in part) because I embody a change-the-system script: in my teenage years I protested against police-state totalitarianism in the 1989 Romanian Revolution. I had the courage to take to the streets (in part) because I had been taught the stories of the Hebrew prophets who spoke truth to political and military power. On the other hand, some of my own family members justify police brutality against black men and have totalitarian leanings. I love and seek the good for my family members (in part) because I have a traditional view of ironclad family-loyalty. I both love and rail against some of my family members. Clearly, the concept of narrative needs refinement or supplementation in order to better capture the interaction among these different self-interpretative perspectives.

I propose that the interaction be understood on the model of *an inner dialogue, a conversation,* or *a dramatic performance.* Practical reasoning can be taken to involve alternately identifying with different interpretative perspectives analogous to the interaction of different dramatic personae in a drama. While the personae or the narrative voices in one's self have clear histories and causal power to form intentions, the dialogue among the personae *also* has a genuine causal power over how the drama goes on: which voices are silenced, which gain ascendency, and how or whether new characters can enter the stage.

One benefit of this proposal is a diversification of our practical reasoning. If various (maybe even antagonistic) virtues reveal to their bearer relevant features of her practical/normative world by finetuning or broadening her ways of seeing it, then she can examine a situation from different axiologically-charged perspectives. Her practical self is axiologically and motivationally enriched by keeping dissonant virtues in dialogue with each other. Agency can thus be characterized as the locus of multiple dramatic personae expressed in terms of multiple and mutually accessible evaluative postures.[30]

---

[30] Intentions as well as decisions could be seen as outcomes of an internal "conversations" taking place anyhow among various interpretative perspectives. Typically, the virtues that enter deliberation

Being conversant with one's repertoire of virtues does not have to lead to a strict motivational unity, or a strict narrative harmony in one's practical life. In fact, if the entrenchment of our various traits is due in part to richly-textured relationships with various friends, experts, past experiences, good art, and fiction, though we may develop a sharper moral vision in specific circumstances, it's likely we will experience multiple points of practical tension between our virtues. A tidy synchronic and diachronic coherence of the self is unlikely and undesirable. Analogous to the way conversations between people can stop, become interrupted, then pick up again, the dramatic/dialogical model of agency allows for a chorus of voices, for dissonance, for interruptions, and for silence. Nevertheless, my hunch is that *multiplying* the evaluative stances in one's practical self is often preferable to either compartmentalizing them or to facilely integrating them. This model of the self thus affirms the value of assorted narrative perspectives *and* the value of keeping these in conversation with one another.

Multiplying dissonant evaluative standpoints in an agent can sensitize a person to aspects of her moral reality she would not have otherwise considered. I want to show this in two ways. First, I will show that the dramatic/dialogical model helps explain how an unwitting oppressor can be sensitized to the reality of the oppressed. Second, I will show that the dramatic/dialogical model helps those oppressed in non-ideal circumstances to *both* effectively hang on to their virtuous anger *and* to enrich their perception of their normative reality by adding affective-evaluative self-interpretative scripts that could transcend anger. In other words, this model gives us a general strategy for meeting the desiderata (D1)–(D3).

First, consider the fictional case of Huckleberry Finn. The contours of the story are commonplace. Resisting the advice of his conscience, Huckleberry Finn befriends Jim the runaway slave.[31] Having absorbed the norms of the nineteenth-century Mississippi valley, Huck's conscience demands he return Jim to his rightful owner. But when the time arrives for Huck to act decisively toward this end, he is first paralyzed by indecision. When he is finally capable of acting, Huck facilitates Jim's escape, suppressing the voice of his conscience. Jonathan Bennett sees in Huck's incapacity to turn Jim in a classic case of weakness of will, an irrational failure to act on general moral principles: "Huck doesn't weigh up pros and cons: he simply *fails* to do what he believes to be right—he isn't

---

are diachronically stable, and one measure of such stability is given by the virtues' tendency to constitute the agent's modes of self-understanding. When things go well, an agent's internal conversation translates well into an ability to articulate public reasons for action. But idealized conditions should not be taken as entailments or even probabilities. People with a rich internal conversation may not be able to articulate their reasons to others, and many of those capable of expressing their practical reasoning may display flagrant failures in self-knowledge.

[31] Huck's conscience seems largely shaped by the moral beliefs of pre-Civil War, small-town, slave-owning American South. Twain is masterful at ironically describing Huck's own interrogation and mistrust of his conscience.

strong enough, hasn't the 'spunk of a rabbit.'"[32] For Bennett, Huck's "unreasoned emotional pulls" cannot reveal any aspect of self-awareness, thus they cannot properly enter into dialogue with his "general moral principles."

In a more plausible interpretation, Jennifer Rosner argues that Huck does not really display weakness of will. She observes that early in the decision-making process Huck vacillates between determining his will with respect to his Southern morality and with respect to his desires to help Jim. But the fact that Huck fails to become unified in his volition with respect to commonly-accepted morality does not entail that Huck fails to have *any* volitional determination. Revealingly, Rosner quotes Huck's own account:

> I was a-trembling, because I'd got to decide, forever, betwixt two things, and I knowed it. I studied a minute, sort of holding my breath, and then says to myself: "All right then, I'll *go* to hell" ... I would take up wickedness again, which was in my line, being brung up to it, and the other warn't. And for a starter I would go to work and steal Jim out of slavery again; and if I could think anything worse, I would do that, too; because as long as I was in, and in for good, I might as well go the whole hog.[33]

For Rosner this monologue indicates that Huck identifies wholeheartedly with the desire to help Jim, expressing thus a fundamental commitment inherent in an integrated and rational volition. Because he is steadfast in his identification with the desire to help Jim, this "endorsement appears to be revelatory of Huck's real self."[34] Responding to both Bennett and Rosner, however, I hold that Huck's decision to help Jim is better explained by a dramatic/dialogical agency. For the sake of simplicity, I identify four different *dramatis personae*, four agential traits. Each of these underlie a distinct intentional strand, each tied to a self-understanding mode, and each contributing to Huck's final decision.

First, Huck is a *congenial adventurer*. Huck's love of adventure gets expressed in his steady association with Jim during their flight, but not elevated all the way to friendship just yet, or at any rate, not the type of friendship that would risk much for the sake of the beloved. As a casual adventurer, perhaps Huck sees in the alliance with Jim an occasion to skip out on the banality and restrictions of provincial life. The second trait expresses Huck's *love of neighbor*, more precisely, his pity for Mrs. Watson and the related feelings of shame and guilt for having stolen Jim from her. Though Huck's neighbor-love rests upon an abhorrent cultural assumption—that human beings can be possessed as objects—it certainly appears that he is strongly disposed to pursue Mrs. Watson's wellbeing by not depriving her of her owned goods.

---

[32] Bennett 1974: 127.   [33] Quoted in Rosner 2000: 109.   [34] Ibid. 110.

Huck's third dramatic persona is that of *an apostate* of American civic religion. Huck has internalized the cultural message that outlaws are spiritual renegades, and while his conscience grows more burdensome for "stealing Jim," Huck has fresh reasons to think he's heading to the proverbial hell. But instead of fearing this state of affairs, he endorses it. In other words, Huck is in the process of exchanging the script of a God-fearing citizen for that of the hell-bound renegade. Finally, Huck also develops along the way a *genuine friendship* with Jim. He comes to value Jim's humanity, his suffering, and Jim's projects. This friendship-perspective, resolutely different from his own framing of the adventurous association, and from his internalized cultural scripts, makes its way steadily into Huck's overall sensibility.

There are several moments in the narrative when these four competing voices contend for Huck's attention, creating a healthy discord between alternating perspectives. As he allows each self-understanding perspective a voice, Huck gets a better grasp of the entire situation. First, Huck widens and deepens his view of his friendship with Jim by steadily seeing his own adventure on the Mississippi from the latter's perspective. In Jim's story, of course, Huck functions as the hero, a savior who risks big to help his friend out. As he listens to Jim's account, Huck comes to see himself through the former's eyes; he is not so much a fickle adventurer as he is Jim's devoted rescuer and friend.

Additionally, to the extent that he internalizes Jim's perspective, Huck also begins to question the value of his socially-conditioned morality. Initially, he feels regret for robbing Mrs. Watson, and seems fearful about going to hell due to this trespass. But the reinforcing loop between Huck's friendship-script and Huck's apostate-script helps explain settling on the decision to save Jim. The deeper the friendship with Jim, the more Huck rejects civic religion and suppresses his regret for having stolen from Mrs. Watson. To experience more regret would be perceived as a betrayal of the friendship. And the more confident Huck grows in his identity as a rebel and fiend, the deeper his commitment to Jim becomes. And so, my suggestion is that the iterated play of such alternative perspectives allows Huck, in the end, to settle upon a course of action. I am not suggesting that Huck consciously explores all of these different perspectives, or that he forms particular practical judgments every time he switches evaluative stances. The thought here is that Huck effectively identifies with these perspectives in the course of whatever thought processes he goes through.[35]

The net motivational and normative outcome of the inner dialogue among Huck's various dramatic personae is this: Jim's view of their friendship resonates so deeply within Huck, that the echo blunts the force of culturally-induced virtues, even though Huck continues to experience some residue of fear and regret.

---

[35] I am grateful to Mike Rea for helping me clarify this thought in conversation.

Through his interaction with Jim, Huck comes to interpret himself simultaneously as a loyal friend, courageous white man, outlaw, and eternally damned. And with this cast of characters he *is* prepared to live.

Second, the dramatic/dialogical model helps illuminate the virtuous anger of oppressed people living in seriously non-ideal circumstances. As I am writing this, the United States is in the grip of massive protests against the killing of George Floyd by a Minnesota policer officer, who was video-recorded holding his knee over Floyd's neck for close to nine minutes. The week after the video emerged, the massive public protests against this injustice were punctuated by looting of stores, vandalizing businesses and government buildings, followed by police retaliation, followed by more looting. In some American cities, this situation led to an escalation in police brutality even against peaceful protesters, in the calling of the National Guard, and in curfews. In this context, one of the most momentous statements came from Atlanta-based rapper Michael Render, delivered at the Mayor's press conference, on May 29, 2020, even as the fires were still burning on the streets of Atlanta. I quote at length the beginning of his speech:

> I didn't want to come, and I don't want to be here. I'm the son of an Atlanta City Police Officer. My cousin is an Atlanta City Police Officer, and my other cousin, [a] police officer. I got a lot of love and respect for police officers down to the original eight [black] police officers in Atlanta that, even after becoming police, had to dress in a YMCA because white officers didn't want to get dressed with n*****s.

> And, here we are, 80 years later. I watched a white officer assassinate a black man, and I know that tore your heart out. I know it's crippling, and I have nothing positive to say in this moment because I don't want to be here. But, I'm responsible to be here because it wasn't just Doctor King and people dressed nicely who marched and protested to progress this city and so many other cities. It was people like my grandmother, people like my aunts and uncles, who are members of the SCLC and NAACP.

> So, I'm duty bound to be here to simply say that it is your duty not to burn your own house down for anger with an enemy. It is your duty to fortify your own house so that you may be a house of refuge in times of organization. Now is the time to plot, plan, strategize, organize, and mobilize. It is time to beat up prosecutors you don't like at the voting booth. It is time to hold mayoral offices accountable, chiefs and deputy chiefs. Atlanta is not perfect, we're a lot better than we ever were, and we're a lot better than cities are.

> I'm mad as hell. I woke up wanting to see the world burn down yesterday, because I'm tired of seeing black men die. He casually put his knee on a human being's neck for nine minutes, as he died like a zebra in clutch of a lion's jaw. And we watched it like murder porn over and over again. That's why children are

burning it to the ground. They don't know what else to do. And it is the responsibility of us to make this better. Right now. We don't want see one officer charged. We want to see four officers prosecuted and sentenced. We want to see the system set up for racism burnt to the ground....[36]

Clearly, Michael Render gives voice to distinct and dissonant normative-motivational personae. Seeing how he brings them in dialogue with each other is both moving and compelling. He is the son of a system-representative, but has a keen consciousness of how black police officers were discriminated against by white officers. A protester against injustices, Render upholds the legacy of the Civil Rights movement through his art and political activism. He resonates with the pain and the fury of black men who want to "burn the city down to the ground," and in fact, his fury has the context and the depth of someone whose historical consciousness connects Floyd's killing to numerous similar injustices. Render's virtuous anger has narrative depth. But Render's anger does not result in violence or incitation to violence. Why? Because *in addition* to his own history of anger and protest, Render identifies strongly with the civic duty to create systemic conditions for the flourishing of black people. And it is this evaluative stance, this commitment—to protect the concrete accomplishments of black people while fighting against systemic oppression—that focuses his anger *away* from burning down Atlanta and *toward* carefully plotting and organizing the demise of the political and legal processes and systems that make racism effective. To wit, Render's focused anger is presumably *directed toward individual actors* within the current racialized or racist political and legal system. And it is precisely the anger with politicians and judges who promote racist policies that drives Render to fight for installing in public office people who promote explicitly anti-racist policies.

It seems to me that Render's multifaceted compassion—for black policemen, for the young people who think violence is an effective political tool, for all those whose conditions will only worsen through the rioting, for young black kids who need to see models of wise courageous resistance—helps focus and strengthen the efficacy of his rage. Alternating between anger, compassion, and civic duty helps focus and strengthen rather than diminish Render's rage. And so, it seems to me that the dramatic/dialogical model of the self can successfully explain the co-inherence of rage and grace, sustained anger and sustained empathy in the same individual.

Before I move on to address the danger of anger-entrenchment, I want to respond to a worry. The worry is that the dramatic/dialogical model implies a virulent double-mindedness, a moral irresoluteness, and a motivational

---

[36] Transcript of "Killer Mike speech," found online at: https://www.youtube.com/watch?v=sG0yrng0eY4&feature=youtu.be. Last accessed August 23, 2022.

indeterminacy. Is there *any* form of psychological harmony available to dramatic/ dialogical agents? Is there a way to prevent the different voices allowed to express interpretative standpoints from collapsing into a cacophony? To dislodge this worry I offer three responses: psychological, normative, and theological.

First, a substantial measure of our psychological integration is already achieved for us biologically and socially. As our virtues and self-understanding scripts take hold in a unified physical organism, and for most of us in pretty homogeneous communities, we cannot help but attain already a high degree of psychological integration.

Second, the dramatic/dialogical model questions the normativity of whole-hearted authenticity that underlies much of the motivation for psychological integration. It seems normatively preferable to cultivate an authenticity by *addition* of different dramatic personae rather than an overly-integrated agential unity through *subtraction*. Wayne Booth expresses his concern about the normativity of "the purity of heart" like this:

> Our true authenticity, in this view, is not what we find when we try to *peel away* influences in search of a monolithic, distinctive identity. Rather it is the one we find when we *celebrate* addition of self to self, in an act of self-fashioning that culminates not in an individual at all but in – and here we have to choose whatever metaphor seems best to rival Mill's bumps and grinds of atomized units – a kind of society; a *field* of forces; a *colony*; a *chorus* of not necessarily harmonious voices; a manifold *project*; a *polyglossia* that is as much in us as in the world outside us.[37]

There are several reasons why I prefer the authenticity of a *polyglossia* over wholeheartedness by subtraction. To begin with, the self as *a colony* or *field of forces* seems better suited to explain our admiration for the diachronic maturation and transformation of the self, alongside our intuitive valorization of a rich inner life. Though the psychological costs of expanding our dramatic personae may be high—inner tensions, unresolved questions, attention to the evaluative stances of others—a robust thread running from the old Greeks to J. S. Mill emphasizes the inherent goodness of an individual's self-development over against the dangers of self-repression or conformism. Famously, Mill argued that a rich variety of "experiments in living" generates productive tensions that stimulate and sustain enduring, fruitful progress in a society, in ways that are foreclosed in a despotic culture. Analogously, a "democratic" self that cultivates various multiple evaluative stances in dialogue with each other, finds in the *unfolding of that dialogue* the seeds and the engine for a richer, ongoing, fuller self-expansion.

---

[37] Booth 1993: 89.

This self-development is difficult for a self in the "despotic" grip of a single, unified narrative. It's the unsettling of that despotic single life-narrative through dialogue that Booth finds particularly valuable: "Every prisoner, every murderer, every torturer shares this potentiality for dramatic change and growth into the future."[38]

I take Booth to say that a self who nurtures even dissonant or outlier voices places oneself in a position to experience a richer life, because through its many narratives held together in a creative tension, she becomes more open to trans-formative experiences such as conversion, repentance, forgiveness, or other par-adigm shifts. And a life more opened to transformation, renewal, refinement, a life continually teeming with an inner dialogue, is richer, fuller, and more fruitful than a life unfolding according to a single, deterministic blueprint.

Additionally, the authenticity of polyglossia is normatively preferable because it fosters a fuller and richer understanding of other people. When we cultivate dissonant voices in our practical self, we acquire standpoints from which to evaluate critically our own subcultures and moral frameworks, and open ourselves up to appreciating values inherent in other people, normative frameworks, and ways of life. When Huck brings his own self-reflections as an adventurer and apostate to bear on his friendship with Jim, he enters all the deeper into Jim's own experiences as an oppressed individual. As the son of a policeman, Render empathizes with the calling to maintain civic order, but as a historical witness to police brutality he also understands the fury of those who want to dismantle that institution.

What should we say, then? Shall personal non-integration abound so that fruitfulness, fullness, and understanding may increase? I don't think so. The dramatic/dialogical view does indeed recommend multiplying the evaluative standpoints with respect to our decisions, patterns of affection, and practical identities. Nevertheless, *I must emphasize that the normative integration of the person is maintained through the dialogue.* Because the various evaluative stances are integrated through and by means of the dialogue, the dramatic/dialogical model does not fall prey to the non-integration typified in a multiple personality disorder model (MPDM). In a MPDM, the guises of the self are mostly autonomous, inaccessible to one another, the switch from one persona to another occurring reflexively and pathologically. By contrast, the dramatic/dialogical model requires that to one degree or another an agent's multiple self-interpretative scripts are mutually accessible, conversant, and rationally assessa-ble. Healthy, sustained dialogue requires not only that each voice is heard now, but that they would have been heard along the way.

Finally, the dramatic/dialogical model does not entail a troublesome *theological* double-mindedness. Biblical writers speak more strongly and consistently against

---

[38] Ibid. 92.

the double-mindedness of idolatry than against the double-mindedness of doubt. Consider the latter. The letter of James famously deplores the double-minded who petitions God while doubting.[39] But two quick things about this kind of dissonance. To start off, the doubt James mentions here goes beyond the cognitive, and must be particularly virulent, for clearly Jesus tolerated and even responded positively to those experiencing ostensible faith-conflict.[40] Additionally, in the verses immediately following James's condemnation of double-mindedness, he seems to presuppose a kind of dramatic/dialogical model of the self: "Let the believer who is lowly boast in being raised up, and the rich in being brought low, because the rich will disappear like a flower in the field" (James 1:9–10). In other words, the poor in church should take the posture of royalty when addressing God in prayer, whereas the wealthy should take the posture of servitude. The poor believer looks at her austerity *by* recalling herself as a fully-endowed child of God, while the rich believer re-examines the advantages of his social status *by* taking the axiologically self-interpretative stance of someone in a desperate and constant need of divine grace. Consequently, the doubt of the faithful poor seems at least partially grounded in failure to acknowledge or dial up the dramatic persona "I'm a royal child of God," over against the self-interpretative script "I'm economically disadvantaged."

The *real* biblical problem with the double-mindedness is idolatry. The idolater professes, even thinks of herself as a God-worshipper, while replacing God as the ultimate target of her love with some other finite thing, property, or event. In central cases, the double-mindedness of idolatry seems rooted in a kind of self-deception and compartmentalization. The rich young ruler publicly avows loving the Torah, but deep down loves his wealth more than the practical implications of the Law. Other religious leaders of Jesus's day seem to love more the public performance of religion and the power of rite-manipulation than the humble worship of God through rite and ritual. But the dramatic/dialogical model does not imply nor presuppose the idolater's self-deception. Instead, it can provide an antidote to it. The model encourages the rich young ruler to bring to the table of conversation his motivational centers in their full heterogeneity. Even the less admirable self-interpretative scripts shaping his desires, each self-guise must be interrogated in light of the others: "I am a Yahweh-worshipper" *and* "I'm prone to cherishing the privilege and comfort that comes from wealth" *and* "I value the canonic interpretation of the Torah that implies that I cannot cherish both God and Mammon." Learning to acknowledge and to give voice to these inner scripts would place him in a better epistemic, motivational, and theological position than

---

[39] See James 1:5–8.

[40] Mark 9 narrates Jesus's encounter with the father of a boy possessed by a mute spirit. When Jesus urges the father to believe, for everything is possible to those who believe, the father confesses: "I believe, help my unbelief." Jesus heals the boy. Jesus's generous encounter with *doubting Thomas* is another great example (cf. John 20:24–9).

a counterpart who integrates his motivations while hiding or compartmentalizing or silencing any of these other guises of the self.

This example illustrates why something like a dramatic/dialogical view of the self is consistent with and may even be required for a healthy diachronic orientation of the self toward the true good, the *summum bonum*, the love of God. To genuinely love God for the long haul seems to require a trained and refined sensibility in detecting the counterfeits that function as practical substitutes for God. We cannot do this effectively or honestly without acknowledging and interrogating the cast of personae that stabilize our motivations or organize our desires over time. Honest confession and repentance of sins seem to presuppose a skilled and active interrogator of self-interpretative scripts, one who brings close to the light of God's gracious love *all* our different scripts, guises, and personae.

I have barely sketched an account of dramatic/dialogical agency. I suggested that even though an intentional strand can be supported by a narrative or script, our agency is formed at the intersection of multiple strands. Our practical agency is more like a drama that brings multiple personae into dialogue, instead of compressing them to a single storyline. As we are accountable to others and as we hold others accountable, our interpretative frameworks would fall under diverse and sometimes incommensurable relational pressures. And consequently, agency matures and grows from the interchange of voices that improvise around some central themes. And so, it seems that a self that multiplies the motivational/normative stances through such dialogue, can allow full range to both the virtue of anger and to forgivingness.

Consider Douglass. For one, Douglass is in relationships with oppressors but also with other non-oppressors and with folks oppressed by masters just like his. Long-lasting virtuous anger against a perpetrator and the system Covey represents is fully compatible with the presence of forgivingness toward other non-oppressive people. In Douglass's non-oppressive relationships, the presence of recurring insults, slights, and hurts can be a catalyst for the entrenchment of forgivingness. Additionally, some dispositions ancillary or supportive of forgivingness in the non-oppressive context may transfer to the oppressive context. As suggested by the example of Michael Render, the compassion and grace at work in one's non-oppressive relationships can function as catalysts for sharpening, focusing, and appropriately channeling rage in oppressive contexts. Consequently, if Douglass examines his anger toward Covey through the lens of his compassion for the humanity of this perpetrator, and if he seeks to understand Covey's own plight, he may begin to focus his rage on the *really* privileged and powerful actors in the slave-owning business—self-entitled and violent men such as Thomas Auld. While the behaviors and affairs of such men do not exculpate Covey, it is clear that these kinds of people had contributed to dehumanizing poor white men, forcing them to work as "slave breakers," turning them effectively into tools of violence against humanity.

Anger-Entrenchment

I have argued so far that for people living under conditions of oppression it is desirable to give full articulation to their virtuous anger or rage. But even for them, and perhaps especially for them, anger should not hold a monopoly over all of their concerns. A virtuous person presumably cares about a number of important things, his diachronic dispositions expressing any number of distinct concerns. But anger naturally tends to be psychologically dispersive and entrenching in ways that gracious dispositions such as curative forgivingness are not. This section argues that it can be consistent with the psychological health and overall flourishing of people living under oppression to develop forgivingness and related dispositions that stand for the good, not only because they sharpen one's anger against evil, but also because they are more likely to prevent the entrenchment and dispersing of chronic anger among the dramatic personae of the agent.

Generally, after being severely wronged, a victim's motivational structures are likely to change. As we will see in a moment, especially in people prone to *ruminating*, the perpetrated injury is internalized and rehearsed in emotional routines that combine the initial justified anger with subtle forms of fear and pride. These routines set in motion other emotional trajectories that direct the interpretations victims cast on their own past and on the past of offenders. Disseminated and entrenched, these resentments will tell us how we should continue to feel about our perpetrators. At the same time, the pragmatic urge to move on with our lives applies pressure that resentment move to a quasi-conscious or semi-conscious level, becoming masked by other mental states. So, *anger ruminating* agents seem to be in the grip of a double psychological pressure: to magnify resentment and the pragmatic temptation to obscure it from sight.[41]

Cognitive studies find that following an insult or provocation, both the spontaneous and reflective brain systems show increased activation.[42] As Thomas Denson shows, it is perhaps expected that the spontaneous brain routines—the so called X-system—"implicit in prejudice, emotional pain resulting from social rejection, and intuition-based self-knowledge" would also be involved in stabilizing emotional reactions in the aftermath of provocations.[43] Interestingly though, following an insult, the process of *anger rumination* increases not only in the X-system, but also in parts of the highly reflective system—C-system—the structure responsible for monitoring emotional states, reflecting on feelings, and reassessing emotional responses to distress.

---

[41] At times victims engage in both tendencies at the same time: manifestly they claim to have moved on and are unwilling to face the hurt and resentment, while secretly the resentment and even hatred is often amplified.

[42] Cf. Denson 2010.   [43] Ibid. 108.

Recent studies suggest then that negative emotional responses to injuries permeate equally through the unreflective and the reflective motivational structures of our minds. But research supports also an interesting feedback loop. Victimization early on in life leads, through sadness and anger-rumination, to an increase in depressive and anxious symptoms later on.[44] Meanwhile, when anxious people attend to their past victimizations, the memory is accompanied by a surge in angry feelings, more rumination, and other negative emotions such fear, sadness, and hostility.[45]

The argument we developed so far shows the normative value of prolonged anger for victims of oppression. But it has not dealt with the problem of the diffusion and entrenchment of diachronic anger. If historically victimized people are, by and large, more predisposed to be anxious, ruminating individuals, and if diachronic anger mixes rather disproportionately and facilely with other negative moods, emotions, or intentional attitudes, then one's apt anger with perpetrators can easily mutate into chronic resentment. It could diffuse through motivationally central modules and exert a pressure over numerous normative concerns. The chorus could be reduced to a single voice. Polyglossia could capitulate to mono-lingual resentment.

Even aside from anger-rumination, I want to give four additional reasons why anger and resentment have, among all other mental states, a unique tendency toward promiscuity and entrenchment. First, resentment seems to have survival value. What Bishop Butler refers to as "sudden anger" seems like a biological defense-mechanism, an efficient alarm-system that protects the organism from harm.[46]

Second, resentment has significant social utility. For Joseph Butler, the proper object of sudden anger is harm, to be distinguished from injury, which although could include harm never describes just a biological happening but contains implicitly moral valuations. Injury and not harm is thus the proper object of what Butler calls *settled* or *deliberate resentment*.[47] This is a form of moral indignation that arises quite naturally in response to cruelty and injustice. This feeling is as naturally intense as it is socially valuable when we witness the plight of others.[48]

Third, resentment has significant psychological and moral value. I won't develop this point since we have already mentioned some of the benefits of anger to protest wrongs and to resurrect the feeling of self-respect and freedom in the oppressed. Finally, resentment has an important role in integrating agency

---

[44] Cf. Peets et al. 2022.   [45] Cf. Mikulincer and Orbach 1995.   [46] Cf. Butler 1993.

[47] Clearly the two responses can coexist in the same person in all sorts of ways. The same event can be an instance of harm and moral injury, thus triggering both sudden anger and deliberate resentment.

[48] Famously Butler claims that resentment arises against "vice and wickedness: it is one of the common bonds, by which society is held together; a fellow feeling, which each individual has in behalf of the whole species, as well as of himself" (Butler 1993: 96).

over time. In parts of his essay "On Resentment," Butler appears optimistic about the role of *settled resentment* in interpersonal relationships. Even so, he takes the time to reveal some of its "abuses."[49] But he makes only a little progress before his enthusiasm wanes, as he bemoans the futile task of labeling the endless deviations of resentment. At this point he makes the following striking observation:

> But there is one thing, which so generally belongs to and accompanies all excesses and abuses of it [resentment], as to require being mentioned: a certain determination, and resolute bent of mind, not to be convinced or set right; though it be ever so plain, that there is no reason for the displeasure, that it was raised merely by error or misunderstanding. In this there is doubtless a great mixture of pride; but there is somewhat more, which I cannot otherwise express, than that resentment has taken possession of the temper and the mind, and will not quit its hold.[50]

According to Butler, over time resentment tends to mix with other emotions—such as pride—in a way that makes it an entrenched reflexive mode. A reflexive guise is a distinctive standpoint through which the agent understands and relates to others and the world, though she may not be aware of this guise. Butler suggests that resentment's tendency toward taking hold of mind and temper—to become a meta or chief reflexive guise—is evidenced in its abuses, that is, in our tendencies to treat either the harm or the excusable injury done to us as *culpable injury*. If resentment infiltrates and cements the mind when the injury is fictional or excusable, its propensity toward entrenchment is no less pronounced when the injury is real, culpable, and systematic. And if resentment deepens and tightens its grip on our psychology in ordinary contexts, it is even more likely to do so in the psychology of people living under systemic oppression.

It might be helpful to understand "taking possession" as a scalar property of a complex—perhaps non-linear—tendency (a) to subsume sudden biological reactions under ingrained intentional dispositions and (b) to subsume intentional dispositions under diachronically stable higher-order outlooks or reflexive modes. If our affections and memories are patterns of salience that direct practical reasoning, and if resentment spreads seamlessly through emotional and memory routines, we can expect resentment to direct stable and *yet* improvisational interpretative scripts, scripts that in one way or another rehearse and keep fresh past harms or injuries. As a measure of its tendency to infiltrate or commandeer diachronically stable and motivationally central self-reflexive guises of the person, we may thus say that resentment is deep, or entrenched.

Recall the biblical story of Joseph the dreamer. Let me re-narrate it in two takes.

---

[49] I disregard here his concerns about the abuses of sudden anger.   [50] Butler 1993: 99.

Take 1: Spoiled by his father's lavish attention, the youngest of the lot develops a superiority complex, or perhaps merely an inability to filter his public speeches. At the more pragmatic hands of his older brothers, the visionary Joseph is sold into slavery. Surely, his anger with his brothers is justified: they nearly killed him, then they exiled him. But Joseph imagines what life is like for a Judah or a Simeon. He recalls Jacob's uneven attention to his elder sons, attends to the hardships a nomadic life places upon the older males of the clan, and pictures how preposterous his self-absorbed dreams might have seemed to them. As he grows in empathy, the brothers' spits of anger become intelligible. Joseph's anger dissolves into a mitigated blame, less blame gives way to more pity, and pity blossoms into compassion. Each of these less vehement passions sets up brand new directives for Joseph's beliefs and desires, so that though the brothers have not changed one bit, Joseph sees them in a new light. Remembering his brothers from a prison in Egypt, Joseph undergoes a change of heart. Joseph develops forgivingness even while his brothers have not moved one inch toward repentance.

Take 2: Imagine the same history of trauma at the hands of his brothers, but with different psychological dispositions forming and informing Joseph's sensibility. Joseph sees that Jacob is lopsided in his fatherly love and that his brothers have reasons for their envy, but the lingering distress of being abandoned in a waterhole, along with his wounded pride, intensify Joseph's resentment. It is easy to see how, guided by this tangled web of negative emotions, Joseph remembers the massacre of the Shechemites or Reuben's bedding Bilhah, instead of critically investigating the sources of Jacob's favoritism. So, instead of mitigating his anger, Joseph now forms this additional judgment: "And who can blame Jacob for prizing me above my brothers? Who in their right mind could love such murderous and lecherous sons?" And so, if in mingling with other emotions, Joseph's initial anger disguises itself and latches on to other attitudes, his settled resentment will be remarkably resilient and tough to root out.

My point now should be obvious. In light of the phenomenon of anger-rumination, and given the Butlerian observations about the tendency of settled resentment to take hold of temper and mind, **Take 2** is more likely than **Take 1**.

That resentment is deep and promiscuous does not mean it always surfaces in our thinking or our feeling. It can also be self-effacing. It can recede for a while, only to re-emerge as a diachronically stable reflexive mode. Revisit Joseph. Decades after their treacherous transaction, under the threat of starvation, the brothers descend to Egypt to buy grain. Joseph has meanwhile become, ironically through his ability to interpret dreams, Pharaoh's mighty treasurer. The meeting scene: "Although Joseph had recognized his brothers, they did not recognize him. Joseph also remembered the dreams he dreamed about them. He said to them: 'You are spies. You have come to see the nakedness of the land'" (Genesis 42:8–9).

It is interesting that *this* memory intrudes at the moment of reunion. It may explain Joseph's initial pretense, the half-feigned harshness at play in locking up his brothers for three days, and the real harshness of keeping his brother Simeon in custody until the others trek back to Palestine to fetch Benjamin. In his dreams, worshipped by brothers, mother and father, Joseph is center stage. And now, after decades, the fate of the family in his hands, his dreams are on the verge of being actualized.[51] Whatever virtues he developed along the way, if Joseph frames the current meeting as a vindication of his teenage visions, his actions show enduring resentment. And a peculiar form of it, one filtered through, and perhaps only kept alive due to a kind of self-importance. Now that the tables have turned, he will show *them* how the "dreamer boy" can play with *their* lives, and he will take his sweet time doing it.[52]

Joseph's resentment seems to endure, embedded and disguised in the reflexive guise of self-importance, and vice versa.[53] Here the standpoint of self-importance provides not an evaluation of Joseph's anger, but a reinforcement of it. The pride articulated in the self-description "I am the dreamer who correctly predicted you will revere me" sustains and is supported by the resentment articulated in this self-description: "I am the victim whom you sold into slavery." I must quickly add that Joseph's resentment does not take possession of his entire temperament; it is local and somewhat contained. When Benjamin is brought to him, Joseph reveals his true identity and embraces his brothers. Perhaps he judges that they have atoned sufficiently for their wrongdoing. Or, perhaps, more interestingly, a subtle change had taken place in some recesses of his heart even as resentment calcified in others.

The extended Joseph-illustration indicates that the dramatic/dialogical model is not sufficient by itself to handle the worry about dispersion and entrenchment of resentment. The virtue of anger may enter into dialogue with "voices" such as self-importance, fear, or anxiety which deepen the resentment rather than focus it and evaluate it. In our imagined case, Joseph's resentment survives for decades because it is embedded in or mixed in with smugness and pride. If in cases such as these resentment gets entangled with smugness and anxiety, it could very well become a reflexive guise of persons, especially those prone to ruminating on past wrongs, or

---

[51] I am not suggesting this is the only way to read this story, or even the primary way. Nonetheless, all I need is that it is a possible interpretation of this story.

[52] It may be replied that Joseph is trying to teach his brothers a moral lesson or test their moral progress. Will they return for Simeon? Or will they leave him to rot in the Egyptian prison, just like they disposed of Joseph in the past? Several quick responses. First, even if this is Joseph's primary motivation, it can still be interlaced with both resentment and smugness. Second, the smugness is particularly evident, if Joseph is described as entitled to track the moral progress of his brothers. Finally, strictly speaking Joseph presents the brothers with a devastating moral dilemma: either abandon Simeon, save Benjamin but run the risk of starvation, or bring Benjamin to Joseph, thus run the risk of hurting Jacob again if anything were to happen to him. Joseph is not making his brothers' lives easy, and runs a high risk of hurting his father.

[53] One intriguing possibility is that for Joseph resentment can be kept alive *only* by the self-reflexive guise of smugness. On this possibility, to the extent that Joseph dissociates himself from the self-conception of a visionary, he will also let go of resentment.

those overrun with anxieties. And if resentment is generally adept at survival mixed among other mental states, simply multiplying the "voices" in our overall psychic economy won't expose it and root it out. We need to multiply *the right* evaluative stances, *the right voices*. And the right voices in the psychology of the oppressed are not those that challenge the intensity or the longevity of episodic angers against injustices, but the ones that subvert the chronic resentment that infiltrates other motivational and normative centers.

I want to suggest that prolonged anger with people is virtuous only if it is accompanied in its bearer by other long-lived dispositions that scrutinize and interrogate it. The interrogatory stances on our different angers will be able to distinguish between anger that resists the bad because it is bad and anger that resists the bad out of malice. They will be able to detect when long-lived virtuous anger begins to encroach upon and undermine the dispositions in our psyche that are oriented toward loving the good. They must *recognize* specifically the rhetorical power of resentment and *aim to undermine* it. If resentment is a skilled rhetorician who propagandizes self-defense and security, resisting it involves listening to voices that prevent past injuries to slip into the gravitational center of our self-conception. And sometimes, these voices lie at the periphery of our attention.[54] And sometimes, perhaps often, we can be more receptive to voices that unsettle resentment by cultivating forgivingness. If our rage is examined through the standpoint of curative forgivingness, and if forgivingness entails cultivating a gracious, blame-reducing, anti-dehumanizing disposition toward our perpetrators, while absorbing the relational costs of the offense, then we gain one more lens through which we can more accurately perceive our offenders *and* we also lessen the entrenchment of our angers.[55]

Let me now turn to one final example that illustrates how such multiple interpretative standpoints can decalcify a resentful heart. This extended illustration comes from literature. There are many reasons to appeal to good literature in developing one's conception of practical agency. The thick and detailed

---

[54] Consistent with our view of the self as polyglossia, a helpful image of resentment in a psyche may be that of a subtle tyrant in a *polis*. Plato describes the tyrant as an omnipresent force incapable of making friends, teetering between the ingratiating and the vengeful, doing all it can to maintain control of the constitution. If the analogy is adequate, resisting resentment would be like guerrilla warfare against a very persuasive but self-effacing tyrant. If Butler is correct, resentment is a main integrator of agency over time. It does this by telling and retelling coherent stories that propagandize the values of self-defense and security. But if I am right, the kind of psychological unity achieved through defensiveness is not worth much, partially because it tends to fictionalize the past, to promote poverty in emotional lives, and to stunt rich self-conceptions.

[55] The process of recalibrating rage to its virtuous setting is neither automatic nor somehow uniquely effective by adopting the standpoint of gracious forgivingness. Since I am recommending the dialogical/dramatic self, the evaluation of rage should happen simultaneously through multiple panels, forgivingness being only one of them. And so, the anxious individual who evaluates her rage through the lens of forgiveness will not drop her justified anger altogether, because she also evaluates it through the lens of condemning wrongs and wrongdoers, and that of proper resistance to insults and injury.

descriptions of actions, the psychological realism, and the nuanced, textured inner lives of the main characters suggest that good novelists care about understanding human agency at least as much as ethicists or analytic philosophers of action. Their tools are just different. Great literature creates believable, realistic agents that in important ways display and amplify dispositions of real agents. So the following should be taken as an attempt at cross-fertilization.

In Margaret Atwood's novel *Cat's Eye*, the aging but famed Elaine Risley returns to Toronto, her childhood stomping grounds, for a retrospective art show in her honor.[56] Physically reinserted in the world of her youth, Elaine pieces together fragments of her traumatic past. The retrospective art, indicative of reflection on the past, shows how ordinary harms, even in the lives of nine-year-old girls, can swell into lifelong resentments that shape memories, emotional reactions, and even guide creative work.[57] In my discussion I limit myself to Elaine's recounting of Mrs. Smeath, the mother of Grace, one of her childhood friends.

The elderly Elaine recalls how in the mind of her nine-year-old self, Mrs. Smeath suffers from "a bad heart." She is severe and judgmental, dispensing upon the un-churched Elaine a combination of smug charity and disgust. For instance, she demands that Elaine memorize Scripture, only to despise her for her excellent performance. The fear of losing Grace's friendship makes Elaine keep returning to the Smeaths, though she feels constantly judged, scrutinized, and watched. Particularly evocative in this respect are Elaine's church visits in the company of the Smeaths. During her first visit, Elaine is impressed with the huge stained-glassed windows. The largest one portrays a "Jesus in white," white bird circling his head, with a thick black inscription underneath that reads: THE. KINGDOM.OF.GOD.IS.WITHIN.YOU. Another has a woman, dressed in blue with a white cover partially hiding her face, reaching out to a man "with what looks like a bandage wound around his head."[58] The inscription underneath reads: THE.GREATEST.OF.THESE.IS.CHARITY.

On White Gift Sunday Elaine brings to church Habitant pea soup and Spam for the poor. The white gifts, "bleached of their identity," look sinister to Elaine, and she worries that the Smeaths would perceive hers as inadequate. Worse, she feels judged for having to read the words to the songs from the screen, while Grace, who knows them by heart, is intently watching her. She reflects: "I want to shine like a candle. I want to be good, to follow instructions, to do what Jesus bids.

---

[56] Atwood 1998.

[57] Atwood's view seems to be that early hurts form robust and lasting self-interpretative scripts. The third paragraph from the book has Elaine contemplate on the nature of her remembering: "But I began then to think of time as having a shape, something you could see, like a series of liquid transparencies, one laid on top of another. You don't look back along time but down through it, like water. Sometimes this comes to the surface, sometimes that, sometimes nothing. Nothing goes away" (ibid. 3).

[58] Ibid. 106.

I want to believe you should love your neighbors as yourself and the Kingdom of God is within you. But all this seems less and less possible."[59]

We catch up with Elaine a couple of decades later. She is now an acclaimed young artist, seemingly a vibrant woman at the forefront of the feminist movement. Still, she is in the grips of her childhood resentment and fear that have now escalated to malice. Her paintings, like her resentments, gravitate around the memory of Mrs. Smeath. The artistic anatomizing and despoiling of the woman may very well represent Elaine's payback for Mrs. Smeath's earlier judgmental gaze. At an all-women artist show she displays her paintings of Mrs. Smeath. In one painting entitled "Leprosy," she appears with half the face peeled off, but the main attraction is "White Gift" which is in four panels:

> In the first one, Mrs. Smeath is wrapped up in white tissue paper like a can of Spam or a mummy, with just her head sticking out, her face wearing its closed half-smile. In the next three she's progressively unwrapped: in her print dress and bib apron, in her back-of-the-catalogue *Eaton's* flesh-colored foundation garment – although I don't expect she possessed one – and finally in her saggy-legged cotton underpants, her one large breast sectioned to show her heart. Her heart is the heart of a dying turtle: reptilian, dark-red, diseased. Across the bottom of this panel is stenciled: THE.KINGDOM.OF.GOD.IS.WITHIN. YOU. It's still a mystery to me why I hate her so much.[60]

Fast-forward again. Elaine is now the acclaimed elderly artist and the mother of two young women. She has returned home, the place of her childhood traumas, for a retrospective show in her honor. Arriving early at the gallery, she devotes the longest time to a re-examination of her "Mrs. Smeath" paintings. In retrospect, Elaine recognizes the fright that had led her to scorn and desecrate Mrs. Smeath in her artistic work, scorn which, in turn, exacerbated her fears:

> Next to them is Mrs. Smeath; many of her. Mrs. Smeath sitting, standing, lying down with her holy rubber plant, flying with Mr. Smeath stuck to her back, being screwed like a beetle; Mrs. Smeath in the dark-blue bloomers of Miss Lumley, who somehow combines with her in a frightening symbiosis. Mrs. Smeath unwrapped from white tissue paper, layer by layer. Mrs. Smeath bigger than life, bigger than she ever was. Blotting out God.[61]

Acknowledging the exaggerated fear leads Elaine to an unexpected confession. What in the mind of the budding artist was merely a mysterious hatred, in the hindsight of the seasoned introspective narrator is a carefully choreographed

---

[59] Ibid. 137.   [60] Ibid. 384.   [61] Ibid. 443.

malevolence: "I put a lot of work into that imagined body, white as burdock root, flabby as pork fat. Hairy as the inside of an ear. I labored on it, with, I now see, considerable malice."[62] Having confessed her fear and malice, she can also confess the grip resentment had on her life and art. The honest self-assessment is concurrent with another perception and self-perception. Elaine recognizes that some of Mrs. Smeath's features were remembered and represented artistically without malice, realistically, even *empathetically*:

> It's the eyes I look at now. I used to think these were self-righteous eyes, piggy, and smug inside their wire frames; and they are. But they are also defeated eyes, uncertain and melancholy, heavy with unloved duty. The eyes of someone for whom God was a sadistic old man; the eyes of a small town threadbare decency. Mrs. Smeath was a transplant to the city, from somewhere a lot smaller. A displaced person; as I was.[63]

Elaine begins to recollect herself as a victim within a patriarchal system of oppression, whose norms were internalized by women even as they oppressed other women. When her best childhood friend, Cordelia, would chide Elaine, she'd do so with the distinctive mannerism of her father's anger. In the magazines of her youth, the ideal, desirable females were pictured as objects of the male gaze: attractive and dutiful housekeepers. Mrs. Smeath practices her piety and discharges her duties under the eye of a God she experiences as "a sadistic old man." No wonder Elaine experiences her freedom in a devotion to Saint Mary, but not to God. And so, Elaine comes to see that while she had been traumatized most *proximally* by this rigidly religious woman, *ultimately*, she is the victim of an inflexible, legalistic, male-dominated set of religious and cultural practices, iconography, and messages. The little girl's anger with Mrs. Smeath is certainly intelligible and morally justified. Even the artist's iconography of Mrs. Smeath creatively expresses a peculiar form of righteous indignation. But the elderly Elaine is in a much better position to recognize and interrogate her resentments. By taking a reflective stance toward the *ur*-object of her anger and fear, the elderly Elaine recognizes features of Mrs. Smeath that hitherto had gone unnoticed. Perhaps a generalized empathy that may have been nurtured in other non-oppressive relationships, is *now* directed toward Mrs. Smeath, recasting Elaine's memories and associations.[64] And when this new perception reframes the evidence that was there all along before Elaine's eyes, fear and malice begin to lose

---

[62] Ibid.   [63] Ibid.

[64] Elaine has occasionally had to turn the paintings facing the walls (she couldn't bear looking at those eyes). Also, on the occasion of her first feminist exhibition, Elaine's artist friend Jody exclaims regarding the numerous depictions of Mrs. Smeath: "It's woman as anticheesecake...Why should it always be young, beautiful women? It's good to see the aging female body treated with compassion, for a change" (ibid. 380).

their grip on her.[65] The movement of empathy explains the acknowledgment of settled resentment, and that *the recognition* of malice-infiltrated resentment helps Elaine deepen her empathy for Mrs. Smeath.

As this reframing of Mrs. Smeath moves from the periphery to the center of Elaine's self-understanding, it reconfigures the relations among the intentional objects conditioned historically by her fear and resentment. The initial perception of Mrs. Smeath as an overpowering divinity with a reptilian heart is supplanted by that of the "transplant," herself the victim of an internalized fear of God. Mrs. Smeath becomes the mirror-image of Elaine, a double of Elaine, whose own need to be loved, protected, and welcomed home was met only by "a sadistic old man," in other words, by the scrutinizing gaze within a male-dominated, legalistic, religious context. Additionally, as the cruel, masculinist religion is the real culprit behind the trauma of both women, Elaine now humanizes Mrs. Smeath even more, viewing herself sympathetically through Mrs. Smeath's eyes. She imagines how she functioned in Mrs. Smeath's own story:

> Now I can see myself, through these painted eyes of Mrs. Smeath: a frazzle-headed ragamuffin from heaven knows where, a gypsy practically, with a heathen father and feckless mother who traipsed around in slacks and gathered weeds. I am unbaptized, a nest for demons: how could she know what germs of blasphemy and unfaith were breeding in me? And yet she took me in.[66]

Recall my account of curative forgivingness. Chapter 5 argues that it is formed by the interplay between a skilled, gracious sensibility and a conception of one's whole life as justifying and motivating absorbing evil. Evidently, elderly Elaine is capable now to perceive of her whole life as in some sense good, despite all the interwoven wounds in it. She is able to contain the hurts, to cauterize their memories, through a perception of the goodness of her life as a whole, a goodness that is now present and perceivable even in the life of her archnemesis. Preserved and nurtured through art, the gracious construals of Mrs. Smeath reframe the conception of Elaine's life as good, and this in turn, allows a continued nurturing of her forgiving sensibility. When set against the context of Mrs. Smeath's hard life, Elaine can finally see herself as the object of Mrs. Smeath's charity. Embedded in Elaine's empathetic stance toward Mrs. Smeath is an empathetic stance she can take toward herself. She is now capable of seeing herself not only as a victim, but also as the recipient of Mrs. Smeath's beneficence. In her own misguided ways, Mrs. Smeath attempted to make a home for Elaine, though she herself had been

---

[65] It is interesting that empathy itself is born out of the reflection on the pictorial representation of Mrs. Smeath's eyes. Also, reflecting on her past representation of Mrs. Smeath, Elaine reflects: "I have not done it justice, or rather mercy. I went for vengeance. An eye for an eye only leads to more blindness" (ibid. 443).

[66] Ibid.

victimized by the same mechanisms through which she extends her charity to Elaine. In effect, by regarding Mrs. Smeath as a displaced person victimized by the language and iconography of a cruel, male-dominated faith, Elaine is capable to deepen the conception of her life as fundamentally good, to interrogate her own resentment, and to redirect her anger toward the ultimate culprit.

Elaine is lucky to have at hand relevant stances from which to launch a corrective reframing of her past. Her paintings awaken a chorus of dissonant voices that enlarge her conception of Mrs. Smeath. The voices of compassion and of sympathy interrogate and dislodge her resentments. Her paintings and her memories serve as advisors and interlocutors, as ways of enlarging the chorus of possible motivational and normative voices, and these in the end allow her to envision her life as shot through with a kind of grace that also contains and contextualizes her past wounds. By listening to these voices her own self-conception is enlarged: she does not regard Mrs. Smeath only as a monster, or herself merely as a victim.

As Elaine, other victims in oppressive contexts are beset by hurts and injuries stretching back to childhood. As Elaine, though clearly victimized in ways that demand the virtue of long-lasting anger, sometimes they also slip naturally into patterns of resentment that dehumanize their perpetrators, obscuring the ultimate causal springs of their victimizations. Unlike Elaine, they might not have under their noses relevant external frames that provide corrective takes on their past. But, if curative forgivingness involves developing blame-reducing, anti-dehumanizing sensibility and reflective habits, then it provides one way of scrutinizing and resisting the entrenchment of resentment. And ways of cultivating habits relevant to deepening forgivingness are often found right under our noses in non-oppressive relationships with friends, family, fictional characters of good literature, prayer, liturgies, Scripture, and art.

Anger and the Faith Meta-Narrative

In this section, I return to address the genealogical concern that anger was traditionally the prerogative of the powerful, not of the powerless. I want to argue that this genealogy does not fit well with the biblical understanding of anger. Instead, I remind the reader about some of the observations from Chapter 4: (1) Biblically, the anger and protest of the vulnerable, especially of those oppressed by systemic power is seen as valuable and noteworthy. (2) Divine anger is often God's way of showing solidarity with the most vulnerable groups of people, and so it re-affirms and justifies the anger of the vulnerable. (3) When set against God's ultimate healing purposes for the world, and within a meta-narrative of anger as a divine-human partnership of resisting injustices, not only does the virtue of anger become more focused and precise, but so does forgivingness.

Chapter 4 highlights a significant biblical theme: God pays particular attention to the cries of the vulnerable and of the victimized. From the blood of Abel screaming from the ground, to the cry of the Egyptian Hagar in the Hebraic captivity, to the cries of the Hebrew slaves in the Egyptian captivity, to the cry of Jesus on the Roman cross, God observes the pain, listens to the cries of distress, and comes down to bring deliverance. We are hard-pressed to find recorded moments when God responds to the cries of the powerful and of the privileged, unless they themselves are threatened by oppression and victimization.[67] This suggests that the anger of the vulnerable plays a particular role in revealing not just the value of human responses to injustices, but highlights a particular value associated with God's response to those responses. I suspect, for instance, that the Hebrew poet who blesses those who smash Babylonian babes against the rocks in Psalm 137 does not preach a normative behavioral script. Rather, he expresses the rage of the captive against devastator Babylon. And that rage is not only validated and affirmed, but also liturgized, canonized, and poeticized.

It is also worth repeating that God's heightened susceptibility to the pain of the oppressed flows out of God's just concerns, which reflect God's very name, and the center of God's moral identity.[68] We have observed that God's loving concern to deliver justice to the powerless and least privileged in Israel is a main theme in the Law, the Prophets, and the Psalms. It is worth emphasizing that if Jesus reveals to us most clearly the center of God's moral identity, we should also expect that he would stand with the powerless against the powerful. This expectation is not frustrated by the Gospels. Matthew opens up a wide-window into Jesus's self-understanding. According to Matthew, when Jesus inaugurates his just and peaceable kingdom, the eschatological viceroys and the inheritors are surprisingly the ones who had shown concrete, practical love for the stranger, the naked, the prisoner, and the malnourished.[69]

Jesus does not only cement his or his movement's commitment to vulnerable groups of people protected by the Torah. More surprisingly, Jesus *identifies* with them! In Jesus, God's concern with justice toward the most vulnerable people, "the least of these," has come so close as to entail not just sympathy with or empathy for, but identification with the plight of the oppressed. And so, to sum up, a main reason why the anger of the powerless and the least privileged is valuable theologically is that it reveals the following: by insulting, harming, and even neglecting the least of these we malign God's very being.

This helps explain why the anger of the vulnerable is biblically apt. But Chapter 4 had also advanced the thesis that the Bible represents divine anger as

---

[67] Powerful Egypt cries out for the loss of their first born, but the biblical narrative conceives of this national tragedy as the natural result of the arrogant policies of the powerful. On the other hand, God sees Leah's victimization by her husband Jacob and gives her kids. And when Leah turns vindictive and victimizes Rachel, God sees Rachel's pain and gives her children.

[68] Deuteronomy 10:17–19.   [69] Cf. Matthew 25:31–40.

a way of reverberating with or echoing the pain and anger of the oppressed. If the least privileged and most powerless are justified in their anger, how could the maximally privileged and powerful person in the universe be justified in her anger? Does *God* have the proper standing to be angry? I believe so. There are two features of God's being that make God supremely qualified to express virtuous anger. First, God is uniquely situated to identify with and stand in solidarity with the powerless and the oppressed. Not only due to a track-record of showing solidarity with the vulnerable, but paradigmatically through the Kenosis of the Son, God has entered into and lived through a particular mode of life that made Godself vulnerable to religious, political, and cultural oppression.

Second, God is uniquely situated to hold to account the agents within systems of power and privilege for their oppression. God is the ultimate righteous judge of the cosmos. And so, in light of these two different strands in the inner divine life, God is an ideal ally that can reverberate and amplify the anger of the oppressed. Thus, even though God is at once maximally powerful and privileged, God's anger is justified *both* because he has the real power to hold to account those responsible for oppression *and* because God's solidarity with all those oppressed is reiterated and refracted through the drama of the powerlessness and humiliation in the Kenotic event.

The Hebrew prophets and poets explicitly identify God's anger as directed toward the powerful and the privileged. Zechariah tells us that Yahweh's anger burns against "the shepherds" and will punish the "leaders." Isaiah 3 portrays a courtroom scene where Yahweh the Judge rails against the malfeasance of Judah's leaders and elites, threatening to humiliate and despoil their daughters and sons for their role in despoiling the vulnerable among God's people. When Psalm 82 depicts God entering the council among divine beings endowed with much more power or privilege than humans, Yahweh urges them in no uncertain terms to "Give justice to the weak and the orphan; maintain the right of the lowly and the destitute. Rescue the weak and the needy; deliver them from the hand of the wicked" (vs. 3–4). Divine lament follows immediately. Yahweh mourns the fact that these gods (the power brokers of the world) are clueless and ignorant. Because the moral fabric of the universe depends upon protecting the vulnerable, should these most prestigious and powerful cosmic beings continually renege or avoid their obligation, they "will die like mortals, and fall like any prince" (v. 7). If virtuous anger is a way to care about or stand against injustice, God singularly can stand with the victims of systemic injustices, in part by effecting a thorough condemnation of all agents, human and non-human, responsible for their oppression.

But then if God contains in Godself this enormous capacity for resonance with the pain of the oppressed and with the condemnation of the powerful and privileged, how is that reconcilable with divine forgivingness? Again, there's no need to revert to an either/or. Isaiah gives us a beautiful picture of an incredibly dynamic, supple, and transcendent moral character of Yahweh, that accommodates both gracious forgivingness and anger: "...For my thoughts are not your thoughts, nor are your ways my ways," says Isaiah 55:8. Some take this to mean that the normative gap between humans and God is so immense that humans are positively evil and are therefore proper objects of divine wrath. But the emphasis in the extended argument from Isaiah 55 and 56 is on the expansive and subversive nature of God's forgiveness. God's mercy is so generous and so expansive that there is *no* human equivalent for it. We find out that God is sheer generosity to Israel, a radical grace that does not expect any payback and is not preconditioned on any human action. Furthermore, we find out that this generous forgiveness toward Israel is framed by God's generosity toward creation at large. But the kicker only arrives in Isaiah 56. Two groups of people previously isolated from God's covenantal love now get drawn in as close as possible: the foreigners and the eunuchs. The *ancient ethnical other* and *the ancient sexual other* are now set to be included in the generous cosmic temple, in the closest proximity to Yahweh. Indeed, God's ways are not our ways. God's mercy and generosity are subversive and expansive. The rhetorical move of the passage seems to be this: *God's mercy and generosity are so freely given and so free of contractual obligations as to appear as an alien trait to human perceivers. God's goodness is so surprising, so unconditional, that it outstrips and outstretches human conceptions of goodness.*

If there is a critique of human behaviors in these passages—and in Isaiah as a whole—it is a critique of political and religious power. If there is true wickedness, it seems potently concentrated in the hands of those with power.

> All you wild animals,
> all you animals in the forest,
> come to devour!
> Israel's sentinels are blind,
> they are all without knowledge;
> they are all silent dogs
> that cannot bark;
> dreaming, lying down
> loving to slumber.
> The dogs have a mighty appetite;
> they never have enough.
> The shepherds also have no understanding;
> they have all turned to their own way,
> to their own gain, one and all.
> "Come," they say, "let us get wine;
> let us fill ourselves with strong drink.
> And tomorrow will be like today,
> great beyond measure."
>
> (Isaiah 56:9–12)

It is Israel's political leaders—the sentinels—that have turned beastly toward their own people, and it is the religious leaders—the shepherds—who have turned ignorant, profiteering, and desensitized to the fate of the people. We might say the normative gap from Isaiah 55:8 is most obvious when we pit the surprising hospitality of Yahweh against the beastly cruelty of the political leaders and the inebriation of the religious ones. For as expansive as is God's grace toward the most ostracized groups of people, there are those who through their own pursuit of power and privilege have so descended into subhuman behaviors that their hearts have become self-isolated from or unyielding to God's overtures. Sure enough, God calls out and condemns the ignorant, the lazy, the complacent, the profiteer, and all "the beastly" forces that have effectively desensitized and dehumanized these powerful and privileged guardians. But note the divine pathos in the heart of divine anger. This anger "feels" more like a lament. God mourns the corruption of the leaders. God laments the descent into a cycle of sleep, consumption, and inebriation of truly magnificent creatures endowed with the power to rule, to heal creation, and to detect the holy. These people endowed with power and privilege, these people who could have chosen to cultivate the art of grace and expansive mercy, turned day after day toward occupations that slowly eroded their humanity. And so divine anger does not only express a stance against the injustices perpetrated by the powerful against the powerless, but also a stance against all the injustices that the powerful through their abuses have perpetrate against their own better selves. And so, while this aspect of divine anger is indeed a lament, when heeded, it can also truly be a work of grace.

Conclusion

I have argued here then that we can recommend curative forgivingness to those whose life experiences also demand embodying virtuous anger. I have given a cluster of psychological, normative, conceptual, and theological reasons for this. Living a life colored by sustained anger without forgivingness is on a slippery slope toward lifelong bitterness, resentment, and malice. There *is* a conceptual framework available according to which our agency, our practical self, can be conceived as a field of forces that contains both our virtuous anger and curative forgivingness. Further, if our agency is co-opted into the agency of God, we find in the anteroom both the meta-narrative of God's absorbing evil into God's own being in order to elevate transgressors, and the meta-narrative of God championing the case of the weak against the powerful. And these theological meta-narratives are not mutually exclusive. Christ fights darkness and evil by heroically trusting in the radical goodness of a God to deliver the beloved from the clutches of the enemy, while to onlookers it seems that violence and death win, and hope is gone.

Chapter 5 argued that the conception of one's life as good, as justifying and motivating of absorbing evils, is in part constituted by intrusions of supernatural grace, immersion in God's meta-narrative, and friendship with Christ. There, I emphasized throughout the deep connection between forgiveness and a beauty-ridden graciousness, seen so evidently in Esau's teary embrace of Jacob, in Christ's cooking breakfast on the shore for Peter, and Christ's throwing a feast in the wilderness for the multitudes as an act of symbolic resistance to horrors.

I want to end with hope. The connection between forgivingness and hopefulness is severely under-theorized in the philosophical literature. In the current context, what interests me is the concept of normative hope, the kind of hope in persons that aspires on their behalf, that holds up for them some kind of behavioral norm.[70] It seems to me that it is possible to have normative hope even in agents operating inside of or perpetuating corrupt systems.[71] According to Adrienne Martin, vicious persons operating inside corrupt systems meet the following criteria: (i) they have properties that make them unlikely to do the right, just, or good thing; (ii) they themselves are accountable and responsible for these properties; (iii) it is possible for them to change; (iv) if they changed, that would be a cause for universal gratitude. Isaiah's "shepherds," and Edward Covey are clear examples of such agents. Mrs. Smeath may be a borderline case.

It seems to me that it is not irrational or morally bad to invest hope in the vicious. Even if we don't see how, if they *could* change, normative hope gives reasons to trust the goodness of God at work in that person's life. In addition, a victim immersed in the divine meta-narratives has reasons to trust that there is a divine goodness at work in her own life. This situation is fully compatible with virtuous anger. In fact, the victim's anger with the vicious may deepen one's normative hope in their transformation, and vice versa, the hope may intensify the anger. And the victim's trust in the operative goodness of God may sustain both her virtuous anger with her offender and her normative hope. On the other hand, the victim can still trust that eschatological goodness will prevail against the chaos, even if the vicious never changes. But in this situation, it seems to me virtuous anger would give way to a kind of disappointment or lament.

Normative hope can also and at the same time intensify and deepen curative forgivingness. A keen perception of what the offender could become through grace can expand our sensibility, and provide a larger conception of the goodness of God in our life, one that allows us to contextualize the insult or offense. And vice versa, curative forgivingness can deepen hope. When we see our life under the conception of grace, and the more we become sensitized to dimensions of our offender's contrition, of mercy for his suffering, of our common humanity with him, of the thick bonds that unite us both, the more we resist seeing offenders as

---

[70] Cf. Martin 2014: ch. 5.

[71] Adrienne Martin gives a moving and shocking example from David Dow's book *The Autobiography of an Execution*. The story centers on an utterly failed justice system to exonerate Walter Buckley due to decisive evidence that he was "retarded."

closed projects, incapable of future development. We may very well be able to conceive ways in which they too are capable and liable to change and take responsibility for who they are.

To restate Paul, for all those virtuously-angry downtrodden, now these three remain: trust in the radical goodness of God, normative hope, and curative forgivingness. And perhaps, all of them are interwoven.

APPENDIX

Subverting Retribution in Lamentations

In Chapter 4 I argued that the communicative-restorative framework makes good sense of a narrative arc that begins with the Creation story and ends in the resurrection of Jesus. But I want to emphasize that while this biblical arc trending toward healing and restoration is real and true, the research program into divine retributive justice does not simply fade away.[1] I examine here a fascinating attempt to sustain this program as it unfolds in the book of Lamentations. I show that when Lamentations tries to articulate an account of divine retributive justice, for various reasons, theological, liturgical, and psychological, the account ultimately collapses into incoherence.

Not only on account of its intricate poetic structure or its polyphonic stances, the book of Lamentations offers us dissonant pictures of God's agency with respect to the wayward daughter Zion.[2] For the sake of simplicity, I will isolate two such pictures, which we find primarily at the center of the book in the extended poem from Lamentations 3. The first, embedded in a larger theology of hope, solidifies the conception of restorative divine agency which we find in the other prophets. The second, framed and reinforced by a theology of despair, continues to play with the possibility of a retributivist god. But this conjectural musing leads to liturgical and conceptual incoherence. Or so I will show.

The poetic voice of Lamentations 3—a Strongman according to some, a Weakling according to others, Jeremiah himself according to others still—clearly expresses at times a theology of hope. Through the lens of the Strongman, we are able to empathize with Zion's suffering, and to understand why the narrator from Lamentations 1 and 2 has moved from accusing Zion to empathizing with her. What are the features of a restorative divine agency that kindle such theological hope? First, as some have noticed, verse 33 in chapter 3—the chiastic center of the whole book and of the Strongman's poem—declares that God does not willingly afflict or grieve anyone.[3] Second, immediately following this, through a series of rhetorical questions the Strongman dramatically recalls the God of Exodus, the Liberator who is moved by the plight of the oppressed: "When all the prisoners of the land are crushed under foot, when human rights are perverted in the presence of the Most High, when one's case is subverted—Does the Lord not see it?" (3:34). Third, this

---

[1] See for instance the terrifying pictures at the end of Isaiah. Even as Israel is being installed back in the Promised Land, God takes vengeance on the nations. After their first worship service back in the restored temple, the Hebrews are encouraged to go out to see God's mighty deeds. Here's what they see: "And they shall go out and look at the dead bodies of the people who have rebelled against me; for their worm shall not die, their fire shall not be quenched, and they shall be an abhorrence to all flesh" (Isaiah 66:14). This is the final word in the book of Isaiah.

[2] A wonderful distillation of the current research and a novel interpretation of the book of Lamentations is found in O'Connor 2002.

[3] This is puzzling because the poet of Lamentations 3, consistent with the narrator from Chapters 1 and 2, *also believes God directly causes grief and affliction.* I am not sure how to solve this conflict. Maybe the view is that God is conflicted about the suffering he causes, he is not wholeheartedly behind it; that affliction proceeds not from the center of God's heart. Or maybe the poet has seen so much devastation that he gives alternating and ambivalent descriptions of the agency of God. Either God is ambivalent about the suffering he causes Israel, or the poet is ambivalent about God, or both.

affirmation of God's compassionate judgeship leads the poet to call for a public confession of transgression and for repentance: "Let us test and examine our ways, and return to the Lord" (3:40).

Fourth, it is interesting to note that all these elements—that God causes suffering unwillingly; that God has a distinct and heightened affectability to the oppressed; that national repentance will soften the effects of sin—are framed by recalling the grace-formula. As I have argued, the grace-formula gives us the most intimate biblical portrait of Yahweh. The Strongman is a good, orthodox believer, reciting by rote God's steadfast love, his mercy and compassion, resorting to memory and Scripture even in the absence of experiential knowledge of these attributes of God. Finally, the Strongman finds somehow, quite inexplicably given the extent of personal and corporate devastation, that God answers in the nick of time. God rescues him from the pit and upholds his cause against the accusers. Whether the poet recalls a past divine intervention, or expresses hope in a future delivery, or describes a presently-unfolding action, is not at all clear. What is clear is that this is a God who does not intentionally cause harm, who is faithful and merciful to the thousandth generation, a God who liberates the oppressed, and a God who intervenes when the desperate cry out.

But Lamentations 3 also expresses a set of divine motivations that sits rather poorly with the theology of hope distilled above, and even tends to undermine it. First, the Strongman radicalizes the descriptions of the retributive God presented in Lamentations 1 and 2, and deepens the moral accusation against such a deity. Initially the narrator nails his disapproval of Israel on some strong retributive portrayals of Yahweh, while Daughter Zion interweaves them in her forlorn monologues from Lamentations 1 and 2. For both narrator and Daughter Zion, God punishes with the objectivity of a judge or as some other human agents: God treads on Zion the way farmers liquefy their grapes in presses; God sets fire to Jacob as a soldier attacking a foe with an incendiary device.

However, by the start of Lamentations 2 neither the narrator nor Daughter Zion look approvingly on divine retribution. When the narrator turns from considering the fate of Israel's institutions at the hands of her captors to the fate of flesh-and-blood people, of concrete sufferers, the emotional timber changes. When the elderly suffer humiliation and the young sickly depression, when faint infants hang dying at their mothers' withered breasts, when the starved mothers themselves contemplate the horrifying possibility of eating their young, well, then God is no longer just but stone-cold, and Daughter Zion no longer a sinner, but afflicted. The narrator converts from accusing Zion to accusing God for calculated violence: "The Lord has done what he purposed; he has carried out his threat . . . . he has demolished without pity" (2:17). Later on, Daughter Zion turns toward Yahweh accusing him of lacking an essential divine attribute: "You have killed them, slaughtering them [the young and old, the most vulnerable] without mercy" (2:21).

In light of the human metaphors marshaled to illuminate divine retribution, we are warranted in claiming that Lamentations 2 finds it morally dubious but intelligible. But the Strongman of Chapter 3 finds divine retribution utterly unintelligible. For him, God is a "bear lying in wait, a lion in hiding" (3:10). Divine punitive agency is no longer human and personal. It is below personal. It is beastly.[4] It is as if the Strongman is drawing, at this point, an important theological conclusion: *To the extent that instances of suffering dehumanize people, especially the most vulnerable among them, it also animalizes the gods of these people, if these sufferings came about through divine agency.*

---

[4] This is not to say that all animal metaphors for divine characteristics are suggestive of below-personal behavior. The context helps us determine the meaning of the expression. For instance, when Psalm 91 describes taking shelter under God's pinions and wings, the invitation is to think of a deity who protects the helpless the way a mother hen protects her chicks.

The Strongman's tone is strongly accusatory because the descriptions of God's presumed beastly actions occur in a liturgically rich context. It is as if he has taken deliberate care to unravel and subvert former liturgies of praise and comfort with new liturgies of pain and accusation. To the informed reader, the poet signals in the first 19 verses of Chapter 3 if not a direct attack upon, then at least a thematic subversion of Psalm 23. You give him a shepherd, and he'll raise you a stalking bear and a preying lion. You give him green pastures and still waters, and he'll raise you a cave with a collapsed entrance. You give him a staff that comforts, he'll raise you the wrathful rod that crushes teeth in gravel. You give him a cornucopia in front of your enemies, he'll raise you the cup of bitterness before his own folks laughing and taunting. You give him goodness and mercy, he'll raise you affliction and homelessness, wormwood, and gall. You give him a suite in God's house and he'll show you the bull's eye tattooed on his back.

As if usurping well-known songs of praise is not sufficient, the Strongman also takes on the grace-formula. Recall that the grace-formula reveals at least four fundamental things about God's character: divine mercy is more enduring than divine anger; divine mercy is motivationally deeper—closer to God's heart—than anger; even in anger God suffers alongside his people; and loving kindness and not anger marks the fundamental configuration of God's intentions. Anger is always an aside, a passing disposition. But now look at how the Strongman experiences God after the communal confession of sin. By the way, this is another liturgical subversion. We expect assurance of pardon, right?

> We have transgressed and rebelled,
> And you have not forgiven.
> You have wrapped yourself in anger and pursued us,
> killing without pity;
> you have wrapped yourself with a cloud
> so that no prayer can pass through.
>
> (3:42–3)

The assurance of pardon never arrives. The grace-formula is interrupted. God cannot be invoked as the bearer of Israel's iniquity. And here's a possible explanation for this. Experientially, God and sufferer are hermetically separated. The Strongman and his people are engulfed, walled in, by despair and suffering. God is walled in by wrath and anger. The Strongman experiences God's absence as a willful divine prioritization of anger over mercy. Worse, wrath so shapes the contours of God's motivations that mercy does not have a chance to ignite. This is the anti-grace formula. This signals a subversion of the Exodus memory, and of the divine grace and sin-bearing we find in Jonah. In Jonah, only the traumatized prophet is walled-in by anger, accusation, and despair. In Jonah, God's grace permeates to the ends of the earth, to repentant violator, unrepentant traumatized victim, and even to cattle. In Lamentations, God's grace does not even reach next door to the repentant, traumatized victim.

One way to reconcile the theology of hope with that of despair is to say that the Strongman's own suffering and witness to the anguish of others engenders serious cognitive dissonance. We get in Lamentations 3 more dark clouds than light, more thunder-claps than soothing whispers. God causes both good and evil. The God of my memory is all rainbows and sunshine, but the God of my current experience all thunder and storm-cloud. The God of the Psalms is a shepherd, the God of my reality a bear. Yes, perhaps *I* will be delivered from the bear, but I want it to crush my enemies' bones. Perhaps we might expect all these dissonances from those suffering acutely. But this answer strikes me as a bit too facile.

A more satisfying response is that the Strongman's theology of despair, particularly the conception of God as a retributive judge locked into anger is a decisive *reductio ad absurdum* argument. If God is a retributive deity, he intentionally brings about Israel's devastation as payment for transgression. And if Yahweh brings about the state of affairs where Israel's most vulnerable persons—young mothers, infants, and the elderly—are dehumanized, then Israel's central conception of God is false, all of Zion's Psalms of praise ring hollow, and the only appropriate response is revenge. But the grace-formula tracks the real traits of Yahweh, the songs of comfort encode the real history of a merciful and good shepherd, and this goodness and mercy is a psychological possibility even for the ravaged sheep. Of course, another interesting feature of Lamentations is that the *reductio* never gets explicitly articulated. Unlike the book of Jonah where God speaks up and ratifies the radical priority of divine mercy over anger, here God remains silent. At the same time, this silence also strikes me as appropriate. Lamentations lays out better than any other prophetic book the consequences of accepting a retributivist picture of God. And these upshots are horrifying. God is a moral monster. Theology is incoherent. Liturgies are lies. But while those actively suffering and those who have witnessed atrocities do not have to accept these upshots, they also do not have to accept their denials. *Perhaps to those who suffer atrocities, and only to those, are given at once the grace and the dispensation to feel as if divine retributivism is true, though they also know it must be false.*

References

Adams, Marilyn McCord. 1991. "Forgiveness: A Christian Model." *Faith and Philosophy* 8(3): 277–304.

Allais, Lucy. 2008. "Wiping the Slate Clean: The Heart of Forgiveness." *Philosophy and Public Affairs* 36: 33–68.

Alter, Robert. 1996. *Genesis: Translation and Commentary.* New York: W. W. Norton and Company.

Améry, Jean. 1980. *At the Mind's Limits.* Bloomington: Indiana University Press.

Anderson, Gary. 2009. *Sin: A History.* New Haven: Yale University Press.

Aristotle. 1984. *The Complete Works of Aristotle: The Revised Oxford Translation.* Translated by Jonathan Barnes. Princeton: Princeton University Press.

Aristotle. 2002. *Nicomachean Ethics.* Translated by Joe Sachs. Newbury Port: Focus Publishing.

Atwood, Margaret. 1998. *Cat's Eye.* New York: Random House.

Bakhos, Carol. 2006. *Ishmael on the Border: Rabbinic Portrayals of the First Arab.* Albany, NY: State University of New York Press.

Bash, Anthony. 2011. "Forgiveness: A Re-appraisal." *Studies in Christian Ethics* 24(2): 133–46.

Bash, Anthony. 2015. *Forgiveness: A Theology.* Eugene, OR: Cascade Books.

Bauckham, Richard. 2015. *Gospel of Glory: Major Themes in Johannine Theology.* Grand Rapids, MI: Baker Academic.

Bell, Macalester. 2005. "A Woman's Scorn: Toward a Feminist Defense of Contempt as a Moral Emotion." *Hypatia* 20(4): 80–93.

Bell, Macalester. 2006. "Review of Lisa Tessman's Burdened Virtues: Virtue Ethics for Liberatory Struggles." *Notre Dame Philosophical Review*, edited by Christopher Shields. June. https://ndpr.nd.edu/reviews/burdened-virtues-virtue-ethics-for-liberatory-struggles/.

Bell, Macalester. 2009. "Anger, Virtue, and Oppression." In *Feminist Ethics and Social and Political Philosophy: Theorizing the Non-Ideal*, edited by Lisa Tessman, 58–77. London: Springer.

Bennett, Jonathan. 1974. "The Conscience of Huckleberry Finn." *Philosophy* 49: 123–34.

Bleeker, C. J. 1966. "Guilt and Purification in Ancient Egypt." *Numen* 13(2): 81–7.

Bommarito, Nicholas. 2017. "Virtuous and Vicious Anger." *Journal of Ethics and Social Philosophy* 11(3): 1–27.

Booth, Wayne. 1993. "Individualism and the Mystery of the Social Self; or Does Amnesty Have a Leg to Stand On?" In *Freedom and Interpretation*, edited by Barbara Johnson, 69–101. New York: Basic Books.

Bratman, Michael E. 1987. *Intention, Plants, and Practical Reason.* Cambridge, MA: Harvard University Press.

Butler, Joseph. 1993. "Upon Resentment." In *Fifteen Sermons*, 92–101. Virginia: Lincoln-Rembrandt Publishing.

Calhoun, Cheshire. 1992. "Changing One's Heart." *Ethics* 103(1): 76–96.

Callard, Agnes. 2018. "The Reason to be Angry Forever." In *The Moral Psychology of Anger*, edited by Myisha Cherry and Owen Flanagan, 123–37. London: Rowman & Littlefield International.

Carmichael, Calum. 2002. "The Origin of the Scapegoat Ritual." *Vetus Testamentus* 50(2): 167–81.

Carmichael, Calum. 2006. *Illuminating Leviticus: A Study of Its Laws and Institutions in Light of the Biblical Narratives*. Baltimore: Johns Hopkins University Press.

Casey, John. 1990. *Pagan Virtue: An Essay in Ethics*. Oxford: Oxford University Press.

Christian Reformed Church. 1987. *Psalter Hymnal*. Grand Rapids, MI: CRC Publications.

Crisp, Oliver. 2003. "Divine Retribution: A Defence." *Sophia* 42(2): 35–52.

Cuneo, Terence. 2010. "If These Walls Could Speak: Icons as Vehicles of Divine Speech." *Faith and Philosophy* 27: 123–41.

Cuneo, Terence. 2014a. "Liturgical Immersion." *Journal of Analytic Theology* 2: 117–39.

Cuneo, Terence. 2014b. "Protesting Evil." *Theology Today* 70(4): 430–44.

Curley, Edwin. 2011. "The God of Abraham, Isaac, and Jacob." In *Divine Evil? The Moral Character of the God of Abraham*, edited by Michael Bergmann, Michael J. Murray, and Michael C. Rea, 58–88. Oxford: Oxford University Press.

Davis, Ellen. 2001. *Getting Involved with God: Rediscovering the Old Testament*. Lanham, MD: Rowman & Littlefield Publishers.

Denson, Thomas F. 2010. "A Social Neuroscience Perspective on the Neurobiological Basis of Aggression." In *Human Aggression and Violence: Causes, Manifestations, and Consequences*, edited by Phillip R. Shaver and Mario Mikulincer, 105–20. Washington, DC: American Psychological Association.

Dew, Jeffrey. 2007. "Two Sides of the Same Coin? The Differing Roles of Assets and Consumer Debt in Marriage." *Journal of Family and Economic Issues* 28: 89–104.

Doris, John. 2002. *Lack of Character: Personality and Moral Behavior*. Cambridge: Cambridge University Press.

Duff, A. R. 2003. *Punishment, Communication, and Community*. Oxford: Oxford University Press.

Edwards, Jonathan. 1741. "Sinners in the Hands of an Angry God. A Sermon Preached at Enfield, July 8th, 1741." In *Electronic Texts in American Studies*, edited by Reiner Smolinski: paper 54. http://digitalcommons.unl.edu/etas/54.

Fales, Evan. 2011. "Satanic Verses: Moral Chaos in Holy Writ." In *Divine Evil? The Moral Character of the God of Abraham*, edited by Michael Bergmann, Michael J. Murray, and Michael C. Rea, 91–108. Oxford: Oxford University Press.

Feinberg, Joel. 1965. "The Expressive Function of Punishment." *The Monist* 49(3): 397–423.

Field, Tiffany. 2001. *Touch*. Cambridge, MA: MIT Press.

Finlan, Stephen. 2004. *The Background and Content of Paul's Cultic Atonement Metaphors*. Atlanta: Society of Biblical Literature.

Flanagan, Owen. 2009. "Moral Science? Still Metaphysical After All These Years." In *Personality, Identity, and Character: Explorations in Moral Psychology*, edited by Darcia Narvarez and Daniel K. Lapsley, 52–78. Cambridge: Cambridge University Press.

Fox, Everett. 1997. *The Five Books of Moses*. New York: Schocken Books.

France, R. T. 2014. *The Gospel of Mark (The New International Greek Commentary)*. Grand Rapids, MI: Eerdmans.

Frankfurt, Harry G. 1988. *The Importance of What We Care About*. Cambridge: Cambridge University Press.

Frankfurt, Harry G. 1998. "Autonomy, Necessity, and Love." In *Necessity, Volition, and Love*, 129–41. Cambridge: Cambridge University Press.

Frankfurt, Harry G. 2004. *The Reasons of Love*. Princeton, NJ: Princeton University Press.

Fretheim, Terence E. 1984. *The Suffering of God: An Old Testament Perspective*. Philadelphia: Fortress Press.

Fricker, Miranda. 2009. *Epistemic Injustice: Power and Ethics of Knowing*. Oxford: Oxford University Press.

Gallagher, Shaun. 2019. *Enactivist Interventions: Rethinking the Mind*. Oxford: Oxford University Press.

Gerson, Michael. 2015. "The Power of Forgiveness in Charleston." *The Washington Post*. https://www.washingtonpost.com/opinions/the-power-of-forgiveness/2015/06/22/a331c77e-190d-11e5-bd7f-4611a60dd8e5_story.html. Last accessed August 30, 2022.

Girard, René. 1987. *Things Hidden Since the Foundations of the World*. Stanford, CA: Stanford University Press.

Girard, René. 2001. *I See Satan Falling like Lightning*. Maryknoll, NY: Orbis.

Goldstein, Warren. 2006. *Defending the Human Spirit: Jewish Law's Vision for a Moral Society*. Jerusalem: Feldheim Publishers.

Graybill, Lynn and Kimberly R. Lanegran. 2004. "Truth, Justice, and Reconciliation in Africa: Issues and Cases." *African Studies Quarterly* 8(1): 1–18.

Green, Joel B. 2006. "The Kaleidoscopic View." In *The Nature of the Atonement: Four Views*, edited by James Beilby and Paul R. Eddy, 157–85. Downers Grove, IL: IVP Academic Press.

Gregory, Bradley C. 2006. "The Legal Background of the Metaphor for Forgiveness in Psalm CIII 12." *Vetus Testamentus* 54(4): 549–51.

Hamilton, Victor P. 2005. *Handbook on the Pentateuch: Genesis, Exodus, Numbers, Leviticus, Deuteronomy*. Grand Rapids, MI: Baker Academic.

Harris, Angelique. 2018. "Emotions, Feelings, and Social Change: Love, Anger, and Solidarity in Black Women's AIDS Activism." *Women, Gender, and Families of Color* 6(2): 181–201.

Heil, John Paul. 1995. "Jesus as the Unique High Priest in the Gospel of John." *The Catholic Biblical Quarterly* 57(4): 729–45.

Hiebert, Theodore. 1996. *The Yahwist's Landscape: Nature and Religion in Ancient Israel*. Oxford: Oxford University Press.

Holmgren, Margaret R. 2012. *Forgiveness and Retribution: Responding to Wrongdoing*. Cambridge: Cambridge University Press.

Hursthouse, Rosalind. 1999. *On Virtue Ethics*. Oxford: Oxford University Press.

Jones, L. Gregory. 1995. *Embodying Forgiveness: A Theological Analysis*. Grand Rapids, MI: Eerdmans.

Keener, Craig S. 2003. *The Gospel of John: A Commentary (Volume 1)*. Grand Rapids, MI: Baker Academic.

Kennedy, Joel. 2008. *The Recapitulation of Israel's History in Matthew 1:1–4:11*. Tübingen: Mohr Siebeck.

Konstan, David. 2010. *Before Forgiveness: The Origins of a Moral Idea*. Cambridge: Cambridge University Press.

Kraybill, Donald B., Steven Nolt, and David Weaver-Zercher. 2007. *Amish Grace: How Forgiveness Transcends Tragedy*. San Francisco: John Wiley & Sons.

Kynes, William L. 1990. *A Christology of Solidarity*. Lanham, MD: University Press of America.

Leithart, Peter J. 2017. *The Gospel of Matthew Through New Eyes*. Monroe, LA: Athanasius Press.

Lewis, C. S. 2009. *The Problem of Pain*. San Francisco: HarperOne.

Lorde, Audre. 2017. "The Uses of Anger: Women Responding to Racism." In *Sister Outsider*, 124–33. Berkeley: Crossing Press.

McDowell, John. 1979. "Virtue and Reason." *The Monist* 62(3): 331–50.

McFague, Sallie. 1988. *Models of God: Theology for an Ecological, Nuclear Age*. Philadelphia: Fortress Press.

MacIntyre, Alasdair. 1984. *After Virtue: A Study in Moral Theory*. Notre Dame: University of Notre Press.

MacLachlan, Alice. 2010. "Unreasonable Resentments." *Journal of Social Philosophy* 41(4): 422–41.

Maclean, Jennifer K. Berenson. 2007. "Barabbas, the Scapegoat Ritual, and the Development of the Passion Narrative." *Harvard Theological Review* 100(3): 309–34.

Maimonides, Moses. 1956. *The Guide to the Perplexed*. Translated by M. Friedlander. New York: Dover.

Malcom X. 1994. *Malcom X Speaks: Selected Speeches and Statements*. Reprint edition. New York: Grove Press.

Margalit, Avishai. 2002. *The Ethics of Memory*. Cambridge, MA: Harvard University Press.

Martin, Adrienne. 2014. *How We Hope: A Moral Psychology*. Princeton: Princeton University Press.

Merleau-Ponty, Maurice. 1968. *The Visible and the Invisible*. Translated by Alphonso Lingis. Evanston, IL: Northwestern University Press.

Mihut, Cristian F. 2014. "Probing the Logic of Forgiveness, Human and Divine." *Studies in Christian Ethics* 27(3): 288–98.

Mikulincer, Mario and Israel Orbach. 1995. "Attachment Styles and Repressive Defensiveness: The Accessibility and Architecture of Affective Memories." *Journal of Personality and Social Psychology* 68(5): 917–25.

Miller, Christian B. 2013. *Moral Character: An Empirical Theory*. Oxford: Oxford University Press.

Miller, Christian B. 2017. "Character and Situationism: New Directions." *Ethical Theory and Moral Practice* 20(3): 459–71.

Mobley, Gregory. 1997. "The Wild Man in the Bible and the Ancient Near East." *Journal of Biblical Literature* 116(2): 217–33.

Montagne, Renee (host). 2016. "A Decade after Amish School Shooting, Gunman's Mother Talks of Forgiveness." *StoryCorps*, NPR, September 30, 2016. https://www.npr.org/transcripts/495905609. Last accessed August 23, 2022.

Morgan, Michael L. 2012. "Mercy, Repentance, and Forgiveness in Ancient Judaism." In *Ancient Forgiveness: Classical, Judaic, and Christian*, edited by Charles Griswold and David Konstan, 137–57. Cambridge: Cambridge University Press.

Morgenstern, Julian. 2002. *The Doctrine of Sin in the Babylonian Religion*. San Diego: The Book Tree.

Morris, Jasmyn Belcher (producer). 2016. "A Decade after the Amish School Shooting, Gunman's Mother Talks of Forgiveness." *StoryCorps*, NPR, September 30, 2016. https://www.npr.org/2016/09/30/495905609/a-decade-after-amish-school-shooting-gunman-s-mother-talks-of-forgiveness. Last accessed August 30, 2022.

Murphy, Jeffrie. 1998. "Forgiveness and Resentment." In *Forgiveness and Mercy*, edited by Jeffrie G. Murphy and Jean Hampton, 14–34. Cambridge: Cambridge University Press.

Murphy, Jeffrie. 2014. *Punishment and the Moral Emotions: Essays in Law, Morality, and Religion*. Oxford: Oxford University Press.

Neu, Jerome. 2011. "On Loving our Enemies." In *The Ethics of Forgiveness: A Collection of Essays*, edited by Christel Fricke, 130–42. New York: Routledge.

Nussbaum, Martha. 1990. *Love's Knowledge: Essays on Philosophy and Literature*. Oxford: Oxford University Press.

Nussbaum, Martha. 1994. *The Therapy of Desire: Theory and Practice in Hellenistic Ethics.* Princeton: Princeton University Press.

Nussbaum, Martha. 2018. *Anger and Forgiveness: Resentment, Generosity, and Justice.* Oxford: Oxford University Press.

O'Connor, Kathleen M. 2002. *Lamentations and the Tears of the World.* Maryknoll, NY: Orbis Books.

Orchard, Helen C. 1998. *Courting Betrayal: Jesus as Victim in the Gospel of John (The Library of New Testament Studies).* Sheffield: Sheffield Academic Press.

Panchuk, Michelle. 2018. "The Shattered Spiritual Self and the Sacred: Philosophical Reflections on Religious Trauma, Worship, and Deconversion." *Res Philosophica* 96.

Peets, Kätlin, Tiina Turunen, and Christina Salmivalli. 2022. "Rumination Mediates the Longitudinal Associations Between Elementary-School Victimization and Adolescents' Internalizing Problems." *Journal of Interpersonal Violence* 37(17–18). https://doi.org/10.1177/08862605211025020.

Pettigrove, Glen. 2012a. "Meekness and Moral Anger." *Ethics* 122(2): 341–70.

Pettigrove, Glen. 2012b. *Forgiveness and Love.* Oxford: Oxford University Press.

Pinker, Aron. 2007. "A Goat to Go to Azazel." *Journal of Hebrew Scriptures* 7(8). https://doi.org/10.5508/jhs.2007.v7.a8.

Plato. 2004. *The Republic.* Translated by C. D. C. Reeve. Indianapolis: Hackett.

Ratcliffe, Matthew. 2008. "Touch and Situatedness." *International Journal of Philosophical Studies* 16(3): 299–322.

Ratcliffe, Matthew. 2013. "Touch and the Sense of Reality." In *Hand, the Organ of the Mind,* edited by Zdravko Radman, 131–58. Cambridge, MA: MIT Press.

Rea, Michael. 2019. "The Ill-made Knight and the Stain on the Soul." *European Journal for Philosophy of Religion* 11(1): 117–34.

Richter, Sandra. 2020. *Stewards of Eden: What Scripture Says About the Environment and Why It Matters.* Westmont, IL: IVP.

Roberts, Robert C. 1995. "Forgivingness." *American Philosophical Quarterly* 32: 289–306.

Roberts, Robert C. 2012. "Narrative Ethics." *Philosophy Compass* 7: 174–82.

Rosner, Jennifer A. 2000. "Reflective Endorsement and the Self: A Response to Arpaly and Schroeder." *Philosophical Studies* 101(1): 107–12.

Rowlands, Mark. 2003. *Externalism: Putting Mind and World Back Together Again.* Montreal: McGill-Queen's University Press.

Sarna, Nahum M. 1986. *Exploring Exodus: The Origins of Biblical Israel.* New York: Schocken Books.

Schabas, William A. 2003. "The Relationship Between Truth Commissions and International Courts: The Case of Sierra Leone." *Human Rights Quarterly* 25: 1035–66.

Schmidt, Alvin J. 2004. *How Christianity Changed the World.* Grand Rapids, MI: Zondervan.

Schwartz, Daniel R. 1983. "Two Pauline Allusions to the Redemptive Mechanism of the Crucifixion." *Journal of Biblical Literature* 102: 259–68.

Shriver, Donald. 1995. *An Ethic for Enemies: Forgiveness in Politics.* Oxford: Oxford University Press.

Singh, Raghvinder. 2015. "My Father was a Victim of a Mass Shooting. Here's Why Forgiveness Offers Freedom from Hate." *The Washington Post.* https://www.washingtonpost.com/news/acts-of-faith/wp/2015/06/23/my-father-was-a-victim-of-a-mass-shooting-heres-why-forgiveness-offers-freedom-from-hate/?utm_term=.73d0a3df16f5. Last accessed August 30, 2022.

Sommers, Benjamin D. 2009. *The Bodies of God and the World of Ancient Israel.* Cambridge: Cambridge University Press.

Srinivasan, Amia. 2018. "The Aptness of Anger." *The Journal of Political Philosophy* 26(2): 123–44.

Stassen, Glen H. 2008. "The Ten Commandments: Deliverance for the Vulnerable." *Perspective in Religious Studies* 35(4): 357–71.

Staub, Ervin, Laurie Pearlman, and Vachel Miller. 2003. "Healing the Roots of Genocide in Rwanda." *Peace Review* 15(3): 287–94.

Steiker, Carol. 2008. "Murphy on Mercy: A Prudential Reconsideration." *APA Newsletter on Philosophy and Law* 8(1): 10–16.

Stökl Ben Ezra, Daniel. 2003. *The Impact of Yom Kippur on Early Christianity: The Day of Atonement from the Second Temple to the Fifth Century.* Tübingen: Mohr Siebeck.

Strabbing, Jada T. 2020. "Forgiveness and Reconciliation." *Australian Journal of Philosophy* 98(3): 531–45.

Stump, Eleonore. 1988. "Sanctification, Hardening of Heart, and Frankfurt's Concept of Free Will." *Journal of Philosophy* 85(8): 395–420.

Stump, Eleonore. 2012. *Wandering in Darkness: Narrative and the Problem of Suffering.* Oxford: Oxford University Press.

Stump, Eleonore. 2020. *Atonement.* Oxford: Oxford University Press.

Tessman, Lisa. 2005. *Burdened Virtues: Virtue Ethics for Liberatory Struggles.* New York: Oxford University Press.

Thomson, Susan. 2001. "Whispering Truth to Power: The Everyday Resistance of Rwandan Peasants to Post-Genocide Reconciliation." *African Affairs* 110: 439–56.

Urbach, Ephraime E. 1975. *The Sages.* Jerusalem: The Magnes Press.

Van Ness Daniel W. and Karen H. Strong. 2010. *Restoring Justice: An Introduction to Restorative Justice.* New Providence, NJ: Matthew Bender & Company.

van Wijk-Bos, Johanna W. H. 2005. *Making Wise the Simple: The Torah in Christian Faith and Practice.* Grand Rapids, MI: Eerdmans.

Vanhoozer, Kevin J. 2012. *Remythologizing Theology.* Cambridge: Cambridge University Press.

Verbin, Nehama. 2010. *Divinely Abused: A Philosophical Perspective on Job and His Kin.* London: Continuum.

Volf, Miroslav. 2005. *Free of Charge: Giving and Forgiving in a Culture Stripped of Grace.* Grand Rapids, MI: Zondervan.

Volf, Miroslav. 2006. *The End of Memory: Remembering Rightly in a Violent World.* Grand Rapids, MI: Eerdmans.

Walen, Alec. 2014. "Retributive Justice." In *The Stanford Encyclopedia of Philosophy*, edited by Edward N. Zalta. Summer 2014. https://plato.stanford.edu/entries/justice-retributive/.

Walker, Margaret Urban. 2006. *Moral Repair: Reconstructing Moral Relations after Wrongdoing.* Cambridge: Cambridge University Press.

Walton, John H. 2009. *The Lost World of Genesis One: Ancient Cosmology and the Origins Debate.* Downers Grove, IL: InterVarsity Press.

Warmke, Brandon. 2017. "Divine Forgiveness I: Emotion and Punishment-Forbearance Theories." *Philosophy Compass.* September. https://doi.org/10.1111/phc3.12440.

Watts, Rikki E. 2000. *Isaiah's New Exodus in Mark.* Grand Rapids, MI: Baker Academic.

Williams, Rowan. 1982. *Resurrection: Interpreting the Easter Gospel.* London: Darton, Longman, and Todd.

Williams, Rowan. 2002. *Writing in the Dust: After September 11.* Grand Rapids, MI: Eerdmans.

Wöhrle, Jakob. 2009. "A Prophetic Reflection of Divine Forgiveness: The Integration of the Book of Jonah into the Book of the Twelve." *The Journal of Hebrew Scriptures* 9: 1–17.

Wolterstorff, Nicholas. 1988. "Suffering Love." In *Philosophy and the Christian Faith*, edited by Thomas V. Morris, 196–237. Notre Dame: University of Notre Dame Press.

Wolterstorff, Nicholas. 1995. *Divine Discourse: Philosophical Reflections on the Claim that God Speaks*. New York: Cambridge University Press.

Wolterstorff, Nicholas. 2011. *Justice in Love*. Grand Rapids, MI: Eerdmans.

Zehr, Howard. 2002. *The Little Book of Restorative Justice*. Intercourse, PA: Good Books.

Zevit, Ziony. 1976. "The Priestly Reduction and Interpretation of the Plague Narrative in Exodus." *The Jewish Quarterly Review* 66(4): 193–211.

Index

For the benefit of digital users, indexed terms that span two pages (e.g., 52–53) may, on occasion, appear on only one of those pages.